The Little Theatre in Williamstown, A History 1946 - 2021

Robert E Glass

The Little Theatre in Williamstown, A History, 1946-2021

Williamstown Little Theatre, 2 Albert Street, Williamstown, Victoria
Enquiries: contact@wlt.org.au

The Little Theatre in Williamstown, A History, 1946-2021, a revised and extended version of Robert E. Glass's *A Small Intimate Theatre of Our Very Own: A History of Williamstown Little Theatre 1946-1996*, published by Williamstown Little Theatre, 1998.

Copyright © 2024 Robert E Glass and Williamstown Little Theatre
Cover Design by Robert E Glass

All rights reserved. No part of this book may be reproduced, stored in a retrieval system, or transmitted in any form or by any means, electronic or mechanical, including photocopying, scanning, recording or otherwise without permission in writing from the copyright owner.

National Library of Australia
A catalogue record for this book is available from the National Library of Australia.

ISBN 978-0-6486156-0-6

Published by Blue Koala Publishing:
info@bluekoalapublishing.com

Table of Contents

Foreword		1
Introduction		3
1) 1946 - 1956:	From Imported to 'All Local' Productions	8
2) 1957 - 1968:	Challenges posed by TV and Mechanics' Closure	48
3) 1969 - 1976:	A New Home and a Crisis	81
4) 1977 - 1986:	Recovery	112
5) 1987 - 1996:	'If Amateur Can be Termed Professional'	148
6) 1997 - 2006:	Consolidating	176
7) 2007 - 2016:	The Loyalty of Subscribers	218
8) 2017 - 2021:	Making Covid an Opportunity for Renewal	262
9) 1946 - 2021	Looking Back on 75 Years	290
Appendix 1	Productions of Williamstown Little Theatre	297
Appendix 2	Winners of the Cordell, Stewart and Craven Awards	310
Appendix 3	Winners of the Grahame Murphy Award for Excellence	321
Appendix 4	Williamstown Little Theatre and the Victorian Drama League Awards	323
Appendix 5	Presidents, Secretaries and Treasurers of Williamstown Little Theatre	331
Appendix 6	Life Members of Williamstown Little Theatre	335
Bibliography	List of Newspapers, Magazines and Books	337

see if he would be kind enough to do an update – a revised edition which would incorporate the subsequent twenty-five years. Thankfully, he agreed! The original idea was that it would be launched in our 75th year – in 2021 – but Covid-19 put paid to that. Not only were we unable to hold an appropriate celebration, the mere act of accessing records and archives proved impossible. The closure of the theatre for two years due to the pandemic did, however, provide an appropriate point in our history to end this revised edition.

Like the original, this new edition is the result of countless hours of research and discovery by Bob. The stories in this book are captured with Bob's trademark attention to detail, his natural warmth, and his love for the theatre community.

In Bob's introduction to this revised work, he acknowledges the many people who have contributed to this edition. WLT members and friends also extend our heartfelt thanks to these people for their contributions.

As Newton alluded to, a clear understanding of our past means we can look to the future with confidence. Our job, as the current stewards, is to ensure we hand over to the next generation something valuable and relevant – just as it was handed to us.

We hope you enjoy the read.

Williamstown Little Theatre Committee, 2023

Foreword

WLT acknowledges the Yalukit-willam people of the Kulin Nation as the traditional custodians of the land on which Williamstown Little Theatre was built. We celebrate them as the first story tellers and creators of culture.

Sir Isaac Newton is quoted as saying:

If I have seen further than others, it is because I was standing on the shoulders of giants.

In many ways, this is how those of us who are part of the Williamstown Little Theatre (WLT) family feel. Our written history is a reminder to us of those giants who have come before us and worked tirelessly to establish something unique and cherished.

We are the current stewards of a theatrical movement which started more than seventy-five years ago. Over that time, that movement has left an indelible mark on the social and artistic soul of Williamstown and surrounding communities.

Social researcher Robert Putnam refers to the importance of people having *a third place* – a place that isn't home and isn't the workplace – a community place instilling a sense of creativity, well-being and belonging.[1] WLT has been that place for hundreds of people, for more than seventy-five years.

To many of us over many years, Bob Glass' documented history of the first fifty years of WLT – entitled *"A Small Intimate Theatre of our Very Own"* – has been a godsend. It, along with our extensive archives, has been our go-to source for data, facts and stories.

Several years ago, as our 75th anniversary loomed, we approached Bob to

---

1   Putnam, Robert D. (2000) *Bowling Alone*. Simon & Schuster New York.

Introduction

On the evening of 23 May, 1946, nine thespian residents of Williamstown gathered at that City's Mechanics' Institute and formed the Williamstown Little Theatre Movement. Their immediate aim was to bring to the bayside suburb groups of good standing to provide plays, ballet and music of some cultural value. Ultimately, they hoped to 'encourage the actual production of drama in Williamstown'.

This book tells the story of how, over the subsequent seventy-five years, the Movement established that Thursday evening, now the Williamstown Little Theatre Incorporated, (hereafter referred to as WLT), pursued and largely successfully achieved those aims. The book's primary purpose is to record and, in the context of the Theatre's seventy-fifth anniversary in 2021, celebrate the achievement of the men and women responsible for its growth and development into one of the leading non-professional theatres in Melbourne.

The book extends, updates and, as necessary, revises *A Small Intimate Theatre of our Very Own*, my history of the first fifty years of the theatre published in 1998. The primary source material for this book, as with the earlier version, remains the extensive archives of WLT held at the theatre's premises at 2-4 Albert Street, Williamstown. Since the original work was published, successive committees of the Theatre, especially in the context of preparing for celebrations of the Theatre's sixtieth and seventieth anniversaries in 2006 and 2016 respectively, have made major efforts to make those archives even more complete and comprehensive than they were in the mid 1990s.

As a result, new material relating to the period back to 1946 has been unearthed, some of which casts additional light on the Theatre's story, requiring amplification or modification of the original work. The Theatre's archives have again been supplemented by a range of reviewers and commentators in publications as diverse as the *Western Suburbs Advertiser, Williamstown Advertiser, Williamstown Chronicle, Hobson's Bay Weekly, The Listener-In* (and its successor after the advent of television in Melbourne, *Listener-In TV*), *Catholic Advocate*, *VDL Magazine* and its successor, *Theatrecraft*. In addition, I have drawn material from the long-running theatre review program *Applause, Applause* and its successor *Curtain Up* on Melbourne's Community Radio 3CR.

Modern writers about theatre (for example Edwin Wilson) stress how the effective staging of a single play requires the integration of the collaborative efforts of the playwright, the director and the actors, designers and technicians.[1] Performers on stage, those working backstage, and front-of-house staff need to form an integrated team. Six months after he was elected WLT President in 2013, Peter Newling calculated that 103 people could be involved in a single Williamstown production.[2] As Anthony Parker once wrote, 'The Play may be the jewel, but the Front-of House is the setting which can show it off to best advantage.'[3]

Amateur and professional theatre face the same challenges. The differences, as Frances Reid has noted, 'are largely a matter of scale'.[4] An annual playbill, such as those issued by WLT since the early 1960s, requires an individual or group to select the plays to be performed over a year: as John Sumner once wrote, 'Choosing plays, a repertoire, is the key to the success of any theatre company.'[5] Theatre, moreover, requires Drama (a script), Stage (where actors interpret the script) and Audience.[6] Securing and accommodating an audience requires firstly that there be a building fit for the purpose, and people to do marketing, ticketing, front of house, and ushering. This history covers what has happened both on and off stage at 'Willy', as it is affectionately known by many of those with long associations with the Theatre, including the support

---

[1] Edwin Wilson, *The Theatre Experience*, 5th edition, (New York, McGraw Hill Inc., 1991), p.396

[2] *Cues and News*, August 2013.

[3] Anthony Parker, *Amateur Theatre as a Pastime, A Comprehensive Guide to the Stage*, (London, Souvenir Press, 1959), p.111

[4] Frances Reid, *Theatre Administration*, (London, Adam and Charles Black, 1983), p. 138

[5] John Sumner, *Recollections at Play*, p.25

[6] *Drama, Stage and Audience* is the title of J.L. Styan's standard 'textbook' on theatre published by Cambridge University Press in 1975. Styan summarises the multiple elements of theatre in his first chapter 'Communication in Drama', especially at pp.6-14

Introduction

activities necessary to ensure the Theatre's ongoing functioning and survival for more than seventy-five years.

I should like to make three further introductory points.

Firstly, a comment made on both *A Small Intimate Theatre of Our Very Own* and an earlier draft of this update was that there was a risk that the story could be hamstrung by a narrative framework which said simply that 'WLT did this, and then they did that'. But this approach reflects the essential rhythm of life at WLT, and indeed other theatres.

The table on page 6 is a representation of the broad features of this rhythm as it has worked at WLT for a long time. For each play there is a cycle of auditions (usually during week two of the previous show), rehearsals (over eight weeks), set construction and set bump-out (currently on the Tuesday after closing night).

My second introductory point relates to the photographs included in this volume. One has to use the photographs available. Despite the best efforts of the Committee and others, there are no extant photographs of the 1959 production of *The Women*, which other sources suggest was extremely important for the theatre. Nor are there usable ones of Grahame Murphy's November 1964 production of *The Boy Friend* which attracted WLT's largest ever audience at the Mechanics' Institute.

Thirdly, the Coronavirus Covid-19, which first became evident in Melbourne in February 2020, has impacted this work in three ways. Firstly because of the lockdowns imposed in Melbourne to limit the spread of the virus, my access to the WLT archives (on which, as noted above, the details of the book are substantially based) was restricted for many months. Secondly, the absence from Melbourne of the author and key players at WLT for substantial periods of time in 2021 and 2022, further delayed completion of the research underpinning the work. These delays raised the question of whether the work should extend beyond 2021. The Committee determined, however, that the appropriate point to conclude the story was with the official opening of the remodelled and refurbished theatre in December 2021 - though there remain a few minor references to 2022 (mainly in the Appendices).

In preparing this history, I have received assistance from many people, some now deceased. Those deceased who contributed details of, and perspectives on, the history include Brian Crossley, Ray Hare, Doug Lindsay, Joan Lindsay,

A Year in the Life of WLT

Play Selection Committee (PSC) chooses the repertoire	• PSC appoints directors (up to 2 years before any 'year') • Directors submit plays for consideration • PSC recommends to WLT Committee • Committee approves, secures rights for plays • Playbill produced for distribution on November 1
Securing the Audience	• Taking Whole of Year Bookings • Bookings for Individual Shows
Delivering the Plays	• Play 1: February-March • Play 2: April-May • Play 3: July-August • Play 4: September-October • Play 5: November-early December
Celebrating and Sustaining	• Cordell Awards Day (early December) • Presidential Working Bees (January)

Introduction

Ron Little, Grahame Murphy, Dorothy Porter and Ivor Porter. Others who have influenced my work, and to whom I express my heartfelt thanks, are Chris Baldock, Brian Christopher, Judi Clark, Damian Coffey, Graeme Cope, David Dare, Ellis Ebell, Janine Evans, Roger Forsey, Laurie Gellon, John and Caroline Gunn, Ness Harwood, Barbara Hughes, Mary Little, Celia Meehan, Peter Newling, Frank Page, Jennifer Paragreen, Wayne Pearn, Janet Provan, Tony Tartaro, Bryan Thomas, Shannon Woollard and Sally-Ann Wheeldon.

I am especially grateful to Barbara Hughes for going through my most advanced 'pre-Covid-lockdown' draft with a very fine-toothed comb, resulting in the correction of many errors of fact and punctuation. I owe a special debt to Graeme Cope for his thorough editorial job on the version which incorporated Barbara's suggestions, adding at the same time insights from his own involvement at Williamstown, and his knowledge of the broader non-professional theatre community in Melbourne. Barbara and Graeme's efforts have greatly enhanced the book's quality. In a similar vein, Peter Newling has helped greatly in arranging the printing of the book with the assistance of Karlana Kasarik of Blue Koala Publishing.

Finally special thanks are due to my wife, Frances Devlin-Glass, for her support, insight and shared love of theatre for the fifty-six years since we first stepped out together in August 1967 to a Brisbane Arts Theatre production of *A Midsummer Night's Dream*. Many words in this book are originally Fran's, either from her 'inside' role as adjudicator for WLT's Cordell Awards firstly for the years 2000 to 2002, and then from 2009 to 2014, and for a longer period as a reviewer for 3CR's radio programs *Applause, Applause* and *Curtain Up*.

Chapter One

1946-1956: From Imports to 'All Local' Productions

The nine people who assembled at the Mechanics' Institute in Electra Street on 23 May 1946 were Ted Cordell, Ernest Grieve, Sarah Donaldson, Margaret and Hamilton Mathews, Bruce MacAllister, Alec Sinclair, Win Stewart and Bill Ward. The idea of establishing a theatre in Williamstown occurred to several members of a university extension class meeting in the bayside suburb after they went to see a performance by the Arts Theatre Players at their theatre in Post Office Place in Melbourne. Struck by the paucity of the audience, they decided that their local Mechanics' Institute was far superior to the Playgoers' Hall with as good a stage and an ability to accommodate larger audiences. They reckoned that a theatre movement in Williamstown was a venture worth pursuing.

Dorothy Porter provided an account of the Movement's beginnings in an early (Christmas 1962) edition of *Cues and News*. Dorothy Hughes, as she then was, came to the Movement's fourth meeting. She had attended a course run by the Workers' Educational Association (WEA), which had engaged Max Nicholson, at the time a producer for the Marlowe Society, to conduct a drama course entitled 'From Shakespeare to Shaw'. She wrote:

> *It was as a result of this course that I was asked to join a play reading group that had just started at the Cordells' before the theatre was born. I remember how impressed I was by the urgency - we must start a theatre and we must put on the best plays.*

The Movement got off to a flying start. Within a week of the first meeting, the group had arranged for Gertrude Johnson's National Theatre to bring its production of *The Barretts of Wimpole Street* to Williamstown on 29 June.

This sent the Movement into a flurry of activity. Publicity was organised, admission set at two shillings and five pence, 400 tickets printed and working bees arranged to spruce up the Mechanics' Institute. All four hundred tickets were sold. Many people had to be turned away. Win Stewart, Secretary from 1947 to 1957, recorded in her Theatre scrapbook that the 'house full' sign had to be put out. The Williamstown Little Theatre Movement had achieved overnight success or, as *Williamstown Advertiser* wrote, somewhat understating the impact of the event on the local community: 'The size and keenness of the audience show that a demand for this worthwhile kind of entertainment exists in Williamstown.' Alec Colville noted wryly that the demand might have been inflated by the fact that a projectionists' strike had closed the picture theatres.[7]

The arrival of theatre in Williamstown affected residents in different ways. As Reg Gillam, a well-known National Theatre actor of the time who appeared in that first production, recalled:

> *Ray Lawler, Richard Benyon and I were three of the Barrett brothers. We were dressed in our Victorian costumes, sitting in these huge leather chairs in the ornate library next to the hall, waiting for our cue to go on for our last scene. Then some poor, benighted man came in to change his books. He looked around and saw all these Victorian gentlemen, with side whiskers, staring silently at him. A look of absolute horror came over his face and he fled as fast as he could from the ghosts!*[8]

Flushed with its initial success, the Movement pushed on with great

---

7 The strike related to a claim by the projectionists for double pay and an extra day's holiday for working on Victory Day. The complication was that the decision to strike at all theatres was not announced until close to 7.30 pm on the evening of 29 June when, as *The Age* put it on 1 July 1946, 'most theatres were definitely half full'. Even the *Adelaide Mail* (29 June 1946) picked up the story reporting that 'Many cinemas were filled when the men's decision was announced (and) hundreds of disappointed people then flocked to swell the crowds at stage shows, concerts and dance halls', seemingly confirming Colville's view.

8 Frank Van Stratten, *NATIONAL TREASURE, The Story of Gertrude Johnson and the National Theatre*, (Melbourne, Victoria Press, 1994), p. 97

energy. Its strategy was to bring to Williamstown current productions by the several established semi-professional groups which then existed in Melbourne. Immediately after the Second World War, the borders between amateur and professional theatre in Melbourne were blurred, providing a rich pool of theatrical resources. As Keith Maurice, drama critic of the (now defunct) *Argus*, commented in 1948, 'the theatre conscious public in Melbourne [had] a wide choice of repertory productions to tide it over arid patches in professional theatre'.

Repertory or little theatre in Melbourne was strong in the post-war period because it provided opportunities for aspiring local actors, denied access to opportunities in commercial productions by managements obsessed by imported stars. A lot of little theatres were amateur in the sense that established or aspiring professionals worked there for no money but purely for the love of their craft. Melbourne had three such groups at the time: Brett Randall's Melbourne Little Theatre, Gertrude Johnson's National Theatre, and the radical New Theatre, all of which had been established in the 1930s and had survived the vagaries of the 1939-45 War. It was to these companies and the skills of their directors such as Alf Davidson, Alec Doig and Neville Thurgood that Williamstown turned to lay the foundations of its own theatrical endeavours. By the end of 1946 (as shown in Table 1), four separate companies had brought productions to Williamstown's Mechanics' Institute on behalf of the Movement after their original seasons elsewhere in Melbourne.

These imported productions provided opportunities for members of the Movement to get involved. Members loaned their period furniture for the set of *The Barretts of Wimpole Street*. As Win Stewart commented, 'We got used to seeing our furniture on the stage!', while Trevor McKay who worked at the local library, helped build the set for *Acacia Avenue* and was rewarded by the company with a party to celebrate his 21st birthday.

Persuading companies to perform in Williamstown wasn't always easy. When Alex Sinclair first approached Brett Randall about bringing his Melbourne Little Theatre across the river, he received this note of caution in a letter:

While very glad of the opportunity at all times to create an interest in the theatre by paying visits to various centres, I am very particular about the

Table 1: WLTM: Productions Brought to the Williamstown Mechanics' Institute in 1946

Date	Company	Play
29th June	National Theatre	*The Barretts of Wimpole Street* by Rudolf Besier
17 August	Melbourne University Dramatic Club	*Ghosts* by Henrik Ibsen
14 September	Victorian Operatic Society	*The Beggar's Opera* by Johann Christopher Pepusch and John Gay
5 October	Melbourne Little Theatre	*Acacia Avenue* by Denis and Mabel Constanduros

conditions under which we would have to play, for the reason that theatre must be presented to the very best advantage at a time when really the general public is more or less apathetic. The staging of a play is most important... I don't mean in regard to the size of the stage, but to the atmosphere that can be given to the presentation.

Randall inspected the Mechanics' Institute and was satisfied, thereby vindicating the Movement's view of its superior facilities, and agreed that his company would perform there on October 5th for £20, plus payment for transport of both the company and properties.

Actually, Randall had reason to envy Williamstown for its excellent venue. The Mechanics' stage was much larger than his own theatre's fifteen by twelve feet space, and its large proscenium arch facilitated the construction of impressive sets. The photograph over the page of the set for WLT's first 'all local' production, *Man of Destiny* on 13 November 1948, suggests that this feature of the Mechanics' Institute was effectively exploited from the very beginning. And while the building regularly attracted the attention of the local health department, concerned about the hessian curtains and the

Set for *Man of Destiny* 13 November 1948

lighting arrangements, Williamstown Little Theatre never had to advise patrons to bring cushions, rugs and hot water bottles as colleagues in the Frankston Theatre Group had to in their early days.

By the end of 1946, the Movement had made a very promising beginning. The Committee declared that its aim for the following year - somewhat ambitious as it turned out - was to hold shows 'at intervals of not less than one month'. It approached the National Theatre, Melbourne Little Theatre, the Victorian Operatic Society, the University Dramatic Club, the Tin Alley Players, the New Theatre and the Melbourne Repertory Theatre for contributions. Melbourne Little Theatre started WLT's 1947 season on 1 March with Cyril Campion's *Lady Killer*. This was followed on 26 April by another National Theatre production, *Storm in the Haven*, an early piece by Ray Lawler, described in publicity as a 'rising young Footscray author for whom a bright future is predicted'! On 26 July came the New Theatre production of *Physician in Spite of Himself* and *Woman Bites Dog* by Bella and Samuel Spewack, and on 23 August the National Theatre's staging of *Springtime for*

Henry by Ben Levy. Also on the Movement's 1947 playbill was a music and ballet show, a Gilbert and Sullivan Society of Victoria production of *Iolanthe*, (which surprisingly resulted in a heavy financial loss), a series of three play readings, and a produced reading of J.B. Priestley's *They Came to a City*.

As shown in Table 2, the Movement continued importing shows, though in decreasing numbers, through to 1951. The Gilbert and Sullivan Society's performances of their namesakes' operettas proved highly popular amongst Williamstown audiences. Four Society productions came to the Mechanics' Institute for the Movement between 1948 and 1950.

Table 2: WLTM: Productions Brought to the Williamstown Mechanics' Institute 1948-1951

Date	Company	Play/Operetta
6 March 1948	National Theatre	*Jupiter Laughs* by A.J. Cronin
6 June 1948	Gilbert and Sullivan Society	*HMS Pinafore*
14 August 1948	CAE Drama Group	*The Importance of Being Earnest* by Oscar Wilde
4 December 1948	Gilbert and Sullivan Society	*The Sorcerer*
12 March 1949	*Shell Company Dramatic Club**	*The Quiet Weekend* by Esther Mc Cracken
3 December 1949	Gilbert and Sullivan Society	*Patience*
24 November 1950	Gilbert and Sullivan Society	*The Mikado*
24 August 1951	Melbourne Repertory Theatre	*Cockpit* by Brigid Boland

*This was organised by WLT Treasurer Bill Ward who worked for Shell.

Importing shows gave the Movement plenty of experience in the management of productions, from staging to publicity and box office, to organising front of house and suppers for cast, company officials and members. The group's knowledge of, and interest in, theatre was supported by a play-reading group convened by Alec Doig which met each Wednesday to read playscripts borrowed from the newly established library of the Council of Adult Education (C.A.E). More significantly, the play readings shifted the Movement further towards its stated goal of staging its own productions.

The proportion of 'imported' productions at Williamstown peaked as early as 1947. Over the next four years 'all-local' productions steadily increased, starting with a single one-act play in 1948, building up to two and three night seasons of full length plays in 1950 and 1951. The shows were cast almost entirely with local actors and most sets were designed by Trevor McKay. Productions were overseen by Alf Davidson, a local resident and actor/producer with the National Theatre. Alf continued to produce for the theatre until his untimely death from cancer in 1951.

As already noted, Williamstown's first 'all-local' offering on 13 November 1948 was *The Man of Destiny*, George Bernard Shaw's one-act play about Napoleon Bonaparte holed up in an Italian inn after inflicting a major defeat on the Austrian army. Produced by Alf Davidson, the cast was Ted Cordell as Napoleon, Dorothy Hughes as The Strange Lady, Jim Davey as Giuseppe Grandi and Jack Gravell as a lieutenant. Ivor Porter was prompt and Trevor McKay designed the set. Because it was a one-act play, *Man of Destiny* was combined with a short program of ballet organised by Margaret Frey. This first production was a success and even made a small profit. Receipts totalled £25 18s 9d. Expenditure, including £5 5s each to the Mechanics' Institute for the use of the hall and to Miss Frey for her ballet, totalled £25 15s 8d, leaving the theatre with a princely surplus of three shillings and a penny. It was a start!

On 17 September 1949, Williamstown staged its second 'all local' production, *People at Sea*, a one-act play by J B Priestley with leading roles played by Ivor Porter, William (Bill) Ward and Tony Lindsay. This was followed by two performances of *And No Birds Sing* in November, for which the theatre took the radical step of discounting first night tickets by 50% to encourage attendance. There was drama in the lead up to the production when the original director Alf Davidson had to retire because of illness, but Alec Doig 'ably completed the work'. The twelve-person cast of this comedy by John Fernald and Jenny Laird included many actors who became stalwarts of the theatre on and off the stage: Pamela Silk, Ivor Porter, Dorothy Hughes, Tony Lindsay, Ella Bambery, Ted Cordell, Eric Black and Marion Becroft.

Each won plaudits from the reviewers in both *Williamstown Advertiser* and *Williamstown Chronicle*. Pam Silk, for example, played the role of the unhappy Pauline Banks 'with restraint and skill: her training as a drama student was shown in the carrying quality of her voice'. Tony Lindsay and Dorothy Hughes 'with experienced competency obtained the maximum amount of comedy from their parts', while Ivor Porter as Albert Briggs 'was a most convincing character', and Ella Bambery 'played her part with skill and experience'.

By 1950, the Movement had consolidated its role as a provider of theatrical entertainment in the Williamstown area. Its three productions that year were *Poison Pen* by Richard Llewellyn in March, Philip Johnson's comedy *Lovely to Look At* in July, and *A Murder Has Been Arranged* by Emlyn Williams in October. From the embryonic WLT's point of view, the special value of

People at Sea, 17 September 1949
Ivor Ivor Porter as Ritpon, William Ward as Mills, and Tony Lindsay as Frank Jefferson.

these plays was that they required large casts: *Poison Pen* had fourteen and the other two nine and eight respectively. The productions received generally favourable reviews.

Of *Poison Pen*, for example, 'CAH' wrote in the *Williamstown Chronicle* that producer Alf Davidson had avoided the 'whodunit' atmosphere and thus 'achieved a considerable success'. CAH thought many of the large cast performed well: Gillian Witt, for example, 'gave a stylish performance of the difficult part of Mrs Reynolds', David Witt, Fullergrave-Rees, 'extracted everything possible from his part', and Alec Doig 'though at first somewhat indecisive, warmed up to give a fine picture of a local squire'. In addition, Alf Davidson as Griffin and Eric Black as Hurrin 'convincingly played their parts as villagers caught in the web drawn by the poison pen'. Ron Little noted that Alec Doig's production of *A Murder Has Been Arranged*, which he thought a difficult play, 'held the attention of the audience throughout' with good performances from Marion Becroft and Tony Lindsay.

The role of the critic is generally regarded by most theatre companies as a necessary evil. From the earliest days, Williamstown Little Theatre embraced what many leaders in theatre such as Sir Peter Brook regard as vital to artistic success, the presence within the company of a well-informed, constructive critic with a view of what the theatre could be and should be.[9] In 1950 Williamstown had two people doing the job: Clive Hughes, father of Dorothy, whose reviews signed CAH appeared in *Williamstown Chronicle*, and Ron Little, who reviewed for *Williamstown Advertiser*. Both were well qualified for the job: Hughes was an English teacher at the local high school with an M.A. from Melbourne University, a rare qualification in those days. Little had acted with the Melbourne Little Theatre before the Second World War, and after returning from his war service, he took advantage of the Commonwealth Reconstruction Training Scheme to enrol in a drama course at the Melbourne Conservatorium of Music, gaining a Licentiate in Speech and Drama. Both men were appropriately critical when necessary. Clive Hughes, for example thought his daughter's performance as the frustrated Phryne in *Poison Pen* 'impressive...marred only by her tendency to become strident in moments of emotional stress'. Similarly, whilst Ron Little thought the set for *Poison Pen*

---

9   See Peter Brook, *The Empty Space*, (London, Penguin Books 1990), p.37.

'well done by Trevor McKay...who is showing much skill in this work', the lighting 'particularly from the side and footlights, was not directed to best advantage'. In his review of *A Murder Has Been Arranged*, Ron Little saw room for improvement in the acting of both Dorothy Hughes and Gillian Witt.

The critical reaction to the box office success *Lovely to Look At* (which was booked out the day bookings opened), was more uniformly positive. Clive Hughes commented that director Alf Davidson 'showed commendable faith in the ability of his actors to tackle work which would have taxed far more experienced players'. That he achieved a reasonable measure of success speaks well for his skill, and the ability and industry of his leading players - Marjorie Rae playing Sonia, David Witt as Simon, Ella Bambery who 'brought to the role of Amy Verity her natural verve backed by the experience of a veteran', and Ted Cordell, 'who found, in Robert Verity, a role which exactly suited his vigorous personality'. Ron Little felt that 'the cast did a splendid job'.

Ron Little's early involvement in Williamstown Little Theatre gives a keen insight to some of the dilemmas confronting a fledgling amateur company. The first of three productions staged in 1951 was Noël Coward's *This Happy Breed*. The opening night of the play was marred somewhat by the annual meeting of the Rover Football Club going on next door in the supper room of the Mechanics' Institute. Perhaps the actors had trouble hearing, since Ron noted in his review a 'slowness of tempo (pace being a critical requirement of success with Coward's work), a failure to pick up on cues, and quite a bit of prompting'. After running through individual performances, Ron remarked that greater use of facial expressions and easier deportment would have helped Ivor Porter, cast as the happy-go-lucky sailor Billy, in his love scenes with Queenie, played by Dorothy Hughes. No doubt Ivor took this criticism to heart. By happy chance, he and Dorothy, along with two other members of the cast, Pam Silk and Eric Black, married a fortnight later.

Ron raised another dilemma confronting any theatre company, fledgling or established, in his comments on the next play, William Douglas Home's tilt at British party politics, *The Chiltern Hundreds*. The play had recently been made into a film. In his review Ron discussed the merits or otherwise of a theatre company presenting a work that was currently doing the rounds on the big screen. To his credit, Ron avoided making comparisons (although the Committee didn't entirely think so) and concentrated on performances.

Williamstown Little Theatre

The Chiltern Hundreds, June 1951
Ella Bambery as the Countess of Lister, Marion Becroft as June Farrell (of the American Embassy), Ted Cordell (seated) as The Earl of Lister, and Robert Hawdon as Beecham.

Generally, he thought the cast of Ted Cordell, Lorraine Davey, W. McKee Smith, Robert Hawdon, Marion Becroft and Ella Bambery had coped well, which is more than can be said for some ducks who appeared in the production; they unfortunately died of botulism.

The final production for 1951, J.B.Priestley's *Mystery at Greenfingers* was written specially for an amateur company, and, according to the WLT program, first performed by Bournemouth Little Theatre at the Fortune Theatre in London on 18 January 1938. It was a controversial choice. Little, with a keen eye for what he obviously believed Williamstown to be capable of, thought the play wasn't up to scratch. In a letter to the Movement's then Secretary, Eric Black, Ron raised another important issue for any amateur company:

> *Many people throw up their hands in horror if they hear that an amateur group is doing a play which sounds ambitious. 'My dear, they can't possibly do it.' How often have we heard that? If groups become too obsessed with what they 'can possibly do' they will put an end to their progress.*

Ron went on to state that he believed *Mystery at Greenfingers* to be a 'poor play' because Priestley appeared to be attempting both a satire on the detective story and to enter the field himself '... and he is no Agatha Christie'.

Ron's comments seem to have been vindicated by Clive Hughes' review: a few of the cast failed to appreciate Priestley's intentions, Hughes wrote (to the extent they were clear), but the tempo and ease showed marked improvement. Ever the constructive critic, Ron thought the production smooth and efficient, and the acting generally good, yet with scope for improvement. To quote Little in full:

> *Each member of the Company was well-cast and appeared to have no difficulty in playing the character allotted to them. Eric Black contributed a good character study as the French chief Arnold Jordan with appropriate accent and gesture. He would have done better still if he had refrained from drawing attention to his padding by touching it frequently. Many of the best lines of the play fell to the lot of Marion Becroft as the cynical Miss Edna Saunders, who never failed to register her points.*

Clive Hughes thought Marion Becroft 'played a difficult part with the aplomb of an old trouper'.

Little commented further that:

> *Dorothy Porter and Lorraine Davey were two amusing and well contrasting maids and David Witt (Keith Henley, The Manager) and Ella Bambery (Rose Heaton) gave natural performances...Priestley evidently intended Robert Crowther to be a tilt at fictitious detectives and Edward Cordell played him along these lines. Jenny Stewart could have infused more variety into the role of Miss Tracey if she had varied the tempo of her dialogue, particularly on her exit lines which could have been speeded up.*

1951 saw three important developments for the Movement as theatre managers:

- Firstly, a subscription scheme, the life blood of most amateur companies, was introduced. A single subscription at 10/6 entitled the subscriber to one seat for each of four productions a year, and a double subscription at £1/1/0 bought two seats. Forty subscriptions were sold in that first year. Three weeks before each production vouchers were issued to subscribers which they exchanged for tickets at the booking office, then located at Eddie Marr's Music and Radio Centre in Ferguson Street.

- Secondly, the Theatre also decided it was time for its first audience survey. The simple seven-item questionnaire was included as the back page of the *Mystery at Greenfingers* program. The answers revealed the audience to be interested in 'comedy, drama and the classics'.
- Thirdly, the Theatre secured a grant from the Victorian Government. In his 1948 budget speech, the Premier and Treasurer R. B. Holloway announced an annual subsidy of £15,200 to establish, in conjunction with the ABC, a State symphony orchestra, £10,000 to continue and extend the program of concerts organised under the 'Music for the Peoples scheme', and £25,000 'to assist in such other cultural development as may help enrich the lives of the people of the State'[10]. Williamstown Little Theatre approached Williamstown MLA John Lemmon with its submission, securing a grant of £200. This then not inconsiderable sum bought forty-five framed tier-stack steel chairs with canvas back and seats, which were, by all accounts, very comfortable.

One final event in 1951 which helped put Williamstown Little Theatre on Melbourne's theatrical map was the inaugural conference of the Amateur Dramatic Societies of Victoria, held on October 12. Williamstown was represented at this important occasion by Eric and Pamela Black. An initiative of Colin Badger, the conference determined to form the Victorian Drama League (VDL), an organisation which has served Melbourne's amateur

---

10   *Victorian Parliamentary Debates*, 10 August 1948, p.2225. This 'Premier's Vote for Cultural Development' undermines the oft-repeated view started by A.L. McLeod in his *The Pattern of Australian Culture*, (Melbourne, Oxford University Press, 1963), p.314, that until the 1960s 'there was no expenditure of public moneys ... in support of the drama and theatre'.

theatrical community continuously ever since.[11]

The Williamstown Little Theatre Movement had come a long way in its first five years. Its founding members had largely succeeded in what they aimed to do. Clive Hughes had concluded his review of *Lovely to Look at* in July 1950 with the comment that: 'The excellent audiences obtained at both performances prove that the citizens of Williamstown are beginning to realise that we have in our town an amateur group which can stand comparison with most in Melbourne.'

As already noted, the Movement had one major advantage compared with other fledgling amateur theatre groups in Melbourne – access to the Williamstown Mechanics' Institute with its reasonably large stage and capacious auditorium, together with its cottage at the rear. They did not have to face what Harold Baigent in his survey of Amateur Theatre in Victoria in 1964 described as the major handicap facing other non-professional groups at the time: 'the inadequacy of the buildings in which they have to perform their plays,' most being 'multi-purpose halls ill equipped for the presentation of stage productions'.[12]

From 1952 the Movement's members built on the foundations already laid, enjoying five years of vigorous growth. The company was beginning to get a feel for its audience and build up its repertoire. As noted, the survey circulated during *Mystery at Greenfingers* had revealed a diverse range of tastes but with a preference for 'comedy, drama and the classics.' In an early statement of what might be regarded as a 'play selection policy', the Theatre decided early in 1952 to alternate comedies and more serious plays in its annual playbill. Over the next five years, the twenty plays staged by the company were split almost evenly between these two major genres.

Williamstown's civic historian, Lynn Strahan, is somewhat dismissive of the Movement's choice of plays in the early years, commenting that it

---

11   For the details of VDL's first 50 years see my *The Victorian Drama League 1952-2002*.

12   See Harold Baigent, Survey of Amateur Theatre in Victoria, mimeograph, Melbourne, Council of Adult Education, 1965, p. 30. As Colin Badger noted, (*Who Was Badger, Aspects of the Life of Colin Robert Badger, Director of Adult Education, Victoria, 1947-1971*, p.126,) many regional cities had no public halls at all, and the town halls built before the Second World War (at Horsham, Swan Hill and Donald), 'lacked facilities for stage presentation'.

'offered performances of *Bonaventure... French for Love, The Importance of Being Earnest, The Matchmaker*, and other plays that entertained without disturbing'.[13] The Movement's play selection committee might have responded by noting that several of their early plays, such as *French for Love* and the earlier *Young Mrs Barrington* had been considered of sufficient merit to have been staged by Melbourne Little Theatre in the 1940s, while others were already part of the 'classic' repertoire.

Williamstown attempted such a 'classic' in its first 'all local season', staging George Bernard Shaw's *Arms and the Man* in November 1952. This was followed in 1955 by a much acclaimed production of Thorton Wilder's Pulitzer-prize winning *Our Town*, claimed by some as America's 'most read and most produced play'.[14] In the first half of 1956 the Theatre staged Shaw's *Pygmalion* and Emlyn Williams' psychological thriller *Night Must Fall* in succession as its first two productions. WLT's audiences were getting much more than froth and bubble. Perhaps as a consequence, public support grew. The Theatre's audience in its first 'all local' season in 1952 was around 3,000. By 1955 audience numbers reached 3436 and grew by a further 300 in 1956. To some degree this growth was a result of progressively increasing play runs. In 1956, starting with *Night Must Fall*, Williamstown extended its standard run to six nights, largely in response to audience demand: as *Williamstown Chronicle* noted on 27 April 1956, 'the Theatre had no alternative but to do this'.

The energy Williamstown ploughed into developing talent was one of the key factors in its success between 1952 and 1956. Choosing plays with large casts ensured that its performers were given every opportunity. The company continued an extensive program of play readings, some of which were produced, recognising the important role they play in developing actors' talents and sustaining the interest of members not directly involved in a current production.

The Theatre became increasingly confident of its ability to stage its own

---

13   Lynne Strahan, *At the Edge of the Centre, A History of Williamstown*, (Williamstown, Hagreen Publishing Company in conjunction with the City of Williamstown, 1994), p.397

14   See Martin Banham ed., *The Cambridge Guide to Theatre*, revised paperback edition 1992, p.1073.

shows. From 1952, instead of importing productions, it imported talented producers (as directors of plays were then called), notably Paul Hill and Alan Money who between them directed three quarters of Williamstown's productions between 1952 and 1955. Alan Money was also responsible for the highly successful *Pygmalion* which opened the 1956 season. These men were then two of the most experienced directors of theatre in Melbourne. Hill had been a member of Brett Randall's Melbourne Little Theatre, a music and voice production teacher at the Melba Conservatorium of Music, and a producer at Northcote Dramatic Society for seventeen years, as well as at Box Hill and in Tasmania. Money was equally well known. He had studied drama at the Conservatorium and was known as one of its most accomplished performers. There he met Ron Little who enticed him to Williamstown.

It was, however, Neville Thurgood who kicked off the 1952 season. Thurgood was an experienced actor and director, having started his stage career at the age of twelve in England performing for ENSA, the forces wartime entertainment unit. He was associated with the National Theatre, was Victorian president of Actors' Equity for more than eighteen years and later founded Plinge's Music Hall, which toured Victoria and New South Wales in the 1970s and 1980s.[15] Such background stood Williamstown in good stead as it staged the Australian premiere of Joan Temple's *Deliver My Darling*.

Ron Little was gratified to see the company take a 'bold step to attempt a play which is much deeper than the average popular play', and felt the audience's reaction justified the choice. Little continued: 'The prologue, played by Jenny Stewart (Martha Kinsey) and Marion Becroft (Lydia) effectively created the dramatic atmosphere of the play, and the dimly lit scene provided good contrast for the séance that followed. Mr Thurgood's introduction of music at each curtain further enhanced the atmosphere.' All the actors, Little thought, had scope for improvement. Marion Becroft in the leading role 'gave a competent performance…although her voice was a little light for some of the more dramatic passages'. Although Gordon Young's performance as Sammy, the village idiot, 'lacked the polish of an experienced performer, it was detailed and convincing'. Gillian Witt's Miss Glee was 'an excellent

---

15   For this information on Thurgood, see his own book on the history of music hall entertainment, *Good Evening, Ladies and Gentlemen*, Richmond, Spectrum Publications, 1988.

little character study which could have been improved by a little more facial expression during periods when she had no dialogue'. Ivor Porter as Jim 'had sincerity, although he was a trifle wooden' and 'Pamela Black made a dignified Mrs Frayis but had some difficulty conveying middle age'.

Clive Hughes basically agreed with Little about the variable quality of the acting. He noted, however, that 'the local audience had shown its approval by filling the house on each of the three nights of the play' and reiterated his earlier view that 'this company is reaching a standard equal to that of any amateur troupe in Melbourne'.

Ron Little directed the next two Williamstown productions, challenging the fates by staging Noël Coward's *Blithe Spirit*, then familiar to audiences though the cinema. Clive Hughes thought the production 'thoroughly enjoyable' though he thought the tempo could have been improved a little. Hughes gave Little credit for choosing Australian playwright Betty Roland's *The Touch of Silk,* originally written in 1928, as his next offering. This play, which Hughes regarded as 'somewhat loose and flimsy', concerns the relationship between Jim, a sheep farmer in the Mallee struggling in a drought, his homesick French war-bride Jeanne, and Jim's mother. Jim is also suffering the psychological effects of his involvement in the First World War. Jim's mother and the townsfolk are suspicious of Jeanne's 'foreign' ways. In a moment of despair, Jeanne buys some silk lingerie from a travelling salesman who knows Paris. This provokes a brawl where the salesman Cliff is killed. Jim is charged with his murder.

Reviewing the production, Clive Hughes thought that Ron Little hadn't quite achieved the deftness of touch required to make 'a gloomy and savage study of the effects of prejudice, intolerance and the hard conditions of pioneering life,' such as *The Touch of Silk*, work. The first act he thought was 'painfully long', but that 'Mr Little's tempo for the second and third acts was worthy of all praise, and audience reaction clearly showed his success'. The acting was mixed, though Joan Melmoth in the lead role scored Williamstown's first acting triumph. To quote Hughes:

> After the last show, the Chronicle suggested that we hoped to see more of Joan Melmoth, but even the producer must have been amazed to see an inexperienced girl lift a mediocre play to the level of real drama. Miss Melmoth is to be congratulated on a competent and restrained performance

of a part that could easily be overplayed. As Jeanne, she made this play.

Mary Little began her long, still-continuing association with WLT in *The Touch of Silk*. Nell Colville was originally cast in the role of Mrs Davidson, but became ill. Mary was asked to stand in by the director who was already in love with her - her husband Ron. Mary had met Ron at the Melbourne Conservatorium where she was studying an Associate Art of Speech part-time after being considered too young to start teacher training. The daytime Licentiate course members (which, as noted above, included Ron) and the evening classes used to combine to do Shakespearian plays. 'One word led to another' to quote James Joyce,[16] and Mary and Ron married in 1951. Simultaneously with their early involvement at Williamstown, Mary and Ron played a major role in the foundation and development of Strathmore Theatrical Arts Group (STAG); the early meetings of this group were held in their home in Bruce Street.[17]

The final production for 1952 was Bernard Shaw's *Arms and the Man*. Enter, centre stage, director Paul Hill. In a 'hurried note' (of four typed pages!) he wrote to Ivor Porter about 'one or two aspects of the production', Hill revealed himself to be the 'complete director', concerned with every aspect of his production. He wanted to 'make this a ding-dong show', and knew well that he was extending the company:

> *...the method I am using is new to the Movement, and it is exhausting, and yet great fun, and the cast is welded together in one division, everyone pulling their weight and no feeling of division, which is a great thing behind stage. I want the stage staff to be the same...*

Like all good directors, he was prepared for the worst:

> *I shall probably pass out on the last night – but who cares? Several of the cast are already sharpening their knives and preparing ground glass!*

---

16   James Joyce, *Portrait of the Artist as a Young Man*, Penguin Edition, London 1992, p.75.

17   See Cheryl Threadgold, *In the Name of Theatre, The History, Culture and Voices of Amateur Theatre in Victoria*, p.258.

Arms and the Man, 1952: L to R: Lorraine West as Louka, (Seated): Ella Bambery as Catherine, Jim Davey as Major Paul Petkoff (Standing at Back): Eric Black, as The Man, Gillian Wadds as Raina, Peter Henry as Major Sergius Saranoff. (Standing at Front) Keith Craven (blurred) as Major Peechanoff, and Gordon Young as Nicola.

Hill's dedication and commitment was rewarded by a most successful production. The season was extended from three to four nights. Ron Little thought it delightful and Clive Hughes considered it the Movement's best show of 1952, congratulating the company for 'showing that the city (Williamstown) can produce a body of competent actors and experienced actors capable of handling all types of drama'. Though Hughes thought the acting to be of 'even standard', the honours went to James Davey as Major Paul Petkoff, 'a first-rate comic characterisation'. Ella Bambery as his wife Catherine 'gave a competent performance'. Likewise Peter Henry 'making a very effective debut at Williamstown' as Major Sergius Saranoff, offering a splendid contrast to Eric Black's Captain Blunnchli, the professional soldier who 'fights when he has to and is glad to get out of it when he hasn't'.

By the end of its first 'all-local' season, the Williamstown Little Theatre Movement could look back with considerable satisfaction. As well as successfully mounting four main productions, the Williamstown Thespians continued with their weekly play readings, several of which were transformed into produced readings, setting a pattern which continued for several years.

The first of these occurred on 30 May 1952 when Ted Cordell produced a program of three one-act plays: Harold Chapin's *It's the Poor That Helps the Poor*, T.B. Morris's comedy *Apple Pie Order*, and Stanley Houghton's *The Dear Departed*. In 1953, the Northcote Dramatic Society brought to the Mechanics' Institute a produced reading of Frederick Lonsdale's *Canaries Sometimes Sing*, directed by Paul Hill. The extant records suggest that in 1954 there were four such events, usually held in the reading room of the Mechanics' Institute. Another followed in 1955 and two more in 1956 (see Table 3).

Patrons could see the Movement's leading actors and others strut their stuff for a donation of 2/6. The presentation of *The Strolling Clerk from Paradise* enabled the Movement's local audience to view the play with which it had secured fourth place in the VDL drama festival (see Table 4 p. 38).

The nineteen-fifties also saw the Movement regularly taking productions 'on the road'. This practice had commenced in 1950 when *Lovely to Look At* travelled to Bright where the father of the Movement's Secretary, Eric

Table 3: Produced Play Readings by
the Williamstown Little Theatre Movement 1954-1956

Date	Play/Operetta
26 February 1954	*The Late Edwina Black* by William Dinner
9 April 1954	*Fumed Oak* and *Hands Across the Sea* by Noël Coward
3 June 1954	*Love in Albania* by Eric Linklater
10 September 1954	*A Phoenix Too Frequent* by Christopher Fry and *The Strolling Clerk from Paradise* by Hans Sach
25 March 1955	*The Wind of Heaven* by Emlyn Williams
29 April 1956	*Fountains Beyond* by George Landen Dann
8 June 1956	*Venus Observed* by Christopher Fry

Black, was the local bank manager. Subsequently, their last production for 1951, *Mystery at Greenfingers*, was staged in St Albans and at the Greenvale Sanatorium.

All 1952 productions toured as did *Young Mrs Barrington* and *Mountain Air* in 1953. The practice continued for several years, travelling as far afield as Eltham and Ballarat, where the company staged performances for the patients of the Ballarat Mental Hospital in 1957 and 1958.

Another tradition established early in the Theatre's life was an annual informal gathering of members in the 'off-season'. Win Stewart's record of the first ten years includes photographs of 'WLTM's picnics' in February at places as diverse as the Lakeside at Emerald in February 1953, Eltham in 1954 and Toorourrong Reservoir in February 1956. There is no record of such a picnic in 1955, but a Christmas Party was held at the Mechanics' Institute for members and supporters on 18 December 1954.

In the week before its staging of *Arms and the Man*, in October 1952, the Williamstown Movement, along with seventeen other amateur theatre groups from across Victoria, participated in the first festival of one-act plays organised by the just established Victorian Drama League in cooperation with the Frankston Theatre Group[18]. Williamstown's contribution was Geoffrey Skelton's *Have You Seen My Lady?*, directed by Neville Thurgood. The cast for this play was Nell Colville, Joan Melmoth, Ken Withers and Alec Colville. The rapid growth of the VDL festival from seventeen entries in 1952 to thirty-one when hosted by Williamstown in 1956 was one indicator of the burgeoning significance of amateur theatre around Melbourne and Victoria in the first half of the 1950s.[19]

Williamstown's 1953 program started with W. Cheetham Strode's *Young Mrs Barrington*, a drama about the difficulties married couples face adjusting to living together again after years of separation during the Second World War. The theatre publicity noted that the play, first staged at London's Wintergarden theatre on 5 September 1945, had been a London success, though Clive Hughes regarded it as 'somewhat loose and flimsy'. Paul Hill had some

---

18 The League was formed on 3 May 1952. See my *The Victorian Drama League 1952-2002*, p.4

19 See Ibid., pp12-13.

difficulty choosing which of *Young Mrs Barrington* and *The Barton Mystery* he should produce but, having taken *Young Mrs Barrington* to Hobart with him to read ('smuggling her in my luggage'), he 'felt that it had something to say' and so recommended it to Ivor Porter as the first play for 1953.

Young Mrs Barrington launched Williamstown's second 'all local' season very well. As *Williamstown Chronicle* reported: 'The attendance at the first Little Theatre production for 1953 broke all previous records. Over the four nights a total of nearly 850 people were present.'

The play, however, presented several problems. Whilst very topical in the immediate post-war period, and, in Ron Little's opinion, 'far from dated' in 1953, the piece is very wordy in the early scenes. In Little's view, this caused problems in the Williamstown production which 'was rather accentuated in this presentation by a slowness on the part of the cast. They did not reach the right tempo until the play began to build up to its climax'. Moreover:

> *There was also a tendency for the players to be too subdued and intimate for a theatre as large as the Mechanics' Institute. This applied chiefly to Jenny Stewart and Joan Melmoth as Mrs. Barrington and Nancy Barrington. No doubt they were heard everywhere, but more volume would have given them greater strength and made them sufficiently larger than life.*

The balance of the cast was considered generally good. Little thought that Neil Fitzpatrick, as Arthur Barrington 'provided an object lesson in all branches of acting for the whole cast'.[20] Second only to him was Gordon Young, 'whose characterisation of an amiable drunk Tim Acland compared favourably with many Guy Middleton has done in films'. David Witt invested 'Martin Barrington with all the charm and personality that the author implies.' These views were generally endorsed by Clive Hughes who added that 'Ruth Thorsen, as Jo, showed great promise in her debut with the company'.

---

20   Fitzpatrick was perhaps demonstrating the skills which took him to England on an Australian Elizabethan Theatre Trust scholarship in 1964, and thence to The National Theatre in London between 1964 and 1969, before he returned to Australia to act with major theatre companies in the 1970s and 1980s. See Philip Parsons with Victoria Chance eds., *Companion to Theatre in Australia*, (Sydney, Currency Press, 1995), p.230.

Paul Hill also directed Williamstown's second production for 1953, Mary Hayley Bell's *Duet for Two Hands*. As *Williamstown Advertiser's* advance notice for this production noted, this play is 'a drama of the highest suspense, where knowledge of the final outcome undermines the impact of the play'. Hence, as *Williamstown Advertiser* reported: 'Nobody, except the cast and those directly concerned with the production, is allowed to attend rehearsals (because) the producer feels that the fewer the number of people who know the ending of the play, the better the audience reaction.' *Williamstown Advertiser* regarded the play as 'one of the cleverest pieces of dramatic writing that has been presented for many years'. It reported that the noted British actor John Mills 'took London by storm' when he played the lead role in the play in June 1945. Williamstown's cast for the play included five of its best actors of the day: Lorrie McManus, Ngaire McCutcheon, (both making their local debuts), Marion Becroft, Ted Cordell and, in the lead role, Neil Fitzpatrick.

Critical reaction to this production was favourable. As the *Williamstown Advertiser* reviewer put it:

> *This dramatic fantasy set in an 18th century castle in the Orkney Islands, presents many difficulties, but all concerned with the production took them in their stride, and achieved a smooth and in every way impressive interpretation. With the mechanics of the play well taken care of by an efficient back-stage staff, the small cast of five players was able to approach the unfolding of the strange story with full confidence, and each player pulled his or her weight.*

The *Williamstown Advertiser* reviewer thought that the acting honours again went to Neil Fitzpatrick:

> *The plot revolves around Stephen Cass who has his hands amputated after an accident, and a dead man's grafted on in a unique operation. He is haunted by curiosity about this man and feels that he (Cass) is influenced by his personality. This part with all his complexities was expertly handled by Neil Fitzpatrick... His diction was good, and he focused attention on his all-important hands.*

This reviewer also thought that although Ted Cordell had played his role 'strongly, ... (he) could have unfolded the sinister aspects of the character more subtly'. By contrast, *Williamstown Chronicle* awarded highest marks to Cordell for his 'virile playing of the role of the surgeon, Edward Scarlet. By the strength of his performance, he held the play together, and was an inspiration for the more junior players'.

Williamstown's production of *Duet for Two Hands* was sufficiently impressive for the *The Listener-In*, in its annual review of theatre in Melbourne, to nominate it as one of the best amateur productions of 1953. The next production, Ronald Wilkinson's comedy *Mountain Air*, was similarly nominated. *The Argus* reviewer was also impressed, concluding that the production 'compensated for the trek from the City to that part of the hinterland'. The local reviews of this production were also positive with Hughes commenting that 'the Williamstown Little Theatre Movement gave large and appreciative audiences their best laugh for years'. Ron Little's introduction to his review was poetic: 'The play's title is appropriate, as the effect it has on an audience could be compared with a breath of 'mountain air'.' Over the next three years, Williamstown continued to present four plays a year. Consistent with the policy enunciated in 1952, the annual playbills in these years consisted of two comedies and two more serious plays. The reviews suggest that the quality of the productions was progressively improving with WLT's productions regularly receiving honourable mention in the *The Listener-In's* annual review of theatre. Of Williamstown's 1954 program, for example, both Paul Hill's production of Phillip King's *Without the Prince* and Alan Money's staging of Noël Coward's *Red Peppers* were nominated by *The Listener-In* as amongst the best amateur presentations of the year.

The second night of *Without the Prince* generated one of Williamstown's special backstage dramas. As *Williamstown Advertiser* of 20 August 1954 told the story:

> *Miss Gillian Witt opened the back-stage door of the ladies dressing room and challenged a 'peeping Tom'. When the man took refuge in some nearby bushes Miss Witt called for assistance. A London policeman complete in uniform and helmet appeared on the scene and the startled peep went for his life hotly pursued by the law. The policeman was Bruce McAllister, who*

had just changed into his costume for the role of Constable Hawkins.

Of *Red Peppers*, (one of three plays on a single program with Coward's *Still Life* and Gordon Daviot's *Remember Caesar*) Ron Little reported that 'Outstanding performances came from Edward Cordell, Lorrie McManus and Marion Becroft'. After impressing with particularly good period movement as a judge of Charles II reign in *Still Life*, Edward Cordell proved equally at home as the music hall comic, complete with song and dance partner, in *Red Peppers*. His partner in this was Marion Becroft, 'who cut a dainty figure in a sailor's uniform and later in white tie and tails'. Lorrie McManus displayed versatility of a different kind in the leading role in *Still Life* and as the ageing actress 'Mabel Grace' in *Red Peppers*.

Williamstown started 1955 on a high note. Its production of Scottish writer Aimee Stewart's play *Lace on Her Petticoat* attracted the largest audience ever up to that point - 1023. As Win Stewart wrote to Paul Hill when forwarding his production fee and expenses cheque: '*Lace on Her Petticoat* seems to have been one of our most popular plays - people have gone out of their way to tell me how good it was... Marion (Becroft) and Lorraine (Davey) did such a good job that some of the audience had tears in their eyes at the parting scene.' Reviewing the play for *Williamstown Advertiser* on the other hand, Ron Little pointed out some limitations in the production, some arising from the faults in the play itself such as 'long periods of dialogue with little action', and some from the inconsistent Scottish accents. There were two special local aspects of the production noted in the program: a father and son Tom and Keith Craven appeared on stage together, and 'this will be Marion Becroft's last appearance on stage for some time as on April 24 she is sailing for England'.

The next two plays staged by Williamstown, Thorton Wilder's drama *Our Town* and the Moss Hart and George Kaufman comedy, *You Can't Take It With You*, both directed by Alan Money, were particularly important to the company. Both plays require large casts (*Our Town*, twenty-three and *You Can't Take It With You*, nineteen) and quality ensemble playing for their effect. In Williamstown's case, both plays received high critical acclaim.

Our Town came first. As *The Listener-In* reviewer put it, under the headline: 'Top-Class Work in *Our Town*.'

1946 -1956

Our Town August 1955
L to R: Doug Lindsay as The Stage Manager, Gillian Wadds as Emily Witt, and Neil Fitzpatrick as George Gibbs.

The naturalistic technique used by Wilder in this series of dramatised pictures of life in an American country town in the early years of the century was thought very revolutionary when the play was first staged (in 1938). It has since had so many imitations that the novelty has worn off.

Under Alan Money's direction, the Williamstown players succeeded in rolling back the years and creating a realistic reproduction of the homely American scene of the period. They got their effects largely by giving the play naturalistic treatment and avoiding self-conscious staginess.

On the acting side, it seems that the company delivered a real ensemble effort. The *Williamstown Chronicle* reviewer commented that:

The play and the producer demanded maximum effort and ability of the large cast and they unquestionably gave it!

Whilst there was not one weak link in the play there was also no star. Included in the strong cast were popular Little Theatre artists, Lorrie Mc Manus, Winifred Miller, Neil Fitzpatrick, Gillian Witt, George Nichols, Dennis Wain, Jenny Stewart, Doug Lindsay, Ted Cordell and Graeme Murdoch.

It is to the credit of these players that they established the character they were portraying, worked as a team and did not at any stage make the fatal mistake of stealing the show and jarring their audience out of the atmosphere of Grover's Corners, New Hampshire, USA.

You Can't Take it With You scored a special review from Peter O'Shaugnessy, then becoming established as one of Australia's leading actors.[21] He commented in *The Argus* that the company had developed a 'genuine repertory spirit' where 'the actors shone as individuals, not because they aimed at shining, but because they had rooted themselves in the soil of the play until the time came round for them to grow out of it'. O'Shaugnessy thought Williamstown 'should take the plunge and acquire professional status'. Clive Hughes in *Williamstown Chronicle* thought this a 'brilliant production' for which director Alan Money 'must be congratulated on being able to find a cast so large as the play demands and raising it to professional standard. Throughout the play his meticulous care for detail was evident, while timing, lighting and decor was efficient and interesting'. Other reviews were similarly positive. The audiences loved it; it was necessary again to put up the 'House Full' sign on the final night. As *Williamstown Chronicle* reported: 'The Box Office had no alternative but to knock back over fifty prospective bookings on the Saturday morning. Two extra rows were fitted into the theatre on the last night and were snapped up within minutes.'

If things had been going well up until then, 1956 was to prove a bumper year

---

21   O'Shaugnessy had started in amateur theatre in 1941, aged 17, had professional training in England, was a member of the Union Repertory Theatre Company (forerunner of the MTC) in 1954, but became famous for his one man shows that he wrote and devised in the 1950 and 1960s, before going to England again in 1959 to work with the Old Vic in London Bristol. See *Companion to Australian Theatre*, p.420.

for the Theatre. The season opened with George Bernard Shaw's *Pygmalion*, another hit with local audiences as the 'house full' sign went up on the last two nights. In a rare display of munificence, the *Williamstown Chronicle* reviewer had no reservations about the production and particularly praised the leading actors:

> *Newcomer Sue Wilson gives a splendid portrayal of Eliza the flower girl and is equally convincing as Eliza the Princess ... Miss Wilson was always well in control and turned in a brilliant performance. Another newcomer, Murray Tuck, gives just the right comedy touch to Alfred Doolittle, Eliza's father ... So realistic is Doug Lindsay's [as Professor Higgins] clever interpretation that by the end of the performance every female in the audience could cheerfully cut his throat.*

There was an even rarer acknowledgment of the efforts of costume designer and maker Nell Colville and her team of local seamstresses.

> *The frocking ... throughout the whole show is most colourful and it was interesting to learn that all the ladies' frocks were made backstage under the direction of Nell Colville.*

Pygmalion was followed by the drama *Night Must Fall* by the Welsh writer Emlyn Williams. It was a significant production for one of WLT's most promising young actors, Vin Foster, in his second appearance for the company. The *Williamstown Advertiser* reviewer thought Foster 'balanced his ingratiatingly suave manner against the sinister undertones of his purposeful entry into the Bramson household. Never caught out of character, his whole performance was something of a masterpiece'.

The August 1956 production of *Widows are Dangerous*, a flimsy comedy which Judy Garland had made her own, attracted WLT's biggest audience in its first five years - 1,143. The play was directed by Veranne Irving, then a leading Melbourne director and speech teacher. The theatre had made several unsuccessful attempts to entice Ms Irving to direct before finally running her to ground in 1956. She was extremely sympathetic to the Theatre's financial plight, accepting the director's fee without any expenses.

From dangerous widows, WLT went to the other end of the dramatic spectrum with the Australian drama *Pacific Paradise*, a play conceived only two years earlier. At the time Dymphna Cusack wrote it, a hydrogen bomb had just been tested on Bikini Atoll, as a result of which Japanese fishermen were said to have been killed some eighty miles away, and the film *Children of Hiroshima* had just been banned. The play concerns Simon Hoad, a deeply religious man who inherits a Pacific Island from his grandfather and is under pressure to hand it over for atomic experiments. *Pacific Paradise* featured Ted Cordell as Hoad, with Joan Gill as his half-caste daughter, and was directed by David Reid, who received praise for his judicious cutting of what was an otherwise wordy play.

From the comments of various local and 'outside' reviewers, it is apparent that the quality of acting at Williamstown Little Theatre progressively improved between 1952 and 1956. So too did many other aspects of production, in particular the quality of the sets for which Trevor McKay was largely responsible. McKay had no formal training in set design, taking it up as a hobby. Early in the 1950s, he was fortunate to meet the chief designer at Her Majesty's Theatre who became his mentor.[22] Remarkably, he was colour blind, but no matter the extent of his visual handicap from very early on his sets for WLT drew admiration.[23]

Ron Little set the pattern when he complimented McKay on his sets for *A Murder Has Been Arranged* staged by WLT in October 1950. Of the set for *Mystery at Greenfingers* in September 1951, Little commented that: 'Trevor McKay provided an appropriately colourful décor to represent the staff room at a large modern hotel in which the play is set.' Later, of the set for *Mountain Air* in 1953, Clive Hughes suggested that: 'A word of praise must be said for the scenery of Trevor McKay. "A thing of beauty is a joy forever" and Mr McKay has given us something to remember.'[24] In his review of *French for Love* in February 1954 Hughes wrote: 'As usual Trevor McKay's decor was beyond reproach. The company is fortunate to have the services of

---

22 The details about Trevor McKay's extensive involvement in the Arts in Melbourne over many years are taken from Dorothy Porter's obituary on Trevor in *Cues and News*, June 2002

23 The photograph of the set of *French for Love* on p.40 has been chosen to illustrate Trevor McKay's sets and is the best photo of the several available.

24 See *Williamstown Chronicle*, 21 August 1953.

1946 -1956

McKay's set for *French for Love*, February 1954.

so fine a scene expert.' Agon in *The Listener-In* thought that McKay's set for the next production *Ladies in Retirement* 'one of the best sets I have seen for the play, which had genuine period atmosphere for the 1885 story'. McKay's set design activities extended to the Williamstown Light Opera Company and The Ballet Guild. His professional training as a librarian was also useful in developing and maintaining WLT's own collection of plays.

One event in 1956 which helped raise the profile of the theatre in Williamstown and beyond, was its hosting for the first time of the annual Victorian Drama League (VDL) festival of one-act plays. Since its inception in 1952, the festival had always been held at Frankston. However, in 1956, Frankston was rebuilding its theatre and so another venue had to be found.

Williamstown had always been active in the festival entering a play each year (see Table 4 p. 38), achieving equal 4th place in 1953, and, when approached to host the festival, jumped at the opportunity. The festival stretched the company's resources, but with the Mechanics' Institute stage

Table 4: WLTM Entries in the VDL One Act Play Festival at Frankston 1952-1955

Year	Play	Director
1952	*Have You Seen my Lady* by Geoffrey Skelton	Neville Thurgood
1953	*The Strolling Clerk from Paradise* by Hans Sach	Paul Hill
1954	*Remember Caesar* by Gordon Daviot	Paul Hill
1955	*Nelly Lacey and the Bushranger* by Charles Porter	Margaret Hetherington

having just been extended (courtesy of Williamstown Council), the Theatre was particularly well-placed to help the VDL. Thirty-one groups from as far afield as Heyfield, Seymour, Nagambie and Camperdown took part in the festival, with the Frankston Theatre Group, the New Theatre and the Therry Society securing places. Williamstown's own entry was Anton Chekhov's *The Anniversary* directed by Alan Money.

Earlier in 1956 (from August 20 to 25), WLT had also hosted the initial VDL junior one-act play festival, one of the several activities organised by the Williamstown community as part of the celebration of the centenary of the designation of the suburb as a municipality. This festival drew nineteen entries from schools, and junior groups associated with some other Melbourne amateur theatres such as Heidelberg Repertory Group and Belgrave Group Theatre. WLT's entry was *After The Tempest* featuring Grahame Murphy in his 'debut' for the company. Winifred Moverley adjudicated, awarding first place to Heidelberg's entry *Sunday Costs Five Pesos*. Unfortunately, audiences were smaller than expected, 'due to the inclement weather',[25] *The Listener-In* reported.

Perhaps even more satisfying for the theatre was its successful participation

---

25 Melbourne's weather in that week was characterised by regular cold west-to-south-westerly winds and showers, sometimes heavy. The maximum daytime temperatures hovered between 50 and 56 degrees Fahrenheit (10 and 13 degrees Celsius) - see p.7 of *The Age* newspaper for each day of that week.

in the festival of Australian plays organised by the VDL as part of the program of entertainment associated with the staging of the Olympic Games in Melbourne from 22 November to 8 December 1956. Theatre groups were invited to nominate the plays they intended to enter. Foreshadowing the awards system instigated by the VDL in 1997, the nominated plays were performed in the group's own theatre as part of a standard season and a VDL adjudicator visited to assess them. The best three productions were chosen to be repeated at Coppin Hall in Prahran on November 21, 22 and 23. Williamstown's entry was Dymphna Cusack's *Pacific Paradise*, which was chosen to be in the final presentations along with the New Theatre's *Under the Coolibah Tree*, and Canberra Repertory Society's *The Day Before Tomorrow*. Commenting on these productions Laurie Landray, in *Listener-In TV*, noted that whereas the winning play, Canberra Rep's production, had some substance, *Under the Coolibah Tree* was 'a naively old-fashioned piece a bit like *On Our Selection*', and WLT's choice 'undisguised propaganda plus a thin flavour of romance'.[26]

As well as progressively improving the quality of its productions, the Theatre worked hard in other ways to build its audience. *Williamstown Chronicle* helped by making available free of charge its weekly 'Music and the Arts' Column. The Theatre leased a box on the North Williamstown Railway Station to post information about forthcoming productions and other activities, and promoted itself among local clubs and societies, such as the Mission to Seamen, Hobson's Bay Yacht Club and the Animal Welfare Society. Special concession rates were offered to such clubs and societies for Wednesday, Thursday, and Friday night performances: of the 3/6 full ticket price, 1/3 was retained by the group and 2/3 paid to the theatre.[27]

Eddie Marr provided a ticket agency for the Theatre at his radio shop in Ferguson Street. It was here that subscribers could redeem their vouchers for seats and people could make casual bookings. But there was the perennial problem of subscribers and others making group bookings and failing to turn up on the night. Marr proposed a new system from early in 1955, but

---

26 See *Listener-In TV*, December 1-7 1956, pp.1-7

27 The details are contained on page 14 of the program for *Remember Caesar, Still Life and Red Peppers* in November 1954.

still there were problems. The Secretary of the Williamstown Lodge Social Club complained in a letter, that although he'd been advised there would be no problems seating his party, even though the Institute was booked out, 'apparently this was not so'. Nell Colville, then ticket secretary, tried to ameliorate the situation by suggesting a sub-committee be set up to address the problem:

> *Several of our groups have approached me in a definitely hostile manner and I understand the booking clerks have had similar experiences. All this is contrary to the usual friendly atmosphere at the theatre and I feel something must be done.*

Something was indeed done. A new system was set up and, after a trial during *Pacific Paradise*, it was pronounced a success.

The company also attempted to progressively improve facilities at the theatre, particularly for audiences. This was difficult since the Theatre was not responsible for maintaining and upgrading the Institute and had to rely on Williamstown Council. Late in 1952, the council agreed to provide up to £5,000 in its next loan program for reconstruction and general improvements, providing it could obtain authority to place the land and buildings under its control. This took a long time to organise, but with an appropriate sense of theatre, Williamstown's Mayor announced to the inaugural meeting of the Williamstown Arts Council on February 11, 1955 that the council would assume control and spend the promised money. His words were greeted with loud applause.

Soon afterwards, the Theatre pressed the council for urgent repairs to the roof. Heavy rain in March had damaged flats, water poured onto the stage and the tier-stack chairs which had cost the company so much money were being ruined. As the Committee pleaded:

> *Our next production will have to go on without scenery as our decor artist considers that it would be a waste of time and money to do the scenes as it would completely ruin his work. The players and property are likely to need umbrellas if it rains during our next production.*

True to its word, the Council responded promptly and after inspecting the building agreed to repairs being carried out at once. And it didn't stop there. A combined effort of voluntary labour, the Committee of the Mechanics' Institute and the council saw the stage extended five feet and renovations made to the backstage area and the kitchen, all in time for the VDL one act-play festival in November 1956.

Notwithstanding these efforts, the WLTM committee was already on the lookout for its own space. The Committee was discussing the idea of establishing a building fund as early as January 1954, and by the end of that year it had put aside £35 from the 'dues account' into such a fund. When the Free Gardeners building came up for sale in 1955, a special meeting of the Committee was held to discuss the idea of the Theatre making a bid for the property. Such a building could be used for rehearsals, play readings and rehearsed play readings, though there would be a down-side – the Theatre's chairs would still need to be stored at the Mechanics' Institute. Ivor Porter was authorised to bid up to £250 for the property but was unsuccessful.

Lighting at the Institute also needed regular attention. At the first meeting of the Committee in 1952, the matter of lighting was described as 'urgent', and it was reported that electricians were working at the Institute that very evening. The first step was to purchase several 200 watt globes! In June 1953, the Committee agreed to buy extra spotlights, two 500 watt dimmers, four 1,000 watt dimmers and a portable stage switchboard. Permanent wiring between the switches was installed in June 1954. All this work had the desired effect. Bruce McAllister, Williamstown's lighting specialist, was very pleased, reporting that 'people were amazed at the quality of the lighting in an amateur theatre'.

There is an insight into the challenges faced by WLT's early lighting technicians in Alec Colville's lighting report for the August 1956 production of *Widows are Dangerous*. Colville particularly appreciated the work of Veranne Irving, who directed the production.

[Ms Irving] made it apparent that timing, especially at curtain fall, was most important to audience reaction. She went to the trouble of going over the lighting cues until she was sure her requirements were understood. [She was] precise in her requirements and complimentary when good results were

achieved. [However], due to the fact that operation of all the equipment needs the use of two pairs of hands and only one pair of eyes can see the stage, some of the end of act lighting effects were a bit ragged, but apparently this generally went unnoticed by most of the audience.

There were more serious problems, however, which Colville described in some detail in a section of his report titled 'faults':

The most serious fault during the running of the show was the loss of all front of house spots and some of the front borders in the first five minutes of one performance. The lights were supplied by three different boards within the Institute, distributing the load over three internal fuses. Unfortunately, two of the boards came from the same phase of the Williamstown City Council supply. The Gospel Hall over the road, the supper room and the library of the Mechanics, plus at least one private house, were all supplied by the same WCC fuse. The combined load was too much.

Lighting operators worked under some bizarre conditions at that time. Again, the redoubtable Colville provided an extensive description in *Cues and News* in January/February 1972. The Institute's lighting originated from the days of the gasworks in Florence Street, 'which piped its product all the way to Electra Street', Colville recalled:

By the late 1940s ... an elaborate, but somewhat hazardous system of drainpipes, string and saltwater was set up to regulate the energy going to the stage lights. It worked and the expenditure on stage electricians was remarkably small considering the crudeness of the apparatus.

By the 1950s, a nine-outlet board was built. It was so valuable it was locked away above the proscenium between shows and brought out with great ceremony for each 'corroboree'. During the show it was suspended from the rafters on chains, with long leads snaking above the stage and around scenery to various lights. Sliding resistance dimmers were added yearly.

But modern technology didn't take away all the fun. The main source of supply backstage at the Mechanics was a power board from the 1920s. When he wasn't making mental calculations of watts, volts and amps, Colville was praying that the rain would hold off until curtain time.

> *When it rained the gutters overflowed and water ran down the back-stage wall into ... and usually out of ... the main switchboard, doing some quite uncontrollable things to the lights, not to mention the lighting technician's language.*

Things did improve. The Mechanics was re-wired, and equipment steadily upgraded. By the late 1950s, recalled Colville, 'there were as many knobs and levers as there would be in a steam era railway signal box and at times it took all the hands and feet of two lighting men to cope with a lighting plot'.

Improvements on stage and behind the scenes were helped considerably by the Theatre's improving organisational abilities. At the 1952 Annual General Meeting a new constitution was adopted, which spelled out the duties of the executive, the responsibility of committee members to attend meetings, and the duties of the finance, production and social sub-committees, as well as the role of the property officer and stage manager.

Another factor in its success was the quality of WLT's financial management. Unlike many theatre companies, Williamstown was never phased by what Doris Fitton once described as 'the sordid principles of bookkeeping'.[28] Perhaps because of the banking or accounting background of early treasurers such as Harry Conradi and Ivor Porter, and the financial experience of other key members such as Eric Black, from the outset Williamstown took a cautious systematic approach to financial management.

Early on, the Theatre negotiated a 'rise and fall' contract with the Mechanics' Institute Committee in which rental was related to the surplus made on individual productions. The professional accountants within Williamstown's midst were able to keep a close watch on finances. In 1954, for example, Ivor Porter's balance sheet showed that ticket sales were only just above expenses, then averaging £111 per show. It was clear that profits were to be made on

---

28 Doris Fitton, *Not Without Dust or Heat, My Life in Theatre*, (Sydney, Harper and Row, 1981), p.86.

teas and sweets sold during the intervals. In the following year, however, Porter presented the Committee with an analysis of the expenditure and receipts for each show that year: all had made a profit - ranging from £49 for *Our Town* to £ 62 for *Granite*. Later, in1958, Porter demonstrated that the theatre was losing almost £6 on each Monday night performance, which led to those performances being discontinued in 1959.

On 28 July 1956, starting a practice religiously observed (almost[29]) every ten years since, the Theatre celebrated the conclusion of its first decade of life with a party at the Mechanics' Institute. By the end of that year, Williamstown Little Theatre Movement was well established as a key player in the cultural life of its city, and in the emerging and progressively strengthening network of non-professional theatres in Melbourne. When the Movement was first formed, *Williamstown Advertiser* pronounced the venture 'new in suburban enterprise', being either unaware of, or ignoring, earlier ventures in Hartwell in 1938, Frankston in 1942, and in Ferntree Gully[30] and Mordialloc in 1945. These theatres were different in scope and purpose from the Catholic-based Therry Society founded in 1936, and the Tin Alley Players set up by Keith Macartney and Maurice Belz at Melbourne University in 1939.[31] When Hugh Hunt, the first director of the Australian Elizabethan Theatre Trust, arrived in Australia in 1955, he commented that Melbourne was as well off for theatre as English cities of corresponding size. (New 'little theatres' similar to Williamstown's had been formed in Box Hill in 1951, Heidelberg and Mitcham in 1952, Beaumaris in 1953 and at The Basin in 1954.)

The base of the Williamstown Theatre at this stage, both in its active membership and its subscribers, was unambiguously local. The 1951 audience survey showed that all but two of the respondents lived in Williamstown or the immediately adjacent areas of Newport, Spotswood and North

---

29   Except in 1966, when the Theatre was effectively homeless – see pp.68-70

30   What started as the Ferntree Gully Arts Society in 1945 evolved to become the 1812 Theatre. For the story see Angela Ellis, 'The 1812 Theatre-60 years and Growing', *Theatrecraft*, October 2005, p.4.

31   See Geoffrey Milne, *THEATRE AUSTRALIA (UNLIMITED), Australian Theatre Since the 1950s*, Monograph 10 in *The Australian Playwrights Series* (General Editor Veronica Kelly), (New York, Rodolpi, 2004), pp.76 & 97.

Williamstown. There was a simple reason for this: in the early 'fifties few people in Melbourne had cars and theatre members were no exception. Williamstown Little Theatre Movement in its first ten years was very much a 'community theatre', not in the modern sense of the term which focuses on a particular style of theatrical presentation, but in the sense used by Peter O'Shaugnessy when describing Williamstown's thespians in 1955. The theatre then was 'rooted in Williamstown's soil', as O'Shaugnessy noted, because that is where the actors, managers, set designers, technicians and costume creators lived and (largely) worked: either in the case of the men in industry, commerce and places like the SEC or, in the case of most of the women, in the home raising their families.

Aiding the Theatre's growth was the fact that Williamstown was on the fringe of the rapidly growing western suburbs of Altona and Werribee: Altona's population increased fourfold between 1947 and 1961 and Werribee's doubled, courtesy of the major industrial developments such as Vacuum Oil Company's oil refinery being progressively built in the area[32] This growth provided a new market for the Movement's theatrical wares and a source of new members such as Gwladys Winfield, who arrived from England with her husband and two sons in 1955[33]

The major factor contributing to the Theatre's growth in the 1950s, though, was the talent, energy and dedication of the core group of actors, technicians and administrators who drove the Theatre's development. The actors included Marion Becroft and Lorrie McManus who each appeared in eleven productions at Williamstown between 1952 and 1956, Ted Cordell and Gillian Witt who appeared in nine, Doug Lindsay in eight, and Ngaire McCutcheon and Dennis Wain who each appeared in seven. Members often took advantage of opportunities to improve their capabilities. In 1954, for example, Marion Becroft, Neil Fitzpatrick and Gillian Witt participated in

---

32   Construction of Mobil's refinery at Altona commenced in October 1946. It commenced operations in June 1949, initially making lubricating oil and bitumen from imported crude oil. An expansion of the refinery completed in 1955 extended its product range. For the details see https//www.exxonmobil.com.au/Who are we?. See also Susan Priestley, *Altona, The Long View* (Hagreen Publishing Company in conjunction with the City of Altona, 1988), pp.213-233.

33   See note in program for WLT's August 1964 production of the *Chalk Garden*, which was directed by Gwladys.

the drama section of the annual C.A.E. Summer School, that year held in Albury.³⁴

Behind the scenes were people such as Ivor Porter and Alec Colville, whose appearances on stage were rare,³⁵ but who contributed, in Ivor's case as treasurer, and in Alec's in multiple roles including the building of sets, coordinating cast and back-stage crew, and lighting technician. Nell Colville was secretary, self-described as 'Nell the Procurer', and the leader of a great team of seamstresses responsible for the costuming of all Williamstown's productions and for making the red gowns worn by the usherettes in the early days. Eddie Marr, as well as providing a ticketing agency, helped with sound in 1952 and 1953, while Tom Craven, dapper in evening suit and bow tie, was the almost permanent front of house manager and the driving force behind the Theatre's touring efforts. Millie Craven ran the highly profitable sweets stall.

The prime mover, however, was Ted Cordell. His home at 18 Esplanade, Williamstown, was the focus for the Theatre's early activities. As Dorothy Porter recalled in 1961, it was at the Cordell residence that the play reading group which led to the foundation of the theatre met. On the pavement outside his house, plans for the development of the Theatre were made. His lounge became a rehearsal room and lines were learned in his kitchen. A capable actor, Cordell played many different roles, and is remembered by many as a man of diverse tastes, an omnivorous reader, a dedicated bush walker, especially fond of Wilson's Promontory, and a compulsive renovator of houses. His baked bread became the focus for many an impromptu evening meal at his home, coupled with soup made by his wife Alice, counsellor to many from the theatre community.

Cordell developed an extensive network of contacts in the theatre world and

---

34   I am indebted to Gillian (now Gillian Senior) for providing me with information about this event. A photograph of Gillian 'studying her lines' appeared on page 34 of *The Weekly Times*, January 13, 1954.

35   Famously, Alec appeared on stage as an islander in *Pacific Paradise*. His single line was 'The pigs was perfect, except that they was dead' – a line he would repeat on many future occasions when he considered it appropriate. This from the obituary on Alec in *Cues and News*, November 1988, by his daughter Christine Saunders, after his death on 14 October 1988.

was the Victorian Drama League's delegate to the 1957 national conference of the New Theatres of Australia. Appropriately, at the theatre's tenth annual meeting in January 1956, Cordell was made the first Life Member, rendering him speechless, an apparently rare event. The minutes of the meeting record that after the then President, Tom Craven, presented Cordell with the Theatre's first life membership certificate which was accompanied by much acclamation, 'Mr Cordell was so overcome he could not reply'.

Chapter Two

1957-1968: Challenges posed by TV and Mechanics' Closure

At the end of 1956 a new challenge to theatre emerged. Television transmission commenced in Melbourne on 19 November 1956, and it was immediately popular. By mid-1957 there were 45,000 television sets licensed in Victoria, which grew to 270,000 in 1959, and to more than half a million four years later. In Geoffrey Blainey's words, television 'was an instant addiction' and its impact on social life was dramatic:

> *Ten years after the end of the Second World War the media was dominated by radio, the newspapers, books, the cinema, the pulpit and the classroom, but their hold was quickly loosened by television. People crowded into neighbours' houses to watch Graham Kennedy ... In Elizabeth and Bourke streets – still magnetic as a centre of retail trade – people crowded the pavements to watch television programs in the window of shops ... Toddlers played all day in front of the television set, parents ate their evening meal in front of it.*[36]

There were varying views about the likely effect of television on theatre. Melbourne actor and theatrical entrepreneur Frank Thring believed television attracted people to see the real stage. On the other hand, many feared its impact. In September 1955, three hundred stage, radio and screen stars, including luminaries such as Lewis Casson, Garnett Carroll and Sybil Thorndike, signed a declaration arguing that the 'present television plans are a grave threat to the future of musical acting and allied talents' in Australia, and advocated strict rules about local content. However, it appears that as far

---

36 See Geoffrey Blainey, *Our Side of the Country, The Story of Victoria*, (Melbourne, Methuen Hayes, 1984), p.206.

as amateur theatre in Victoria was concerned, the optimists were eventually proved right. Harold Baigent, of the Council of Adult Education, conducted a survey of amateur theatre in Victoria in 1964 and found that a third of the active drama groups had started up between 1956 and 1962, 1959 being the peak year. At Christmas 1959, a Melbourne theatregoer could choose between twenty-four separate plays all produced by amateur groups. And up until 1959 the advent of television had little effect on the popularity of the annual VDL one act play festival.[37]

As repertory theatre in Britain also found, staving off the challenge of television was long, hard work.[38] At WLT the threat was reflected in audience numbers from 1957 into the early 1960s. Total attendance at Williamstown's productions was 3,436 in 1955 and 3,715 in 1956. Only once in the next seven years were these figures topped, in 1961 when audience numbers totalled 3,533, largely because of the record-breaking attendance (1,338 persons) at the last production for the year - Vin Foster's production of Hennings Nelms' *Only an Orphan Girl*. After that, the Theatre had to wait until 1963 before it was able to put up the 'house full' sign again, for Vin Foster's next production, *The Ballad of Angel's Alley*.

It seems production standards cannot explain these lower audience numbers. Critical reaction to Williamstown's productions was still favourable. Individual productions had their strengths and weaknesses, but critics saw as much good and improving theatre as they had between 1952 and 1956.

The downturn in Williamstown's audience numbers did not happen overnight. Indeed the first production for 1957, David Reid's staging of the Agatha Christie mystery *Murder at the Vicarage*, attracted 1,143 people, though the *Listener-In TV* reviewer gave it a rather lukewarm review thinking, for example, that whilst Ngaire Mc Cutcheon 'carried off the role of Miss Marple well ... she was not quite the spinsterish type Miss Christie intended'. Whilst 'Neil O'Halloran as the vicar and Pam Black as his wife did good work', Margaret Burdon was 'not always articulate' as the maid, though the *Williamstown Advertiser* reviewer thought Burdon warranted 'special mention'

---

37   For the details see Robert E. Glass, *The Victorian Drama League 1952-2002*, pp. 12-19.

38   For some details on the British situation see John Elsom, *Theatre Outside London*, (London, MacMillan and Co., 1971), pp.63-70.

for 'her excellent comedy study.' Numbers were, however, down for the second production, George Bernard Shaw's *Major Barbara*, directed by Alan Money, which similarly received a mixed review with *Listener-In TV* writing it was: 'a plucky but not altogether successful attempt to steer a course between Shaw the comedian and Shaw the propagandist'. The main trouble, *Listener-In TV* went on, was 'that the players mostly tend to prate rather than to converse. The characters must be brought to life as real people, in spite of their extravagant and near farcical background'. Only Jenny Stewart, playing the role of Lady Britomarte, achieved this. Indeed, so impressed was the *Listener-In TV's* 'Agon' with Miss Stewart, that she won Agon' s weekly 'Oscar' for the best performance that week in amateur theatre in Melbourne.

There was a further decline in audience numbers for the next show, Paul Hill's production of R.F. Delderfield's *Orchard Walls*. Numbers recovered for the final production of 1957, *My Three Angels*, despite the fact the play was late starting every night partly, because of the difficulty of doing Marion Becroft's hair, but also because some members of the cast did not arrive early enough to allow time for make-up. The recovery was not, however, sufficient to offset the earlier downturn, and in 1957 WLT incurred its first and largest ever loss (£348) for the year.

The years 1958, 1959 and 1960 were three of the leanest for WLT in the whole of the time it performed primarily at the Mechanics' Institute. It incurred another loss in 1959-60 despite engaging some of the best amateur theatre directors available in Melbourne at the time: David Reid, Margaret Hetherington, Neville Thurgood and Lorna Kirwood-Jones, for example, and apparently continuing to give audiences the mix of plays which had proved so successful in earlier years.

After *Bell, Book and Candle* in 1958, Hetherington wrote to Nell Colville indicating that 'I have enjoyed working down there again, and the cast has been absolutely wonderful (and) so has backstage - under difficulties which I appreciate'. She was worried that too much was falling on too few:

> *I have rather felt, on this show, that the whole responsibility of management and actual set construction rested on about three individuals, who performed most of the stage operations during the show. This is not entirely satisfactory from the point of view of the producer or the stage crew.*

1957 - 1968

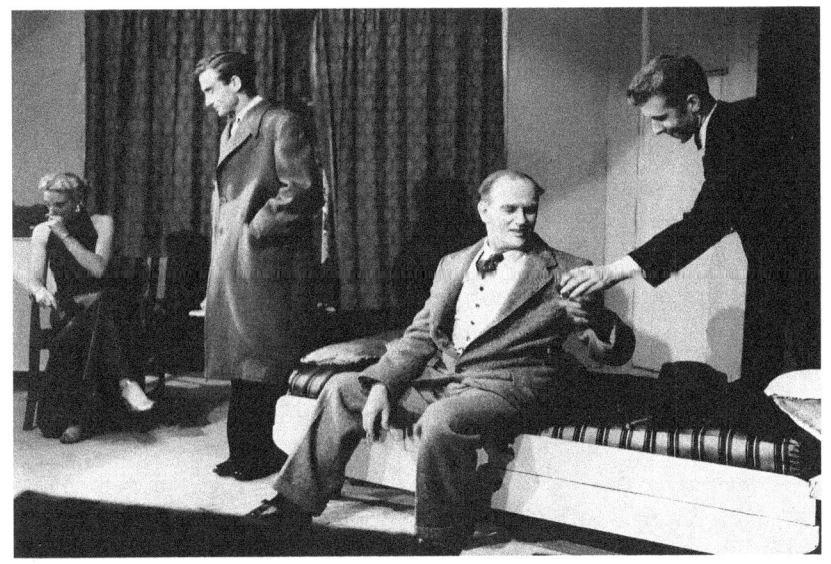

Bell, Book and Candle, March 1958
Lorrie McManus as Gillian Holroyd, Neil O'Halloran as Nicholas Holroyd (Gillian's brother), Ted Cordell as Sidney Redlitch and Frank Maas as Anthony Henderson.

She had some specific suggestions about lighting:

At whatever the cost in effort, time and rent a producer should be able to have one session with the backstage boys in the dark on setting and plotting lighting cues, however simple. It will save producers many a heartache and the clients many a sore eye.

After her production of *The Heiress* in 1958, she had more useful suggestions:

1. 'Suggest that, on future shows, particularly costume ones, the W.L.T.M. works to a budget of sorts (estimated sensibly of course, and not just hopefully)'.
2. 'Somehow you bribe a wardrobe mistress. Multiple costumes are too much of a chore and a responsibility for busy people who also have many lines to learn.'

Dorothy Porter volunteered to be Williamstown's first wardrobe mistress early in 1960, but the practice of budgeting for all productions was not introduced until the early 1980s, and then not strictly adhered to.

Even in these difficult years, however, there were always productions which were artistic and financial successes, and which contributed to the ongoing development of the company. Such indeed was the case with *The Heiress* with *Williamstown Chronicle* commenting that the Theatre had 'lifted itself from a rut of mediocre productions', noting that Gillian Wadds as the heiress 'showed that she had not lost any of the qualities that made her popular a few years ago', and that Ted Cordell as Dr Austin Sloper had 'given her good support'. *Small Hotel* in June 1958, directed by David Reid was also 'a first-class production', as was his production of Clare Booth's comedy *The Women* in August 1959. This play about smart American women in the 1930s has forty-four different roles which, with appropriate doubling-up, can be played by a slightly 'smaller' cast – in WLT's case, thirty-five. On WLT's stage, the principal roles were played by the female mainstays of many a Williamstown production through the 1950s: Ella Bambery, Marion Becroft, Margot Harper, Joan Lindsay, June Lownds, Ngaire McCutcheon, Dorothy Porter, Judy Sippo, Jen Stewart, Win Stewart, Gillian Wadds, Lorraine West, and Gwladys Winfield.

The *Listener-In TV* critic thought that: 'Williamstown Little Theatre tackled a task that had never before been attempted by an amateur group here and brought it off with a considerable measure of success.' Locally, *Williamstown Advertiser* commented on 'the smoothness of the production', seeing it as 'a triumph of cooperation between him (Reid), his cast, and backstage staff - all of the latter being men'. Margot Harper 'scored all the way as Sylvia Howard ... Gillian Wadds ... opposed to her as Mary Haines ... used her quiet charm ... as bad woman'. As Crystal Allen, Lorraine West 'gave us an excellent picture of how a "man trap" can behave towards other women'. Audience numbers for *The Women* rebounded to 1,051, the most attending a production for more than two and a half years, including the largest first night audience since the advent of television. It would be a another two and a half years before the total audience for a WLT production again topped 1,000.

The Women was also important from a production point of view. Aside from the need to coordinate such a large cast and crew, there were problems in the development of the set. As well as reorganising the dressing rooms to accommodate the large female cast, staging the play required considerable innovation backstage as it was the first production in which a revolving stage, specially constructed for the play, was used at Williamstown.

Alec Colville's Stage Manager's Report on the production captures both the nature of the backstage challenge and the Williamstown team's ingenuity in meeting it. His report was divided in two parts: preparation and running of the play. It is worth quoting at length.

Under 'Preparation', Colville wrote:

A great deal of the preliminary construction work including furniture, the revolve and the 6'0" by 8'0" book wing, was carried out by working bees at Ron Bird's workshop. The tempo stepped up over the last two weeks by which time the backstage crew were working at top pressure and for long hours. Apart from the woodwork and cardboard construction handled by the male workers, a party of cast and other ladies of the group put in some very useful hours with sewing machines and tack hammer to make the furniture look something more than just old stage props.

About the 'Running of The Play', Colville commented:

After the confusion of the dress rehearsal, all concerned with the staging of the play fell into the way of the scene changes and other work, and generally speaking, the play ran smoothly (as the *Advertiser* review noted). With the aid of the revolve we were able to prepare quite complicated settings while a scene was running and then swing it round to face the audience while the curtain was down. One useful feature was the broadcasting of the play and instructions to cast, to the dressing rooms, which greatly assisted in keeping the cast in touch with the progress of the play, and, at the same time keeping surplus members of the cast out of the hair of the back-stage crew.

Two more artistically important productions stretched the capabilities of the company in 1960. Margaret Hetherington directed a late May production of Thornton Wilder's *The Matchmaker*, which *Listener-In TV* thought Williamstown's 'most satisfying achievement for quite a while'. The reviewer thought there was 'real first-class work' by Margot Harper, Marion Becroft, Vin Foster and Grahame Murphy. The major challenge again was the large cast, sixteen separate characters. The ability to assemble large casts economically is often seen as one of the strengths of amateur theatre, but as Don Reeves noted in his review, the challenge in *The Matchmaker* is to find sufficient actors to be able to allocate roles according to suitability for the part, rather than being driven by necessity. Reeves thought Margaret Hetherington achieved this in her production, presenting the play 'much as Wilder would have wanted it'.

There were similarly positive remarks about the next production *Johnny Belinda*. *Listener-In TV* thought it had been given 'effective staging' with Mary Little's Belinda being 'full of character … she managed cleverly the transition of the miserable domestic drudge of the early scenes to the comparative happiness of young motherhood'. Mary Little had to learn sign language to play her role. There was also praise for Osborne Nettie as the seducer who 'managed one of the most realistic death falls I have seen on the stage for years'.

But for all its artistic progress, Williamstown continued to struggle to rebuild its audiences. The total for 1960 was 2,867, among the lowest for any year after the Theatre went 'wholly local' in 1952. There were various efforts during 1959 and 1960 to market the theatre more effectively, including more paragraphs in local newspapers and a float in Melbourne's annual Moomba procession in 1959. Another suggestion from Gillian Wadds was a monthly newsletter and free tickets to Sunday night dress rehearsals for Williamstown's elderly citizens and the House of Friendship in Footscray.

Win Stewart was made Vice-President for Publicity in July 1960 and she moved quickly. By August a new program format had been designed, and an invitation sent to Williamstown and Altona councils and to the Deaf Institute to attend a gala opening performance of *Johnny Belinda* with supper in the Green Room after the show. In April 1961 ABC television helped by televising a rehearsal of *Separate Tables* and the Apex Club of Altona agreed to patronise the first night of each show as a fund-raising venture. Later in the year, the local papers ran a series of articles on theatre personalities, and a dodger drive was conducted in the area to coincide with the final production for the year, *Only An Orphan Girl*. It worked - 1,213 people saw that production, the largest audience at a WLT production up to that point.

Even when audience numbers were down in the Theatre's second decade and the reaction of audiences unpredictable, several of Williamstown's productions achieved critical acclaim, for example Margaret Hetherington's production of Ben Levy's *The Rape of the Belt* in March 1961. Williamstown took a risk staging this play, since the amateur rights had only just become available. The *Listener-In TV* reviewer commented:

> *This dramatic version of the legendary ninth labour of Hercules which imposes on him the task of wrestling from the Amazons their celebrated royal belt from the goddess Hesa presents many production problems... With the help of a competent cast admirably supported by an efficient back-stage staff, Miss Hetherington overcame all of them... Principal acting honours went to Lorrie McManus for a highly virtuoso performance as Hippolyta. Her transformation into the war-like goddess for the last act was brilliantly done... June Lownds as Antiope, Doug Lindsay as Heracles and Grahame Murphy as Theseus were exactly right (and) sets and costumes were well done.*

G. Kirby, reviewing the play for *Williamstown Chronicle* agreed, thinking that 'for pace and polish, this production could hardly have been improved upon'.

Williamstown was one of the first Australian amateur companies to stage, in August 1961, Ray Lawler's milestone work *Summer of the Seventeenth Doll* (where again, the amateur rights had only just become available). Unusually, perhaps, for an iconic Australian play, WLT's production was directed by Englishwoman Gwladys Winfield, who, as noted above, arrived in Australia in 1955, the year of the play's premiere. (Gwladys had a solid background in theatre, having studied at the Guildhall School of Drama and directed plays for a Royal Air Force group in England.) The production was not without its difficulties. Gwladys had trouble casting the male leads, Roo and Barney, and at one stage almost abandoned the play. In the event the show went on and was quite successful attracting an audience of 798. Frank Murphy in *The Advocate* thought the play generally very well cast, and that Roo and Barney came to life naturally in performances by Graeme West and David Gibson, and that Gillian Wadds' Olive was also real. 'The Doll' produced a special drama. As *Williamstown Advertiser* reported:

> *The Williamstown Little Theatre Movement had a bad break last week. Right in the middle of its five nights' run of Ray Lawler's "Summer of the Seventeenth Doll", David Gibson, who was playing Barney, was stricken with a severe bout of influenza. All seemed lost as amateur groups don't indulge in the luxury of understudies. Fortunately they were able to get experienced actor Lynn Foster to read the part, and a very good job he made of it. Main trouble was the fight in the second act. It's pretty well impossible to stage a real dinkum box-on while one of the adversaries has to hold a book in one hand.*

The final production in 1961 was *Only an Orphan Girl* 'a soul-stirring drama of human trials and tribulations in four acts by Hennings Nelms' as one reviewer described it. Director Vin Foster made a great effort to bring back the spirit of the 'gay 1890s' by displaying old-time playbills, lent by the Historical Society, in the foyer. Both the *Williamstown Advertiser* and *Listener-In TV* reviews were very positive. The *Advertiser* wrote:

> *Grahame Murphy as the hero presented us with an interpretation reminiscent of Lil Abner with a dash of Davy Crocket. He was very funny. Lorraine West's Nellie (the orphan girl), was so sweet that Mary Pickford would have shed a nostalgic tear if she had seen her ... Ngaire McCutcheon and Gary Metcalf were a humorously homespun Ma and Pa Perkins. Gillian Wadds ... frightened the life out of us when she shot the villain with a gun nearly large enough to be in the heavy artillery! Last but not least ... was the funny child, Lucy, presented by Deidre McDonald. With Judy Canova plaits, she bounced like a yo-yo and her business with the sticks of dynamite was a beautiful piece of mime.*

The Theatre's March 1962 production of Philip King's *See How They Run* was something of a triumph since well-known British producer Norman

Marshall[39], on a visit to Australia, had advised amateur groups against tackling farce. *Listener-In TV* commented:

As if to challenge Mr Norman Marshall's advice to amateur groups to avoid farce like the plague, the Williamstown Little Theatre Group made a first-class job of Philip King's See How They Run.

Frank Murphy in *The Advocate* agreed:

Williamstown ... showed that it could handle farce. in a high spirited and hilarious production of Philip King's 'mystifying multiplication' of clergymen in an English vicarage ... Fast moving, split-second timing and unusually good characterisation in most of the main roles ensured success.

Williamstown's next play was *The Multi-Coloured Umbrella*, by now little-remembered Australian playwright Barbara Vernon.[40] Gary Metcalf played the lead role of Ben, the eldest son of the Donnelly family, around which the play centres, delivering what one reviewer described as 'a virile, emotional piece of acting' the 'most complete performance' of a cast which included Graeme West and June Lownds.

For his efforts, early in December 1962 Metcalf was declared the first winner of the Cordell Award for the best performance by an actor in a lead role in a play staged at WLT during the previous year. The award was established by the WLT committee as a memorial to Alice and Ted Cordell who had died within a short time of each other in 1960 and 1961, Alice from cancer, and Ted from a heart attack suffered whilst running. The first adjudicator of the

---

39 Marshall had managed the Cambridge Festival Theatre and the Gate Theatre in London, before forming his own repertory company which toured Europe and India for the British Council from 1949 to 1951. He also played an active role in planning the British National Theatre – see Martin Banham ed., *The Cambridge Guide to the Theatre*, (Revised Paperback Edition 1992), pp.622-623.

40 Vernon's play had run second to Richard Beynon's *The Shifting Heart* in a play competition held by the Journalists' Club in Sydney in 1956, and she was responsible for starting the long-running TV series Bellbird on the ABC - see *Companion to Australian Theatre*, p.623.

The Multi-Coloured Umbrella, May 1962:
L to R: Graeme West as Kevin Donnelly (Dadda), Gary Metcalf as Ben Donnelly, June Lownds as Gloria Donnelly, and at back, Peter Foster as Joe Donnelly and Judy Sippo as Kathie Donnelly.

Cordell Award was Loys Caudwell, well-known in Victorian amateur theatre circles as Secretary of the Victorian Drama League from 1955. According to the Christmas 1962 edition of *Cues and News*, speaking at the presentation to Metcalf, Doug Lindsay suggested that the event represented a deliberate attempt to start a theatre tradition, a tradition which has now continued for sixty years.

But just as things looked as if they were turning around for the better, audience numbers took another dive, despite the Committee's continuing the dodger drives, offering a prize of a guinea, the cost of an annual subscription to the member who sold the most tickets, and contributing a special section 'Curtain Calls from the Little Theatre' to the local papers.

The Committee was particularly disappointed at the failure to increase audiences for the Mary Chase play *Harvey*, its last production for 1962 which received reasonable reviews. The *Listener-In TV* reviewer thought

1957 - 1968

Vin Foster a Dracula, February 1963.

that 'though marred by more lapses of memory than we usually find, *Harvey* should develop into one of Williamstown Little Theatre's major successes' - perhaps the locals were put off by the reported memory losses. *Dracula*, then enjoying enormous popularity on the big screen, was chosen to redress the falling audiences. Despite extensive pre-publicity in the local papers, and quite favourable reviews, with Vin Foster a particularly nasty piece of work in the title role, *Dracula* pulled in fewer people than for every other play in 1961 and 1962. In response, the Committee adopted a new strategy: the first and last shows of each season would be selected for their ability to attract large audiences.

The strategy seemed to work. The last production for 1963, Vin Foster's treatment of *The Ballad of Angel's Alley*, an Australian musical by Bruce George and Jeff Underhill, attracted an audience of 1,058. Set in Melbourne of the 1880s, the play deals with the lawless 'Pushes' that inhabited the dimly lit flagstone alley which ran off Little Bourke Street behind the G.P.O. Frank Murphy in *The Advocate* thought Williamstown's production 'a decided success', and Laurie Landray agreed, noting the 'thoroughly efficient teamwork of the group' with 'uniformly good comic sketches' from both 'the Bloods'- Graeme West, Frank Wadds, Grahame Murphy and Roy McQuade - and 'the Molls' - Lorraine Davies, June Lownds, Margot Harper and Gwladys Winfield.

In the light of this success, the Committee reaffirmed the policy that the first and last shows each year should be chosen with a view to attracting large audiences, with more serious plays being done in between. In December 1963, the Committee endorsed the following program for 1964: *Dear Charles*, directed by Paul Hill; *The Man*, directed by Vin Foster; *The Chalk Garden*, directed by Gwladys Winfield; and *The Boy Friend*, directed by Grahame Murphy.

The soundness of the policy seemed established when 1009 people saw the first production of 1964, Alan Melville's *Dear Charles* directed by Paul Hill. *Listener-In TV* thought Williamstown made 'a pretty good job' of the play. Ruth Thorsen filled 'the key role of the unmarried mother of three grown up children with considerable skill', the 'youngsters were very well played indeed by Judy Sippo, Barry Robinson and Ellis Ebell', while Frank Wadds 'pretty well [stole] the show with his sketch of the excitable Polish pianist'. This production produced a WLT 'first': a long-playing recording was made!

In the winter months, however, it was harder to attract audiences - *The Man* had only 643 patrons and *The Chalk Garden* 592. This despite Frank Murphy in *The Advocate* considering the former 'a genuine thriller' where 'the development and tension were cleverly built up' with June Lownds and Grahame Murphy as the leads 'admirably capturing the necessary effect'. Supporting actors Lorraine West and Gary Metcalf were respectively 'excellent' and 'good'. Grahame Murphy was again 'responsible for a good style set' and 'the production ... attended well to detail'.

Buoyancy returned in October with Grahame Murphy's production of Sandy Wilson's *The Boy Friend*, which set a WLT audience record of 1,401 patrons. The demand for seats forced WLT to open not only for a full week but on the Friday preceding the published opening night. Laurie Landray writing for *Listener-In TV* thought the production 'outstanding for the characterisation brought to the leading roles'. Landray thought Murphy had chosen his cast 'with a sure eye for acting and singing contact'. June Lownds was the 'most outstanding personality on stage'. According to the *Williamstown Advertiser* reviewer, June 'sang like a nightingale'.

The Boy Friend was Grahame Murphy's first production for Williamstown, not that you'd have guessed it, according to *Williamstown Advertiser*: 'For a seasoned producer, *The Boy Friend* would have been fine work; as a first up effort ... it was little short of sensational.' And, in a comment that would become almost standard about Murphy's productions over the ensuing thirty years, the *Williamstown Advertiser* reviewer added: 'It was meticulous ... there can be no other description ... a richly costumed and lavishly lit show.'

Murphy had already established himself as an accomplished set designer and actor for Williamstown. His career started as a member of Williamstown's junior group in their contribution to the VDL junior one-act play festival staged at the Mechanics' Institute in August 1956. Subsequent performances - Stephen in *Major Barbara* (1957), Barnaby Tucker in *The Matchmaker* (1960), the hero in *Only an Orphan Girl* (1961), and Howard Wilton in *The Man* (1964) - attracted wide critical acclaim. Murphy was interested in theatre from an early age, spending his teenage years designing his own stages and encouraged at Northcote High School by a sympathetic teacher, Miss Moody. Later, Murphy met Vin Foster in the city where they worked in separate companies in the insurance industry in buildings across the road from each other. Foster introduced him to Williamstown, first to the Light Opera Company and then to the Theatre. The partnership between Foster and Murphy was rich for the theatre, as subsequent chapters will demonstrate. Early on they made a joint decision not to pursue careers in the professional theatre, preferring, as so many do to take advantage of the opportunities available in the non-professional theatre world whilst enjoying the certainty of income associated with a 'real' job.

Paul Hill's production of *Dracula* in 1963 introduced a new concept for WLT: the Production Meeting. Getting together the director, cast and backstage crew as soon as possible after casting was a great success, contributing greatly to the smooth running of the production, especially backstage. It also revealed unknown talents in Lorraine West, who turned her hand to the foyer display in which she demonstrated a certain feeling for the macabre.

At this time, WLT faced a major problem in its shortage of manpower - quite literally - both on and behind the stage and front of house. As the annual report of 1959 commented: 'Shortage of men has been a great worry throughout the year, often delaying rehearsals and always affecting selection of plays.' It wasn't just WLT's problem, however. As Harold Baigent noted in his 1964 theatre survey, a shortage of men was a major problem throughout amateur theatre in Victoria. Baigent suggested it was because there was still an idea that the arts were 'cissy' and not for the full-blooded Australian male, though the widespread existence of the problem in England[41] somewhat undermines that argument.

Moreover, WLT now had competition from the Williamstown Light Opera Company, which had been established in 1955, and also used the Mechanics' Institute as a venue. At a practical level, both companies had to liaise closely on scheduling of rehearsals and productions. For example, when there was little time between productions of the two groups, it meant there was less time for set construction. However, there was common membership between the groups. Vin Foster and Grahame Murphy both appeared in the Light Opera Company's initial production, Gilbert and Sullivan's *The Gondoliers*, and several other WLT stalwarts, Marion Becroft and June Lownds, for example, were also 'stars' for the Light Opera while, as noted above, Trevor McKay designed sets for many of their productions. Overlapping membership fostered cooperation between the groups and by 1962 the executives of the two groups were meeting regularly, leading to a formal contract over the sharing of properties and a shared fund for the replacement of basic items such as light bulbs.

Indeed, the existence of the Light Opera Company gave WLT an ally in its negotiations with Williamstown Council over the improvement of facilities at the Mechanics' Institute. Putting pressure on the council had always been a preoccupation of the WLT committee. In 1963, the Theatre and the Light Opera Company jointly pressed the council to commit itself to improvements to the stage, dressing rooms and toilets. Letters and discussions followed with the council eventually agreeing to do the work. It would contribute the equivalent of £1 for every £1 provided jointly by WLT and the Light Opera Company up to a maximum of £250 making a total of £500. WLT also tackled the council over the freezing temperatures in the hall, a major disincentive to audiences in winter months. The council pleaded lack of available funds, forcing the theatre eventually to meet a substantial portion of the costs.

Throughout the early 1960s, WLT continued to be an enthusiastic supporter

---

41   As Anthony Parker noted of the British situation in 1959: 'Every Dramatic Group I come across invariably complained bitterly about a shortage of men.' See Anthony Parker, *Amateur Theatre as a Pastime*, (London, Souvenir Press Limited, 1959), p.37.

of the Victorian Drama League. Having hosted the one-act play festival in 1956, Williamstown provided an entry in each subsequent state-wide festival up to 1960, but without success. The VDL festival was organised on a regional basis from 1961[42], with the best production from each of the country regions competing in a 'State Final' in Melbourne with the productions ranked first to sixth in the metropolitan regional event. WLT's breakthrough came in 1963 with a Gillian Wadds' production of G.B.Shaw's *In the Beginning* set in the Garden of Eden with Ian Moore as Adam, Lorraine West as Eve, and June Lownds as The Serpent. *In the Beginning* was placed sixth in the Metropolitan Regional Festival which gave it entry into the State Finals, where it was awarded second place, after adjudicator John Casson (Sybil Thorndike's husband and a speech specialist) had extreme difficulty in coming to a decision, pacing the carpet for ten minutes. He allotted one extra point to Heidelberg and pronounced WLT second. WLT achieved second place again in the State Finals in 1964 with a production by Gillian Wadds of Jean Anouilh's *Madame De*. Gillian, Lorraine West, Vin Foster and Grahame Murphy received honourable mentions in both years. One critic commented that there were times during *Madame De* when the sheer beauty of it brought tears to the eyes. Lorraine West recalled it as one of her greatest moments in theatre. Based on these two successes, the Theatre offered to host the Metropolitan Region festival for the VDL in 1965.

WLT was going from strength to strength, but always faced the challenge of maintaining the interest of members not directly involved in productions and of developing their skills. In September 1958, at the suggestion of Dorothy Porter, a forum was held to discuss theatre in general and ways in which WLT could be improved. A direct result of this forum was the conduct of a series of 'CAE lectures' by Harold Baigent covering topics such as movement, lighting and stage management. So enthusiastic was the response that the Theatre organised more such events: in 1963 for example monthly talks were given by experts such as Ron Little on speech, Ken Woodward on movement, and Herbert Browne on make-up. In 1960 the VDL took the initiative of running a course on production. Kath Hindson and Ian Moore went along from Williamstown, which inspired Kath to produce a one act play for WLT.

---

42   For the details, see *The Victorian Drama League 1952-2002*, Chapter 3.

In the early 'sixties, Williamstown regularly presented one-act plays between major productions partly to keep members' interests alive when they were not directly involved in a production, but also to give new members an opportunity to show and develop their talents. In 1961, for example, there was a double bill of *Landslide* produced by Gillian Wadds and *Intermezzo* by Sue Nette, followed by *The Playgoers* produced by Kath Hindson and a reading of *The White Cliffs* by Margot Harper and June Lownds. As part of the Footscray Council of Churches' celebration of Education Week that year, WLT also presented Thorton Wilder's *The Happy Journey* produced by Kath Hindson. It was repeated at Williamstown with Vin Foster reading from *The Sentimental Bloke* and Margaret Burdon reading a selection of short poems. Finally, there was a double bill of Sue Nette's *Master Dudley* and Gwladys Winfield's *Orange Blossom*. The following year, on 23 June, Graham Murphy produced Peter S. Perston's *The Tri-Color Suite*, a play set in Paris during the fourth republic.

Another initiative, much appreciated by the younger folk of the area, was a series of pantomimes staged in the week before Christmas in each of 1962, 1963 and 1964. Two of these events, *Sleeping Beauty* in 1962 and *Cinderella* in 1964, could be described as 'standard repertoire', but the 1963 offering, *Peter and the Princess* (whose subtitle was 'How to Succeed in Rescuing a Princess without Really Trying'!), was an original piece by Gillian Wadds.[43] As the publicity described it:

> *Peter the Shepherd is our hero, and he and Silly Willie go in search of the beautiful Princess Pamela, who has been captured by the Wicked Sorcerer. They are helped in their search by the Fairy Queen, and after defeating the Sorcerer and old Witch Hazel, everybody, of course, lives happily ever after.*

When you add in thirteen people, (everyone from Ellis Ebell to Mary Little), playing supporting roles as villagers to the cast of fourteen and the four fairies, you have thirty-one WLT members involved in this pantomime, a good and fun way to build the company's camaraderie and visibility. That they succeeded

---

43   I am grateful to Gillian (now Gillian Senior) for supplying me with the program and other material relevant to this event.

was reflected in the *Williamstown Advertiser's* report on 19 December 1963 that the piece had generated much 'delight' in the three packed houses of children and parents from Williamstown and district' who had attended.

In a few short years, WLT had become an extremely vital company. Not surprisingly, by the end of the 1950s, a few strains on the hard core of members were beginning to emerge. In 1960, it was decided to form specialised committees to handle production and publicity. April 1961 saw the adoption of a new constitution and a decision to drop the word 'Movement' from the Theatre's name, so that it became 'Williamstown Little Theatre'. The Theatre was now to be governed by four officers, president, vice president, secretary, and treasurer, and nine directors each responsible for a definite branch of activities. As well as production, stage and house directors to make productions happen, there were to be directors for publicity, liaison, tickets, properties and electrical work, plus an all-important social director to encourage people to have fun!

Not that this was a problem. The WLT community has always had a tradition of being able to relax and enjoy its own company. In the early nineteen-fifties, as noted in Chapter 1, the annual picnic in January/February was an important event in the Theatre's social calendar, a practice which continued for many years: *Williamstown Chronicle* for example reported on 22 Feb 1962 that the group had enjoyed a swim at the newly opened Olympic Pool in Werribee. In the mid-sixties, members indulged themselves in that very popular event of the time, the 'progressive dinner'. The social director's handwritten report of the first one in May 1963 speaks for itself:

The dinner consisted of six courses, the 'right' wine of course being served with each. We commenced at 6.30 at the home of Graeme and Lorraine West, where hors d'oeuvres and sherry were served. After allowing time for all to partake, and for latecomers to arrive, we set off again. At Gillian and Frank Wadds' we were met by a hostess with shining eyes. No! They weren't tears of joy at serving so many of us – she had peeled six pounds of onions, which she made into a rich soup and served with Sauternes.

We then progressed to the home of Mary and Frank Ironside for a tasty fish dish served with Chablis. Everyone, sherry glasses in hand, then found it necessary to walk to McCutcheon's where Ngaire served us with a delicious curry and rice, and re-filled our glasses with Burgundy. By this time a feeling of general goodwill surrounded all who had indulged and in such good spirits we set out for the Colville household, where we were welcomed by Nell and Alec. As we hoped, Nell provided some of her beautiful pavlovas which were served with Muscat. Much later we set off for the cottage, where cheese and biscuits, this time served with black coffee, awaited us. All who joined us agreed it was a most enjoyable night and should happen again soon.

A profit of £15/2/4/ was made on the evening.

The success of *The Boy Friend*, Williamstown's last production for 1964, left the company on a high. It seemed that it had at last kept the threat of television at bay and established itself as a significant player in Williamstown's cultural life. Moreover, compared with other amateur theatre groups in Victoria,[44] Williamstown had more members, was producing four plays per year compared with the average of two or three, had access to better rehearsal space, and achieved better quality design in its productions.

As it looked forward to 1965, WLT planned to stage just three local productions with the usual August production making way for the week-long VDL Metropolitan Region Festival it had agreed to host. It also was planning an entry in the first festival of one-act plays organised as part of Melbourne's Moomba Festival. This inaugural festival, sponsored by the Caltex Oil Company, was held in the Hawthorn Town Hall from 1st to 4th March, attracting entries from twelve groups across the State. WLT's entry was Michael Dines' *Viva Juarez*, produced by Gillian Wadds, with a cast which included Doug Lindsay, Ellis Ebell, Bernadette Twomey, Deidre McDonald and Vin Foster. Interestingly, given his later extensive involvement with the theatre as a director[45], the adjudicator for this festival was Brian Crossley. *Cues and News* reported that Crossley had 'honourably mentioned our play and Douglas Lindsay', but had awarded first prize to Mordialloc Theatre, Group, second to the Tin Alley Players and third to Echuca Drama Group.

---

44   This conclusion is based on information contained in Harold Baigent's mimeographed report *Survey of Amateur Theatre in Victoria*, (Melbourne, Council of Adult Education, 1964).

45   Starting with *The Second Mrs Tanqueray* in 1982 - see page 132.

Fifteen groups from across Melbourne entered the VDL Metropolitan Regional Festival held at the Mechanics' Institute from Tuesday 10th to Saturday 14th August. WLT's entry was Harold Pinter's *A Night Out*, produced by Vin Foster, and featuring a cast of thirteen, most of whom were people who already had, or would have, a long association with WLT.[46] Vin himself played two roles. Adjudicator Lorna Kirwood-Jones declared WLT's entry the winner, gaining it entry to the State Finals held at Russell Street Theatre from 30 September to 2 October, but it failed to gain a place.[47]

Unfortunately, audience numbers were down at all Williamstown's own productions in 1965, despite two of them receiving reasonable reviews. The first show of the year, a Paul Hill production of the Harold Brighthouse comedy *Hobson's Choice*, attracted only 615 patrons. Frank Murphy in *The Advocate* thought Williamstown had given this play a 'worthy performance' with the Lancashire accent 'remarkably well-managed'. Gillian Wadds was 'excellent as Maggie' with Terry Belville as Willlie, and Judy Sippo and Mary Little as the younger daughters 'very good', whilst Vin Foster, though giving an 'impressive performance' could have given the rich dialogue even greater effect. The largest audience of the year (698) came to Grahame Murphy's production of *A Dead Secret*. Again, Frank Murphy was positive about the acting of the large cast with Ellen Metcalf, June Lownds, Vin Foster, Gwladys Winfield, Bernadette Twomey, Frank Wadds and Ellis Ebell being 'outstanding'. The result was satisfying: 'The air of reality was caught and maintained by avoiding any touch of burlesque'. In Murphy's view, the next production Jean Anouhl's *Thieves Carnival* was of lesser quality: 'It succeeded very well in places, but the overall effect was not consistent.' The show attracted an audience of 622 and ran at a loss. The low attendances caused the theatre great concern, but at the end of the year, a new and unexpected challenge emerged.

At the 17 November 1965 board meeting, theatre president Alec Colville dropped a bombshell: The Mechanics' Institute, he reported, had been closed

---

46 The festival program shows that the cast included (in order of appearance) Bob Harsley, Ellis Ebell, Peter Egan, Vin Foster, Frank Wadds, Gary Metcalf, Margot Harper, Lorraine West, Judy Sippo and June Lownds.

47 This festival was won by the Tin Alley Players, with the City of Mordialloc Theatre Group securing second place, and the Morwell Players third.

while a panel of experts compiled their report on its structural condition. The next two shows at least would have to be staged somewhere else. The future of the Institute became a hot topic in Williamstown throughout 1966, receiving extensive coverage in *Williamstown Advertiser*, including a meeting convened in July 1966 by Williamstown Council to discuss its future with the Light Opera Company, WLT, the Williamstown Historical Society and the Rotary Club.[48]

Well before these discussions, WLT's committee necessarily went into action to look for another venue. One suggestion was the unused Mission to Seamen in Nelson Place. A meeting with the padre and treasurer of the mission followed to discuss the idea of renting the ground floor of the building, excluding the chapel, for £100, electricity and gas extra.

One important implication of using the Mission to Seamen building was the seating capacity. Holding only eighty to ninety people, audiences would obviously be smaller. The solution - increase the number of performances from January 1966. The first production was to run seven nights with another held in reserve if bookings were heavy. A sub-committee was set up and allocated the then enormous sum of £50 to build a stage and proscenium.

The move to the Mission meant revamping the 1966 playbill. The first production, which opened on March 10, was Terence Rattigan's comedy *The Sleeping Prince* directed by Grahame Murphy. This play tells what happens when His Royal Highness, the Grand Duke of Charles, Prince Regent of Carparthia, who has come to London for the coronation of King George V in 1911, invites an attractive young American chorus girl, whom he has seen in 'The Coconut Girl' (at a West End Theatre) to the Royal Suite at the Carpathian Legation. Because there are many royal characters in the play, the costumes had to be elaborate. Moreover, the intimacy of the new venue demanded even more attention to detail than normal.

Williamstown characteristically rose to the challenge of this crisis period, as Frank Murphy's review in *The Advocate* of *The Sleeping Prince* demonstrates. It was, he wrote, 'yet another example of the not generally appreciated truth that there was as much pleasure to be had from seeing a good amateur performance of a play as from a professional performance of it'. Murphy

---

48   See *Williamstown Advertiser*, April 7, May 5, and July 28, 1966.

1957 - 1968

The Sleeping Prince, March 1966
Vin Foster as His Royal Highness, the Grand Duke Charles, Prince Regent of Carparthia, and Lorraine West as Mary Morgan.

elaborated:

The role of Mary Morgan was 'played with great charm and nicety of acting by Lorraine West' who 'succeeded in a role made familiar on the screen by Marilyn Monroe'. It was Miss West's show, though there were other fine performances [from] Vin Foster, Ellis Ebell, Grahame Murphy, Margot Harper and Judy Sippo. On a much smaller stage, producer Grahame Murphy and his team worked wonders by mounting the scene in an impressive gilded decor ... costumes too were splendid.

Another reviewer thought that: 'Special mentions must be given to Ellis Ebell for an excellent portrayal of the King and Bernadette Twomey as the as the delightfully vague Grand Duchess.' Lorraine West recalled the positive impact which *The Sleeping Prince* had on the Theatre community: 'It convinced us that the theatre was more about people than about a specific building.'

WLT's tenure at the Mission was short-lived. As rehearsals for the next show, *Sailor Beware*, got underway, the Department of Interior requested that the company move out of the building by June to make way for the Navy. The Mission committee stepped in to plead on the theatre's behalf so that the show could go on, then on June 5, the theatre moved out of the Mission. A group started dismantling at eight o'clock in the morning, while a fleet of cars and trailers transported everything to the cottage next to the Mechanics' Institute where it was stored.

The Theatre had to act quickly, however, to keep the show on the road. Frank Murphy in *The Advocate* of 18 August 1966 wrote that he found WLT 'irrepressible', given the way they had successfully adapted to performance in the stage-less supper room at Williamstown Town Hall for a production of Tennessee William's *The Glass Menagerie*. The acting won praise from Murphy, particularly Judy Sippo's 'sensitive and appealing performance of the painfully shy and crippled girl', and Lorraine West's performance as the mother.

WLT had indeed proved indomitable in the face of crisis, as Nell Colville's Annual Report for 1965-66 reflects:

> *Probably 1965/66 has proved one of the most tempestuous in our career, but from it we have learned much. We have a nucleus of dedicated members who place the welfare of the theatre before every other consideration, a much larger following of members and friends who can be relied on for support, both physical and financial in times of crisis and so many, many people who previously knew us as only 'a good night's entertainment' but now identify us as their personal theatre to be sustained, sympathised or rejoiced with as the occasion demands. Tenure of the Mission has shown that a small, intimate theatre of our very own is the ideal and a goal worth striving for.*

Remarkably, despite the crisis at home, in the middle of 1966, Vin Foster managed to mount as a fund-raiser for the Victoria Drama League a production of *A Midsummer Night's Dream*, featuring a raft of WLT regulars: the cast included Ellis Ebell, Bob Harsley, Mary Little, June Lownds, Gary Metcalf, Grahame Murphy and Frank Wadds. The Theatre later entered John Mortimer's *Collect Your Hand Baggage* in the 1966 VDL one-act play festival securing third place behind Clayton Theatre Group and the Warrandyte Arts Association. Adjudicator Kenneth Woodward commented that WLT's effort was 'a first-class production', with Vin Foster receiving honourable mention for his work and stylish acting. Graham Murphy was similarly acknowledged. Overall, however 'the play proved to be lacking in quality'. *Collect Your Hand Baggage* was repeated in a festival of one-act plays held at the Newport Anglican Hall early in November, and WLT also presented Tennessee Williams' *Auto-da-fe* at Altona City Hall on 11 November.

As the Committee considered the uncertainties facing it in 1967, it was decided that unless WLT could be certain of performing at the same venue for at least the next four shows, it would not be fair to expect people to renew their subscriptions. To lay the basis for a better 1967, the company negotiated with Williamstown Council for the use of the Town Hall Supper Room throughout that year. Agreement was reached on suitable dates and a scale plan of the hall forwarded to council, showing the proposed position and dimensions of a stage with a request that the theatre be allowed to construct one. After what to the theatre members seemed an interminable delay, permission was finally granted in December on a trial basis and work began in January under the supervision of Gary Metcalfe.

Things, however, didn't go entirely smoothly. Relations became a little strained when a Council authority expressed great surprise at the size of the structure and assured the workers that it would not be allowed to remain. Fruitless consultations with the building surveyor followed and finally the Theatre circulated a paper to all the councillors personally, stating its case. At the same time, Williamstown Rotarians persuaded the Council to call a public meeting at which it was decided to explore the possibility of building a community centre. It seemed a reasonable solution, but Alec Colville doubted it would ever happen. He saw it as a 'long term dream'. The building would be able to seat about 500 and rental would have to be around $70.00 to $80.00 a night unless it was heavily subsidised.

Eventually, the Supper Room was made available to the Theatre and in March it staged Andre Roussin's *The Little Hut*, directed by Frank Wadds, a play chosen for its small cast of five - Bill Goode as the husband, Judy Sippo as the wife, Doug Lindsay as the perplexed lover, Graeme West as the Danish Cook, and Bob Harsley as the Lonesome Monkey. The play received excellent pre-publicity with a long article in *Williamstown Advertiser* focusing on Judy Sippo. Reviews were mixed. ARNIS, for *Williamstown Advertiser*, was not impressed, criticising the director for turning the satire into a straight comedy, considering the acting highly variable in quality. On the other hand, Kay Patullo in *Western Suburbs Advertiser* was much more positive, commenting that 'full credit should go to the Little Theatre for once more gracing the western suburbs with theatre of such a high standard'. Judy Sippo had 'performed her difficult role with graceful ease', Bill de Goode's portrayal of her husband was 'exceptional', though Doug Lindsay 'played his part variably'.

Nonetheless, the Theatre community was feeling stretched. The *Western Suburbs Advertiser* of 19 April 1967 reported the Theatre's decision to defer the production scheduled for 7-15 June. The Committee sought to keep members engaged by holding play readings every Wednesday evening in the hut next to the Mechanics' Institute.

On 31 July[49] the theatre contributed Thorton Wilder's *The Happy Journey* to a festival of one-act plays organised as part of an Altona Arts Festival which ran from 29 July to 5 August - the other contributors were the Strathmore Theatrical Arts Group of which, as noted above, WLT stalwarts Mary and Ron Little were founders and leading lights, and Altona Drama Group of which another WLT 'regular' Gwladys Winfield was President. Between 9 and 12 August, WLT presented its own program of one-act plays titled 'Plays of Contrast', in the Town Hall Supper Room. *The Happy Journey* was repeated (directed by visiting Queensland producer Rod Delaney and featuring Gwladys Winfield in the leading role, supported by a junior member of the Wadds family, Philip), as well as Tennessee Williams' *Something Unspoken*, directed by Frank Wadds, and featuring Lorraine West and Gillian Wadds in the lead roles, and *The Mother*, a play by Irish-American-Jewish author Paddy Chayefsky, directed by Gillian Wadds. WLT was back at the Town Hall Supper Room again in September 1967 with a double bill of one-acters: Wolf Mankowitz's *It Should Happen to a Dog*, directed by Gillian Wadds, and *Subway Circus* by William Saroyan, directed by her husband Frank.

Despite the challenges and uncertainties, it seemed that WLT continued to maintain the quality of its productions. Cordell Award adjudicator for 1967, Loys Caudwell,[50] reported that 'As always at WLT there were many excellent performances'. She listed twenty-six as being 'worthy of mention' with Peter

---

49   *Western Suburbs Advertiser,* 13 July 1967, page 5
50   The details are in *Cues and News,* December 1967.

Egan scoring four mentions, Bob Harsley, Doug Lindsay and Judy Sippo three each, and Gillian Wadds two. Gillian won the 1967 Cordell Award for 'an outstanding admirably sustained performance as Cordelia in Something Unspoken', but Caudwell commented fulsomely on Judy Sippo:

> *It has been quite inspiring during the past two years to note the amazing, almost spectacular work of one member. The adjudicator felt that this warranted some form of acknowledgment, and therefore, an Adjudicator's Special Award is made to Judy Sippo for continuous and outstanding improvement.*

Casting the net more widely during the 1966-67 crisis, many WLT members maintained their acting skills and their passion for theatre by taking on varying roles in other theatrical activities organised by Melbourne's burgeoning theatre network. *Cues and News* for November 1966, for example, reported that Grahame Murphy, Ellis Ebell and Vin Foster had just finished a season of *The Sentimental Bloke* at the Regent Theatre. Ellis and Vin were appearing in Maxwell Anderson's *The Bad Seed* with the Pumpkin Players in Richmond, Frank Wadds was concurrently directing *The Shifting Heart* for the Strathmore Theatrical Arts Group, and Gillian Wadds was 'script writing for the ABC, producing Festival Plays for Altona and baby-sitting'. (We need to remember that the core group at WLT were, throughout the 1950s and 1960s, as well as their theatre activities, living 'normal' lives: falling in love, getting married and contributing to the post war baby boom.) In April 1967, six WLT members (Ellis Ebell, Peter Egan, Bob Harsley, June Lownds, Gary Metcalfe and Grahame Murphy) were playing significant roles in a VDL production of *A Midsummer Night's Dream* at the MLC Hall in Kew. Simultaneously with the Altona Arts Festival, Grahame Murphy was directing a production of *The Merry Widow* for the Williamstown Light Opera Company with a cast including WLT leading lights Vin Foster as Danilo and June Lownds as Baroness Zeta.

It was about this time that Colville, riding his bicycle around Williamstown, came across a red brick building in north Williamstown, which appeared to be vacant. It was the former Cliff's Bakery, already run down when Emanuel

Cliff bought it in 1928[51], and used more recently as an engineering workshop. Colville immediately saw its potential. The small complex of old buildings promised storage space at least equal to the cottage at the rear of the Mechanics' Institute, rehearsal rooms and a theatre slightly larger than the Mission building. The buildings were old and in need of repair, but Colville was convinced that, given the Theatre's efforts in converting the Mission to Seamen building into a theatre in a short time, they could undertake the larger task of converting the bakery into a theatre.

Colville's model was Heidelberg Repertory (the original name of what is now Heidelberg Theatre Company). He put it to the Committee that:

> *A visit to Heidelberg Repertory will convince even the most pessimistic that a small Theatre can present drama of a high standard, provided that it has a permanent building and enthusiastic members and patrons. (Heidelberg) has become more vigorous since it took over the tiny Rechabite hall and turned it into a 90-seat theatre. We have a much bigger area to work in, with much more storage and working space, and even enough "off street parking" to cover our normal activities.*

The owners of the building, the Matthews brothers, were tracked down and, to the Committee's delight, were sympathetic to the cause. They did, however, point out that the area was subject to Melbourne Metropolitan Board of Works (MMBW) zoning, restricting its use in a residential area. Once again, the Theatre was caught in the middle: the MMBW required the owners' and the council's approval for the theatre to move in, while the council, after interrogating the theatre's president and treasurer for a whole evening, said it would re-consider the proposal when it had MMBW and health department approval.

A tense three months followed. Finally in October 1967, the MMBW issued an interim development order granting permission to use 2-4 Albert Street, Williamstown, for the production of amateur theatre until October 1969. The reason for the time limit was the issue of parking in Albert Street.

---

51   For the story of the Bakery, see Peter Cliff, *Dare to Dream*, (Melbourne, Brolga Publications, 2015), pp.1-4.

So, WLT had a solid set of buildings with a leaking roof, a lot of rusting scrap and a yard full of waist high weeds. Nevertheless, Colville and the Committee believed 'Cliff's Bakery' had the makings of a magnificent headquarters for Williamstown Little Theatre. With a permanent home the Theatre could provide so much more for its members and subscribers. As Colville commented in *Cues and News* at the time: 'Each time I have been there with committee members, it has been treated with the reverence of a long neglected holy shrine.'

The Committee's plans included a small theatrette, as well as space for rehearsals and activity nights where newer members could learn stagecraft, make-up, movement, mime and other aspects of the theatre. There would be ample under-cover space for Grahame Murphy and his set-building team, and space to store props and costumes collected over ten years.

By July 1967, the owners had quoted an affordable rent on a five-year lease and offered WLT an option to buy either at the end of that period or when, and if, the Theatre could see its way clear to raising the money. They also agreed to having the building rezoned. They were so sympathetic to the company, in fact, that the purchase price quoted in 1967 ($12,000) remained unchanged when the company finally bought the theatre in 1972. Moreover, the rent paid on the lease of the theatre between 1967 and 1972 was credited against the purchase price.

It was all hands-on-deck for five months. Volunteers were conscripted from everywhere. Through its weekly column in *Williamstown Advertiser* 'THE CURTAIN RISES', the Theatre enlisted the help of the local community and kept it informed of progress. Donations from coat hangers to fire extinguishers to a small refrigerator came from many sources. Special help came from Millie Black, the Theatre's new neighbour, who allowed the workers to borrow things and sleep in her spare beds. She also brought tea, sympathy and cold drinks. The Prince Albert Hotel across the road sent over slabs of beer for the workers on days when the temperature exceeded 100 degrees Fahrenheit.

In December 1967, in response to the question: 'What's happening about the bakery?' from 'friends far and near', Alex Colville reported in *Cues and News* that 'the dust is flying at Albert Street and far from letting the grass grow we have removed every skerrick from the cobbled yard'.

A special general meeting was held on November 18 to discuss the bakery, and individuals took on responsibility for specific aspects of the process. Alex Colville reported further that: 'Our plumbers, roofers, tinsmiths, carpenters, electricians, welders, bricklayers etc. can be seen every weekend and some week nights buzzing like the proverbial bees.' A great sense of energy and optimism took over in anticipation of the theatre opening in its new home on Friday, March 21, 1968. *The Sun* newspaper reported on March 19 that the theatre still had twenty people 'working flat out' to finish the job including painter Helen Koefed chosen to play the lead role in the opening production in 'The Bakery'.

A celebratory weekend followed. The audience came formally dressed up for the Saturday night's gala performance. On Sunday afternoon the theatre was officially opened by Peter Randall, director of St Martin's Theatre, and son of Brett Randall, the founding member of Melbourne Little Theatre who had given his blessing to the Mechanics' Institute being used as a venue in WLT's earliest days.[52] Randall junior confessed to being quite jealous of the large rehearsal room upstairs, as well as the storage space for wardrobe and props.

So, WLT put the trauma of 1966 and 1967 behind it as the opening of Albert Street heralded a new wave of optimism. *Barefoot in the Park*, the Neil Simon comedy, produced by Vin Foster, was a triumph despite the chaos going on around rehearsals. The promotional photo for 'Barefoot' suggested an excited cast. Bookings were better than ever, and the season was extended by two nights. Of the 850 seats available for the ten-night season, 821 were occupied, which was 96.6%, a remarkable figure for any theatre, amateur or professional.

Frank Murphy in *The Advocate* thought Williamstown's labours had been handsomely rewarded. About 'Barefoot', he commented that Helen Koefed as Connie 'gave a delicious performance ... as the young impulsive wife ... and she was well supported by Ellis Ebell, June Lownds and Bill Stevenson. All details of the production ... were the capable work of Vin Foster and Grahame Murphy's set (which used well the space on the Bakery's small stage) mounted the play well'. Koefed won the 1968 Cordell Award for her performance.

The second production at Albert Street, *A Loss of Roses* by William Inge, a

---

52   See p.11.

1957 - 1968

Set for *Barefoot in the Park*, 1968
Using the space on the Bakery's small stage well.

Cast of *A Loss Of Roses*, May 1968:
Bernadette Twomey as Mme Olga St Valentine, Peter Egan as Ronny Cavendish, Ngaire McCutcheon as Helen Baird, Lorraine West as Lila Green and Doug Lindsay as Ricky Powers.

play about the hopelessness of the depression years, was something of contrast to *Barefoot in the Park*. Still, perhaps aided by very effective promotion in *Williamstown Advertiser's* column 'The Curtain Rises' on 9 and 18 May 1968, the theatre filled to 85% of capacity and Frank Murphy thought WLT had upheld its high standard with this production by Gillian Wadds. Lorraine West scored another triumph in the role of Lila, while Peter Egan and Ngaire McCutcheon 'completed a trio of first-rate performances.'

William Gibson's *The Miracle Worker* about the blind-deaf prodigy Helen Keller, who had just died at the age of eighty-seven, was very popular amongst amateur groups in Melbourne at the time with Mordialloc Little Theatre having staged a production in March 1968. It was judged by critics to be WLT's most ambitious to date. Audiences warmed to the story of family conflict culminating in teacher Annie Sullivan's break-through in reaching the girl. The role of Helen was played by the ten-year-old Rosalie Livingstone from the Theatre's Workshop Group. The season extended to ten nights with 90% of seats filled. Foreshadowing comments to come from many reviewers,[53] Laurie Landray in *Listener-In TV* commented that Grahame Murphy's setting successfully fitted a multi-level playing area into the limited stage space. Landray was also positive about the actors:

> *Bernadette Twomey as the idealistic Annie and Julie Graham as the spirited older Helen shared the honours in eloquently projecting their anguish and joy. Vin Foster as Annie's teacher, Di O'Connor as the family aunt and Helen Koefed as the coloured nanny stood out strongly and Gillian Wadds gave a restrained performance full of integrity as Helen's mother. Doug Lindsay showed promise as Helen's father and James Chesworth was churlish enough as the captain's son.*

Ron Little, reviewing for *Williamstown Advertiser*, agreed.

Grahame Murphy moved on to Moliere's comedy *The Miser* which also enjoyed good houses, attracting 747 patrons over ten nights, a load factor of 88%. Laurie Landray again 'took great pleasure' in the production, commenting that the play required discipline to achieve a precise effect. Grahame Murphy,

---

53 For example, Diana Burleigh - see page 125.

he observed, had obviously worked it out in detail with this team of enthusiasts. Vin Foster delivered one of his best observed character roles, June Lownds was the epitome of dissolute avarice as the matchmaking Frosine, Ellis Ebell was marvellously colourful as the comic servant La Fleche, and Bill Stevenson was full of hearty fun as the coachman Jacques.

A similar proportion of available seats (605 out of a possible 680) was occupied for Frank Wadds' October production of Shelagh Delaney's *A Taste of Honey*. Frank Murphy in *The Advocate* thought *A Taste of Honey* 'authentically and movingly presented' with 'top performances' by Helen Koefed and Irene Stephenson, and 'strong' ones from Doug Lindsay and Peter Dunleavy.

The final production for 1968 was Grahame Murphy's Australian premiere production of Wolf Mankowitz's *Make Me an Offer*. *Williamstown Advertiser* thought the show a 'great success'. The second night of the play's season generated a special story from Bill Stevenson in the *Advertiser* worth quoting in full:

Friday night at Albert St, Williamstown, the curtain was just about to arise on another performance of the London musical 'Make Me an Offer' and the cast of this Williamstown Little Theatre was assembled on stage. The house lights were dimmed and the front-of-house staff had just shushed their last batch of latecomers to their seats.

Suddenly the evening silence was shattered by a spine-chilling shriek, followed by another and then another. The screams seemed to be coming from the street just outside the theatre's courtyard.

Fearing the worst, Mrs Dorothy Porter, who is in charge of front-of-house staff, raced into the street. She found herself face to beak with a large cockatoo. After giving Mrs. Porter a suspicious once-over, the cocky suddenly took off and alighted on some overhead wires. There, he proceeded to give an impromptu song-and-dance number in competition with the musical efforts in the theatre. The cocky then flew to the Prince Albert Hotel across the street.

However, the bird's owner arrived on the scene and explained: 'He has a lady friend over there'. After being called by his name, Tom, the bird returned to his mistress without further ado and was taken home.

Coinciding with the Theatre's move into the Bakery, and as if to herald a new beginning on all fronts, on 11 September 1968 a special general meeting of the theatre adopted a new constitution. The main effect was to streamline the somewhat cumbersome committee structure established in 1961, and to focus responsibility for production, administration, sales and public relations, and buildings and maintenance in the hands of four vice-presidents, each of whom would be assisted by small committees of two or three persons. The Theatre continued the practice of having separate directors responsible for production, stage, publicity, ticketing, and social activities, and an editor of *Cues and News* (Dorothy Porter, who was also responsible for the library).

Chapter Three

1969-1976: A New Home and a Crisis

Coinciding as it did with an upsurge in theatrical activity in Melbourne both amateur and professional, Williamstown Little Theatre couldn't have timed its move into its new home better if it had planned it. In 1967, some thirty-one individual amateur companies presented eighty-eight plays in Melbourne. Four years later there were forty-eight groups performing 191 plays. At the professional level, Melbourne Theatre Company attendances grew from 93,926 in 1968 to 183,025 in 1972 as its productions grew from nine to thirteen a year.[54] These 'established' groups were being both challenged and stimulated by the innovators at theatres such as La Mama and The Pram Factory whose foundation in 1967 and 1970 respectively laid the foundation of what is widely regarded as a 'revolution' in Australian theatre.[55]

Riding this wave of renewed enthusiasm for theatre, WLT opened 1969 with Neil Simon's comedy *Come Blow Your Horn*, produced by Vin Foster. It played to packed houses over nine nights. Based on this success, the Committee decided to extend Williamstown's season to ten nights. Over the next four years, the theatre filled to an average 77%. 1972 was an especially good year

---

54   The information on amateur theatre is taken from the *VDL Newsletter*, November 1967 and November 1971. Melbourne Theatre Company's data is derived from that company's 1972 Annual Report.

55   See Leonard Radic, *The STATE of PLAY, The Revolution in the Australian Theatre since the 1960s*, (Ringwood, Penguin Books,1991), p.1. In his memoir *Home Truths*, (Sydney, Harper Collins, 2021), David Williamson provides extensive insights into the dynamics of this 'revolution': see especially pp.83-86, and 99-101. Two of his plays - *Don's Party* and *The Removalists* opened on the same night, 22 July 1971 – *Don's Party* at the Pram Factory and *The Removalists* at La Mama.

with attendances at each of the five productions of the year exceeding 750, the highest being for Loris Blake's production of *Relatively Speaking* in December. In January 1973, a confident management decided to extend the standard WLT season to twelve nights, Wednesday to Saturday, over three consecutive weeks.

The second production for 1969, Patrick Hamilton's *Gaslight* attracted smaller numbers than *Come Blow Your Horn*, though Frank Murphy thought the production 'excellent', commenting that the 'five principals give a gripping performance of the thriller in which the sadistic Jack Manningham methodically strives to drive his wife Bella mad in the room where twenty years ago he had murdered an old lady'. Murphy thought Les Terrill as Manningham and June Lownds as Bella were 'admirably played' but there was a 'super performance' of the detective by guest artist Malcolm Phillips, a prominent professional actor from England visiting Australia who had played the role in England in 1938. Murphy had special praise for Bruce Wapshott's 'fascinating period set'.

Come Blow Your Horn, February 1969
Lorraine West as Connie Dayton, Doug Lindsay as Alan Baker, Jill Cordell as Peggy Evans, Lesley Baird as A Visitor, and Ellis Ebell as Buddy Baker.

1969 - 1976

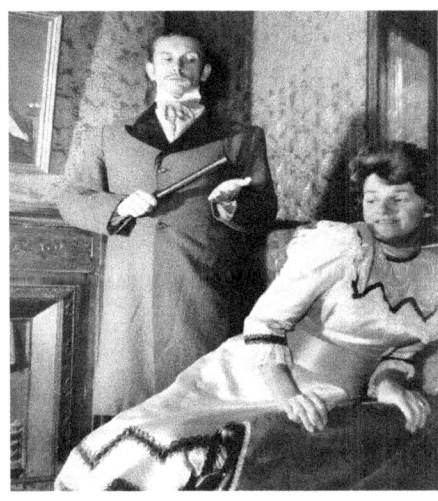

Gaslight, May 1969
Les Terrill as Manningham and
June Lownds as Bella.

A ten-night season was an ambitious undertaking for one of WLT's 1969 productions, George Farquhar's *The Recruiting Officer*, the first play staged in Australia after European settlement. Produced by Eric Donnison who came to WLT with extensive experience gained with Heidelberg Repertory Theatre and the Tin Alley Players, the play required a large cast of fourteen men and four women, plus children and extras, and the making of many costumes. The complicated set involved late-night and early-morning working bees and the company came to the conclusion that six weeks was not long enough to prepare for such a large production. It also decided it should limit its full-scale productions to five a year.

Listener-In TV gave WLT's *The Recruiting Officer* a mixed review. The major issue seems to have been the management of the set changes. The critic thought the changing of the sixteen scenes in Farquhar's play very skilfully done and 'an integral part of the entertainment' but 'the major trouble was that the (changes) held up the action of a long and complicated plot by about twenty minutes so that by the final curtain call at 11.10 pm a bit of tedium had set in'. This, however, was no fault of the large cast, a 'well-knit team (who) maintained an admirable evenness of style'. The cast was a 'who's who' of WLT: in supporting roles were Doug Lindsay, Vin Foster, Lorraine West, Lois Connor, Gary Metcalf and Trisha Watson. Grahame Murphy and Les

Terrill 'revelled in the major roles', with 'spirited support led by Ellis Ebell and Glynis Clod'.

According to reviewer Ron Little, the 'stand-out production' of 1969 was Charles Dyer's *Rattle of a Simple Man* directed by Loris Blake. Noting that though Dyer 'is not one of the better-known playwrights', Little commented that this play 'is very well written with excellent dialogue and character drawing, and a liberal sprinkling of humour and pathos'. The play concerns Percy, a complex if conventional Manchester lad who goes to London with the 'boys' for a football final, gets drunk, picks up a prostitute, Cyrene, and goes to her flat. Little summarised the action with:

> *Percy is too inhibited to do anything about her, but their conversations and the development of this situation reveals an interesting character analysis of two widely contrasting people. The one point of sympathy between them is their loneliness and this brings them together.*

His review was headlined 'Cast of Three Held Play Together', for he also wrote:

> *Les Terrill, complete with a first-class Manchester accent, was excellent in presenting all facets of Percy's character, and Lorraine West's warm-hearted Cyrene probably surpassed her many outstanding acting performances with the Williamstown Little Theatre...(and) James Cassidy as Richard, her brother, gave useful support.*

Little thought that WLT should be 'congratulated for a highly successful presentation'. He commented that 'Loris Blake's production was very detailed and Grahame Murphy's set was extremely stylish and set the right tone for the play'. A good outcome for Blake directing her first show at WLT.

Little's judgment was vindicated, and WLT gained a boost when *Rattle of a Simple Man* won the Best Production Award at the first Moomba Festival of 'full-length' Drama (as distinct from one-act plays) sponsored by Phillip Morris, held at the Northland Shopping Centre Auditorium in March 1970. Loris Blake won the Award for Best Director and Les Terrill for Best Actor at Moomba, thus confirming the judgment of WLT's own adjudicators who had bestowed the 1969 Cordell Award on him. The adjudicator for Moomba,

Joan Morris, also remarked on the attention to detail in the production, and the WLT support crew – the dressmakers, set builders and front-of-house team - also won praise from the Moomba officials.[56]

Les Terrill remembers that on one night of the production, the last line was 'lost'. To quote from his reflection in *Cues and News* for December 2020:

The pair (Percy and Cyrene) argue all night and the play ends when Serene says 'well, are you coming to bed or aren't you'? Percy replies 'Oh I don't know, I'll have to think about it'.

On said night Lorraine West ,who was playing Serene, delivered the penultimate line, but before I could respond a very earnest female voice from the audience shouted 'Go on it will do you good'!

Cast, crew and audience went hysterical, and the last line was lost in the laughter.

Another important initiative in 1969 was the establishment of a children's theatre, a long-mooted idea first suggested by Dorothy Porter at the third meeting of the Theatre in 1946! It was Vin Foster as Production Director who suggested the project be given top priority that year. He saw the program as being an eight-week term covering basic movement and mime, speech, stage geography, basic make up and theatre terms, as well as backstage activities, such as lighting, set design and construction, props and wardrobe. The group got underway and in December 1969 presented the one-act play *The Stolen Prince*, produced by Peter Egan and Ellis Ebell, to a packed theatre of mums and dads, other relatives and friends. In January 1970 Ron Little was made Children's Theatre director and by mid-1970 there were about thirty children enrolled. Unfortunately, the group wouldn't survive in the longer term. It needed more than one adult to maintain some sort of order among so many children and asking anyone to undertake such a large commitment as an eight-week term was a tall order for any volunteer organisation whose members have other jobs and families to take care of. Even so, the initiative continued

---

56   See 'The Curtain Rises', *Williamstown Advertiser*, March 11, 1970.

until 1976 in its first 'life'. It was revived again in 1979, the International Year of the Child, and operated for a further three years.

A Vin Foster production of Peter Shaffer's first play *White Liars/Black Comedy* opened WLT's 1970 season. It was followed by a Loris Blake production of *Woman in a Dressing Gown*, *The Duenna* directed by Grahame Murphy, *Five Finger Exercise*, directed by Bob Karl, and *Semi-Detached* directed by Maggie McInnes.

According to reviewers the quality of these productions varied. Of the first production, *Listener-In TV* thought WLT did 'an excellent job' with *White Liars/Black Comedy*, the latter coming up best giving comic character actors – in this case especially Bob Harsley and Gwladys Winfield – '... acting chances which were taken up with relish and style'.[57] Grahame Murphy was seen to have 'done a Charlie Chaplin' with *The Duenna*, 'directing the show, designing the settings and playing a leading role... his accomplished tenor was one of the musical highlights of the production', though another reviewer, Roy McQuade, thought 'the singing of "When a Tender Maid" by Gwladys Winfield was a highlight of a first-class performance'.

Whilst Laurie Landray in *Listener-In TV* had reservations about the male performances in Bob Karl's production of Peter Shaffer's *Five Finger Exercise*, not so that of June Lownds, who won the 1970 Cordell Award for her performance:

> June Lownds was so right, so superbly controlled, so immaculately modulated in vocal and emotional understanding of the mother's role that the men were dwarfed into relative incoherence. Miss Lownds has done nothing better than this portrait of a frustrated woman who almost unwittingly finds herself seducing the young tutor, only to be devastatingly set back when he asks if he may look on her as his mother. It was the high spot of the evening.

Reviewers of WLT's final production for 1970, *Semi Detached*, seemed to have seen different shows. *Williamstown Advertiser* thought the production 'a roaring success' with a quality performance by Les Terrill in the lead role of Fred Midway, whereas another reviewer thought Terrill's performance

---

57   *Listener-In TV*, March 7-13 1970, p.24.

'over-mannered'.

Person power was something of a problem in 1970. There were difficulties casting *Woman in a Dressing Gown* and *The Duenna*, while Eric Donnison, the original director of *Five Finger Exercise*, had to pull out and it took two months to find a replacement. The Committee eventually decided to pay a director and Bob Karl was recruited from the Council of Adult Education for a fee of $120. Because of Williamstown's perceived isolation, there were also problems getting set designers, as well as a constant lack of labour for working bees on sets, placing a great burden on Grahame Murphy. At Vin Foster's suggestion, it was decided to hold an "at home at the theatre" on a Sunday in May 1970 and to invite members of other theatrical groups around Melbourne. Ironically, it had to be postponed because of a lack of volunteers to help out. Nevertheless, production standards didn't suffer. *Listener-In TV*, reviewing the Melbourne theatrical scene of 1970 included WLT in its list of examples of first-rate companies, the others being Heidelberg Repertory Theatre, Pumpkin Players, Mordialloc Theatre Group, and Clayton Theatre Group.

The early part of 1971 proved a somewhat difficult period at WLT. By February, the Committee still had not determined the annual program, and the first two productions for the year attracted only smallish audiences. On the other hand, Grahame Murphy's production of *The Grass is Greener* received accolades from Laurie Landray in *Listener-In TV*, who wrote:

The high standards of presentation achieved by Williamstown Little Theatre were excelled in Grahame Murphy's production... (it was) a show of professional quality. Landray lamented that: *As so often with a Williamstown show, one cannot help regretting that it comes to pass in relative isolation and deserves the attention of a much wider audience. Vin Foster in the role of Victor was master of the situation, whilst Lorraine West was beautifully relaxed and coolly in character as his wife.*

The third production in 1971, Patricia Ann Jellicoe's *The Knack* directed by Frank Wadds, attracted more people but offended some subscribers who vowed not to renew their subscriptions. *The Knack* tells the story of three young men leading a sparse Bohemian life in London, and their encounter with a girl just arrived from the provinces. The action relates to their fantasies about 'getting' the girl. Laurie Landray in *Listener-In TV* thought *The Knack* 'as tough an assignment as any amateur group could attempt', and unfortunately was 'not perfectly cast'. In particular the girl of the piece, played by Victoria Walden, though in some ways 'well taken', she 'conveyed the naivety and inexperience and the strength of innocence', but 'her lack of acting experience told against her in vocal persuasion'.

Things turned around with the fourth presentation for 1971, *Wait Until Dark*, directed by Loris Blake with assistance from Vin Foster. The production got off to a shaky start. There were casting difficulties, but Ivor Porter was persuaded to return to the stage, even though he was unable to play either the first night or the last two nights. Laurie Gellon, who stage managed the show, also played the role of a policeman and Grahame Murphy, playing the role of Roat, designed the set. Poor bookings led the Committee to cancel the planned first two performances. The show opened on Friday 11 September 1971 with only seventy seats booked for the whole season. Word of the quality of the production soon spread, however, after a review in *Williamstown Advertiser* reported that 'a splendid cast (had given) justice to a splendid play'. In the following week the theatre was fully booked. The stars of the show were Grahame Murphy and Lorraine West. The *Advertiser* thought Murphy was 'brilliant' as Roat: '... from a menacing self-confident criminal he turned into a jabbering coward when Suzy got the upper hand.' Lorraine West as Suzy 'gave a realistic touch to the trying role of the blind girl. The audience was hanging on her every move'. Lorraine won the 1971 Cordell Award for this performance.

WLT concluded 1971 on a buoyant note when, despite Rex Callahan experiencing the 'usual' casting problem of finding suitable men, and a suggestion that his production of *The Happiest Days of Your Life* was a little under-rehearsed, the production proved popular with audiences; the season was extended by two nights to meet demand. Maggie McInnes who played Miss Gossage in this play recounted in *Cues and News* for August 2020, that Ernie Wilson who played the porter: '... had wanted to be on stage all his life, but his wife didn't approve. When his wife died, he enrolled at The National Theatre School, at age seventy-plus their oldest student, ever, and had just graduated when Rex cast him.'

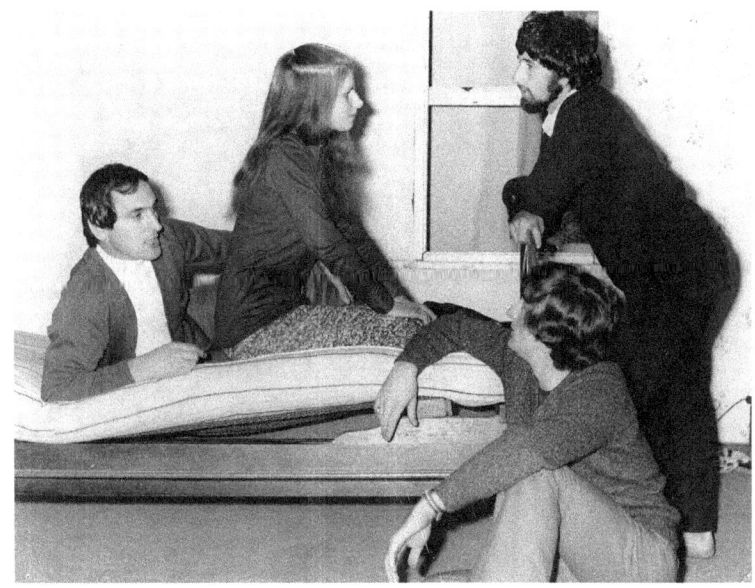

The Knack, July 1971
John Hatton-Davies as The Alfie type, Vicki Walden as The Girl,
Steven Moore as Tom, and Peter Berg as Colin.

On to 1972 and a varied playbill: *The Odd Couple* directed by Loris Blake; *The Shifting Heart* directed by Doug Lindsay; *The Lion in Winter* directed by Grahame Murphy, *The Prime of Miss Jean Brodie*, directed by Vin Foster, and *Relatively Speaking* directed by Loris Blake.

The Reviews of *The Odd Couple* were unambiguously favourable. *Williamstown Advertiser* was especially impressed by Vin Foster and Doug Lindsay as Felix and Oscar, commenting that 'The two actors kept a delicate balance between their personalities, with neither taking the limelight from the other'. In addition, 'Maggie McInnes and Geraldine Dowling gave a fine example of feminine coquetry as the Pigeon Sisters'. In conclusion, this reviewer described the production as 'a first-rate piece of comedy craft, with full value given virtually to every role in one of Grahame Murphy's best-ever settings'. Perhaps the success reflected the hard work with which Loris Blake claimed she always punished her cast!

Richard Beynon's *The Shifting Heart*, WLT's next production, written in

The Odd Couple, March 1972
Gary Metcalf as Murray, Bill Middlemiss as Speed, John Price as Roy and Nick Serpell as Vinnie.

1957, is often grouped with Ray Lawler's *Doll* (1955) and Alan Seymour's *One Day of the Year* (1960) as one of the naturalistic plays that brought Australian language, issues and images successfully to the stage in the late 1950s. Doug Lindsay, WLT's president in 1972, made his directorial debut with this production which the *Williamstown Advertiser* reviewer thought 'first class'. Lindsay, the reviewer opined, 'proved that he was an understanding man at the helm, and his cast built up and sustained a steady dramatic tension and intensity, relieved with joy and laughter which did justice to Beynon's script'. There was praise for the 'strong and perceptive' acting of the whole cast:

> Jim Ramsay has done nothing better than his portrayal of Poppa Bianchi, while Janet Stahl brought out the colour of Momma in a finely controlled performance. The love-hate tension between their daughter and her Australian husband was particularly well wrought by Kaye Butterworth and Paul Tonti-Fillipini, while Ellis Ebell was full of the dramatic brightness of the hapless son. Carmel Behan caught the broad flavour of the harassed

neighbour and Jo hn Saunders gave useful support as her whingeing no-good husband, while Robert Butterworth lent convincing contrast to the unsympathetic detective role.

There was similar praise for Grahame Murphy's following production of *The Lion in Winter*, the subject of a major innovation at WLT in that it was the first of two production exchanges between WLT and the Pumpkin Players in 1972. *Lion in Winter* was staged first at Pumpkin Theatre and then transferred to Williamstown.

Williamstown Advertiser critic Mariann Heimans thought the production at Williamstown 'breathtaking', commenting that 'the story of a tug'o'war between Henry II and his estranged wife Eleanor of Aquitaine was brilliantly handled by the cast'. Heimans had special praise for 'the lion of this strong cast' Gary Metcalf who 'stunned the audience as the expansive and shrewd Henry. He ranted and raved, loved and hated with equal abandon - a dazzling performer'.

Lion in Winter, July 1972
Gary Metcalf as Henry II.

Later, Vin Foster's production of *The Prime of Miss Jean Brodie*, after playing at Williamstown, transferred to Pumpkin's stage in Richmond. Marian Heimans was impressed by the acting, thinking that June Lownds gave an 'electrifying performance' in the title role. June 'thrilled the audience with her characterisation of an emotional, power-hungry teacher, whose daring ideas shock the headmistress of her school'. There was praise too for the performances of Tony Kentuck as Teddy Lloyd, Christine Saunders 'all woman' as Sandy, Teddy Lloyd's girlfriend, Janet Stahl as Helena, and Gillian Wadds as the headmistress who 'scowled with decorous rigidity'. The production also marked a technical first for Williamstown at The Bakery - the use of a revolving stage.

There was, however, some ambivalence about the joint venture. As Gwladys Winfield commented in her production report:

> *'The Prime of Miss Jean Brodie' was reported to have been most successful at Pumpkin and the Pumpkin Players most cooperative and helpful ... however, the Production Director who was also playing the lead in this play feels that this endeavour threw considerable strain on the resources of Williamstown and whilst it had many advantages to the cast and also enabled many people outside our normal audience to see and appreciate WLT's standard of performance, which is in itself excellent publicity and public relations, it is recommended that we don't participate in too many performances outside of Williamstown's own theatre especially if they involve a large cast. This could be said to jeopardise productions from within the group causing casting and back-stage problems and we must at all times put our loyal subscribers and audiences, our constitutional aims and objectives foremost.*

The subscribers and audiences seemed to like the production. *The Prime of Miss Jean Brodie* achieved a record attendance for WLT at the Bakery. Most nights were full, with several people on a waiting list. *Listener-In TV* thought it one of the five most outstanding amateur productions of the year. For her performance as Miss Brodie, June Lownds won the Cordell Award for 1972 and Christine Saunders won the Craven Award for the most improved performance for the second year in succession. The editor of *Cues and News* assured members that the fact that she came the nearest to nudity on the

Williamstown stage ever was irrelevant!

WLT's final production for 1972, *Relatively Speaking*, was also a triumph. It achieved WLT's largest attendance for the year, being almost booked out before the tickets went to Eddie Marr's Music Shop. One audience member, Dorothy Leavings, wrote a long letter, effectively a short review, to *Cues and News* about the production, that is worth quoting at length:

> *The night I saw 'Relatively Speaking' I was in a mood to be amused and was therefore delightfully entertained. It was a pleasant change to see a "piece of fairy floss" easily digested in comparison to the mostly surrealistic and harsh modern plays which seem to be the vogue nowadays… Maggie McInnes took the honours for the night, giving a delightful interpretation of a homely woman with a knack for keeping her man.*
>
> *David Bradshaw, a comparative newcomer to our stage, came a close second, the lack of experience being the only flaw in an otherwise believable interpretation. One small criticism is that he was dressed too young, but this did not detract from a pleasing performance.*

Leavings had reservations about the support actors: Nick Serpell, she thought, 'was over-playing in the first scene', and Jo White 'seemed to miss the author's intent from her interpretation of the young girl'. Leavings' conclusion, however, was that 'All-in-all Loris Blake's production was a great success greatly enjoyed by all audiences and was a pleasant finale to another year of diversified plays.'

Getting *Relatively Speaking* up had not been without its difficulties. Auditions failed to produce a complete cast and one character was not finalised until four weeks before opening night. There were also difficulties finding a set designer. The lack of a designed set meant that sometimes rehearsals didn't start until 9.30 pm. Nonetheless the Committee was very pleased with the outcome. Secretary Nell Colville advised Miss Blake that: 'The Committee was unanimous in its expression of appreciation of your mammoth efforts to overcome all the difficulties which dogged the production.' Colville also reported that: 'As a direct result of the popularity of this play, one new group who bought twenty seats has already booked sixty for March '73 and already we have received two other party bookings which will account for over one hundred seats.'

The theatre made progress in other areas in 1972. An electronic lighting board was installed. Alec Colville was obviously delighted by this advance in technological support. 'Functionally', he reported:

> ... the board is a lighting man's dream with finger-tip control and so much flexibility that our cue sheet sometimes look like a computer printout, ... I am sure that the patrons have noticed the more professional touch in the lighting side of the show ... The flexibility of the board enables the lighting designer to become an artist painting the scene with light.

The Children's Theatre continued to grow at this time. Each Saturday afternoon, swarms of young children took part, supervised by Ron Little. At the end of the last term for 1971, they showed off what they had learned at a Saturday matinee of six one-act plays. As well as the weekly classes, Little ran a very successful two-day school during the May holidays.

Little's underlying philosophy for the Children's Theatre was that while it could be seen as a way towards personal development and did not necessarily have to lead to a production, as a theatrical organisation WLT would inevitably run its classes with performance in mind. He did not share a fear held by some that going on stage made children 'precocious'.

An indicator of the success of the Children's Theatre came with the presentation of five short one-act plays on the afternoon of Saturday 7 October 1972. Notwithstanding that it was VFL Grand Final day, the theatre was packed to the rafters and the appointed critic for the day, Christine Saunders, arriving at the advertised starting time of 2.30 pm was unable to find a seat, and was forced to witness the performances with other enthusiasts in the foyer.

As well as the Children's Theatre, 1971 also saw the start of a theatre workshop for teenagers. The workshop was established so that the young folk attending would gain experience through play readings, and visits to see plays both professional and amateur, including those staged at WLT. The plays that were tackled were those that were 'different' from those generally performed, with an emphasis on experimental or social drama. The workshop met at 8.00 pm on Wednesday night in the Albert Street theatre and most of the members were under twenty-five years of age. The theatre workshop was the brainchild of Peter Curtis, a schoolteacher qualified to teach both acting and production.

Peter's interest in theatre began in England where he was a member of a theatre company in Portsmouth. He moved and became a founding member of the New Theatre in New Zealand in 1955. Subsequently coming to Australia, Peter lived initially in Cooma and then moved to Melbourne where he was employed as a technical representative with Sydney Cook Chemical. For a one-act play season in July, the workshop group met for rehearsal three times a week, constructed its own set and presented a melodrama at Kew Repertory Theatre and the Methodist Club Rooms in Canterbury. Curtis obviously remembered his time at WLT fondly: in 1998 the theatre unexpectedly received a bequest of $27,515 from his will.[58]

For the Cordell Award day in December 1971, the group presented a one-act play *There's No Business*. The cast included Philip Wadds, Stephen Tuckett, Andrew Davies, Lyn Ashlin, Conrad Wadds, John Meehan, Jan Whitburn, Colin Stephenson, Karyn Wilson, Helen Lundberg and Robin Kenny. In the two and a half years it existed the group provided an introduction to the stage for more than thirty teenagers.

By the end of 1972, it appeared WLT had extracted itself from the hole into which it had been dramatically cast by events well beyond its control. Public support was high, and the theatre was well on the way to achieving the major milestone which would make it the envy of many of its amateur theatre colleagues. At the beginning of 1972, President Alec Colville declared it the 'Buy the Bakery' year. The Committee took a formal decision to purchase the property and negotiations with the owners Matthews Bros, Engineering Pty. Ltd. commenced. The transaction was completed at the WLT's annual general meeting in July 1973 when Colville and Ivor Porter signed the documents formally transferring the bakery into the Theatre's ownership.

It was the culmination of many years of effective financial management by the WLT. The idea of having a theatre of its own had been in the minds of WLT's managers from very early on. As noted in Chapter 1, they set up a 'building fund' in 1954 with an initial allocation of £35, to which was added

---

58   See page 179.

£97/10/8 in 1955, £107/4/4 in 1956 and £42/8/6 in 1957. The Theatre's balance sheet for 1962 records that the building fund had by then grown to £396/8/5. By the time Alec Colville found the bakery the fund had grown to almost £500. From then on, any spare money was invested, and surpluses were directed towards the goal of purchasing the bakery. Soon after the purchase Roy Matthews wrote to Nell Colville:

Allow us to congratulate you and your willing band of helpers over last five years efforts to secure your premises. To the Porters and Colvilles and others, you may now look back with pleasure in pride of a job well done.

The boon to WLT from concluding the purchase of the bakery, however, proved somewhat of a false dawn. In June 1973, Doug Lindsay, then President of the Theatre, was worried, so worried that he wrote to all WLT members:

Dear Friends of the Theatre,

Not so long ago we faced a crisis which threatened to seriously curtail, if not completely close down, our activities. The loss of the Mechanics' Institute and the problem of finding alternative accommodation daunted even the staunchest theatre supporter. However, through perseverance, foresight and damned hard work, we have overcome this problem and gone on to become one of the most successful theatres in Melbourne.

Now we face a problem of a different kind. Many of the small core of hard-working members who have served on administration, front of house, backstage etc. are now feeling the strain of keeping up the high standard that we have attained. Quite a number have expressed the view that it is about time they had a rest. If this happens, what will we be left with? A fine theatre, bought and paid for, with no one to run it!

Lindsay was not being melodramatic. He and the committee decided to call an extraordinary meeting to resolve the problem. He added a postscript to his letter:

If you are interested in the theatre and feel as I do that to shut up shop would be a tragedy, then come to this meeting armed with suggestions. If you don't attend, then it may well be the last meeting of this group that you will have the opportunity to attend.

In fact, the Theatre faced several different problems. There was a real shortage of people willing and able to take on key jobs, such as lighting, set design and construction. The final production for 1972, *Relatively Speaking*, for example, was a traumatic experience for production manager Wal Philpott. The choice of play was a last-minute change from *Goodnight Mrs Puffin*. Philpott had organised Gary Metcalf to supervise set construction, but he was without a set designer and time was running out.

Wal collected materials during the day, and also worked on the set, while Gary came in the evenings to work on the main construction. June Lownds, Doug Lindsay and others pitched in, sometimes when Gary was not able to be there, to paint, paper and decorate. Nell Colville did the soft furnishings. It was a multiple 'Cox and Box', with people leaving little notes for the next shift. As Colville reflected, the theatre may have got away with it, but it could not afford to let it happen again. The experience proved that WLT had a pool of workers, but urgently needed people with artistic flair and skill to design scenery so that Wal and his construction team had a blueprint to work from. The Committee advertised for set designers in both the professional and amusement columns of *The Age* on Wednesday 2 and Saturday 6 December, authorising Grahame Murphy to offer up to $1,000 to a suitable applicant. Not one enquiry was received. The problems continued into 1973. Set construction for the first production *Goodnight Mrs Puffin* ran behind schedule as it did for the May production of *Eden House*.

The problem was compounded by organisational problems in the Theatre. In January, the second production for the year had not been finalised and there were doubts about productions for later in the year. Tension had been running high for a while. During the production of *The Odd Couple*, for example, cast members were left a note complaining about their non-attendance at working bees, a move which sent producer Loris Blake flying to their defence, saying that the many hours spent rehearsing was sufficient evidence to show a more than strong interest in the company.

It was a dramatic build up to the June 1973 crisis meeting called by the Committee. About thirty people turned up and there were numerous apologies from people who could not attend because of exams, rehearsals or other prior commitments. Doug Lindsay outlined the situation: a number of long-standing committee members wanted to stand down to give new blood - young or old - a chance to help run the theatre. The meeting revealed a general feeling that in the drive to create a living, efficient theatre WLT had lost its 'club' atmosphere. It was suggested that the Workshop Group, then meeting every Tuesday night, might provide a new focus for such activities.

When Lindsay mentioned the need for volunteers to stand for various committees at the forthcoming annual general meeting a dozen willing hands went up. This apparent enthusiasm was not, however, translated into action at the AGM. Only three nominations emerged for the thirteen available committee positions, though the remainder were filled from the floor - often a risky practice since the enthusiasm of the moment isn't always translated into an ongoing commitment.

Hence, while it appeared the meetings had generated new enthusiasm, the theatre's underlying problems remained. Nevertheless, productions throughout 1973 and 1974 continued to attract good audiences. Indeed audiences for all productions in 1973 were larger than for any in 1971 and 1972. The season for *Goodnight Mrs Puffin* was extended by three nights before it started and played to more than 90% capacity audiences, despite receiving only a lukewarm review from Laurie Landray in *Listener-In TV*. Ella Bambery played the title role, supported by Helen Jackson, Mary Little, Lyn Ashlin (a graduate of WLT's Theatre Workshop productions making her mainstage debut), Val Wilson, Nick Serpell, Stephen Moore, Gary Cameron, Doug Lindsay and Damien Dugan.

WLT's next production, *Eden House*, was a special play for the Theatre. Written by Australian author Hal Porter who taught in Williamstown in the 1930s,[59] the play was reputedly set locally. It concerns an ageing actress, Maxine, who refuses to sell Eden House because it represents to her a past golden age before her son Abel drowned at a nearby seaside. The subject was highly topical in Williamstown at the time, because of a proposal to demolish

---

59   Mary Lord, *Hal Porter, Man of Many Parts*, (Sydney, Random House, 1993), p.75.

a nineteenth century mansion, Maritimo, to make way for town houses.[60] The season was almost booked out, and the Theatre scored a minor dramatic triumph. Laurie Landray, writing in *Listener-In TV* under the headline 'Williamstown finds the real Eden House', described Lorna Kirwood-Jones' production as 'far and away the most satisfying complete account of this Melbourne bayside drama ever staged'.

There had been a small hitch in the run-up to the production when in it was discovered that the rights to the play had not been secured. On advice from contacts in St Martin's Theatre, they approached Porter, then living in Gippsland, directly. Porter graciously replied:

I'm never certain what to charge small amateur groups because it would be unfair to embarrass them. So I'll do what I usually do: suggest a fee (in your case $70) and leave the rest to you. If the fee is more than you are able to afford, I'll be content with what you can afford - it would distress me to know that the good work done by groups such as yours was hampered by unfair demands of mine... $70 or whatever you can honestly afford will satisfy.

The Theatre sent Porter a cheque for $120, based, as Secretary Nell Colville noted, 'on our practice of allowing $10 a night for royalties', concluding that 'it has been a great pleasure to establish this personal contact with you - this happens very rarely'.

Sean O'Casey's *Juno and the Paycock*, WLT's next production, was also admired by many locally, even though Laurie Landray again had many reservations. Jim Shaw won the Craven Award in 1973 for his part as Joxer. The production was also memorable for a 'surprise' birthday party for Shaw. Believing it to be his birthday one night during the season, Shaw celebrated with the rest of the cast in the dressing room, only to return home to his wife after the performance to find no birthday present and no party. She seemed to have forgotten completely. The surprise came when his wife calmly informed him that it wasn't his birthday at all; it was the following day. All, however, was not lost, as Shaw celebrated again at the last night party.

---

60   Maritimo was in fact demolished in 1973. See Lynne Strahan, *At the Edge of the Centre, A History of Williamstown*, pp.380 and 457.

There was a lot of controversy over the final production for the year. It was originally intended to be *Patate*, but there were casting difficulties. After nearly three weeks of searching, *Patate* was almost cast, only to be abandoned for the lack of a suitable actor to play the lead role.

Frank Wadds was hastily engaged for a fee of $100 to produce *See How They Run* and Grahame Murphy for a similar amount to construct the set. This production also ran into difficulties, which led to Laurie Gellon being called in to direct Lewis Carlino's *Cages* for a fee of $100 and for the set to be designed by Grahame Murphy, also paying him this amount. Gellon's production of *Cages*, two companion plays about the walls people build to protect themselves from the outside world and the outside world from them, was the first time they had been presented in Melbourne as the playwright intended, that is on the same program with the same two actors in each play. The production, Laurie Gellon's first for WLT, won many accolades.

Williamstown Advertiser thought the play highlighted Lorraine West's versatility, and celebrated Steven Moore's 'superb performance', for which he won the Cordell Award for best actor of the year. The *Listener-In TV* reviewer agreed that *Cages* was an 'outstanding success' and commented that it 'should encourage the group to cater further for theatregoers who seek enlightenment on the more bizarre aspects of human behaviour than is usually chosen by committees with constant eyes on what will offend conservative playgoers'.

WLT combined its extraordinarily high standard of productions with some mild risk-taking throughout 1974. Joe Orton's *What the Butler Saw*, directed by Loris Blake, was considered a little more earthy, risky, and daring than earlier productions. The real issue was nudity in theatre. The production was highly successful. As Secretary Don Joiner wrote of *What the Butler Saw* in his annual report for 1973-74:

> *Typical Williamstown, typical Loris Blake. What more can one say. A wonderful play of a very high standard greatly enjoyed by the audience. The cast teamed perfectly under Loris' well known and truly great direction, a production that sent everyone (all 952 who saw the show) home feeling warm and happy and having had a great night.*

Another hit in 1974 was *A Funny Thing Happened on the Way to the Forum*, directed by Grahame Murphy. Building on the successful shared venture with Pumpkin Theatre in the previous year, this was a genuine joint production which played at Williamstown from June 26 to July 13 and then at Pumpkin from July 27 to August 10. At WLT, the play attracted an audience of 923, being booked out most nights. In a flashback to a Williamstown tradition, the production toured to Maryborough in Central Victoria as part of that city's Golden Wattle Festival, for a performance in the Maryborough high school assembly hall on 24 August. The Maryborough community was most appreciative, and the cast and crew had a great time. Bernadette Twomey reported in *Cues and News* that 'It was funnier than it had ever been, quite the best performance we had done ... [it] went off with a bang'.

The cast celebrated mightily at the local pub. Twomey again:

> *Joan Evans wins the award for the night with a rendition of Goldilocks and the Three Bears (Boldilocks and the Gre Tears) something to be heard to be believed ... Then ... the French farce with lots of doors and people going and coming, and getting in the wrong and then the right room ... the corridor of the 'Bull and Foot' would have equalled any farce the French could have conceived. I never did find out who slept in Goldilocks' bed.*

WLT's final production for 1974, Alec Coppel's 1958 comedy thriller *Gazebo* received mixed reviews. The play concerns a TV thriller writer who plans to knock off a blackmailer and bury the body under the concrete foundations of his actress wife's latest folly – a gazebo or summer house. *Listener-In TV* thought Gwladys Winfield's production 'over-sentimental and too lovey-dovey for my taste where a stronger satirical edge would have been more appropriate'. Nonetheless, the reviewer thought that June Lownds and Les Terrill in the lead roles had done well: 'Mrs Lownds' honeyed tones and fetching array of gowns for all occasions, and Mr Terrill's nervous energy of a man in a mess were the most entertaining ingredients in the show.'

Throughout this period, the Children's Theatre continued to meet regularly on Saturday afternoons supervised by Ron Little and Val Wilson. Every October, it performed to full houses of enthusiastic parents and in 1973 presented a program of plays, sketches and poems including works by Noël

The Gazebo, November 1974 Les Terrill as Elliott Nash and June Lownds as Nell Nash.

Coward, Lewis Carroll, A.A. Milne and Banjo Patterson. The following year, the children presented two plays plus an improvisation, and there were more in 1975. Sallyann Wilson, a teacher newly appointed to the North Williamstown primary school, took over the Children's Theatre in 1976 and in August that year produced the three-act play *Under the Sycamore Tree*, a comedy set in an ant colony. The local newspapers reported that audiences were delighted with the performance.

Meanwhile, the youth theatre came under Grahame Murphy's wing in 1973, with help from Alec Colville and June Lownds. The workshop met on alternate Wednesdays and covered subjects such as deportment, mime, creating situations and memorising lines. This group also worked towards public performance. Originally Murphy planned to present a program of three one-act plays, including one by Tennessee Williams. However, when one of the workshop members wrote his own piece, *The Gumshuck Prison*, Murphy decided to present this as a produced play reading instead.

One very positive outcome of the youth group was that it was agreed that the age for membership of WLT should be lowered to sixteen, a move which enabled Philip Wadds, son of long-standing members Frank and Gillian

Wadds, to be appointed to the Committee for 1974-75.

The group continued into 1974 under the supervision of Kerry Cordell and invested great energy in work-shopping a play titled *Interview*. The cast and crew gave up their Sundays to rehearse and one Sunday afternoon even painted the gate to the theatre in their spare time. The group also attracted the attention of people like Simon Hopkinson and Jenny Janson, Hopkinson, in 1975, had just completed a stint as writer in residence with the Melbourne Theatre Company. Simon work-shopped an Australian play called *After Z* with the youth group, while Janson, voice coach with the Melbourne Theatre Company for four years, conducted voice classes on Thursdays.

Behind the scenes, however, there were still difficulties. More volunteers were needed. Doug Lindsay repeated his message that the theatre had reached a stage when office-bearers had decided they needed a rest. These were people who loved the theatre and want to see it go from strength to strength, but they also wanted time to devote to their first love: acting. The theatre needed more people who were willing to give their time behind the scenes to administration and organisation.

New people did emerge to contribute their skills. For example, Suzette Neilson, an American-trained drama teacher at Williamstown High School, ran creative drama workshops. There was also a major new publicity push. The publicity team raided the Theatre's wardrobe and paraded around Williamstown's shopping centre handing out leaflets. The team scored quite a coup when Angela and Patricia Klaniscek happened to turn up at the Strand Hotel talent quest one night dressed in clown costumes and proceeded to walk off with the first prize, though they were unsure if the audience was applauding their talent or their courage. The Theatre also began accepting paid advertisements in its programs to help cover costs and negotiated a regular free fortnightly theatre news column in *Footscray Advertiser*.

Amid all the trauma, there were determined efforts to try and improve things. In 1975 the Committee set itself a goal of establishing a 'growth spiral', initiating more activities which would draw in more people. A major initiative was an 'Instant Marathon Theatre', an idea hatched at a highly successful working bee at the theatre on the weekend before the 1974 Melbourne Cup. The plan was that an acting team would work in shifts, starting at 2 pm on Saturday, April 5, and attempt to run a continuous performance for thirty hours. Writers, scribbling away at the theatre, would create scripts for the actors on the spot, adding to the excitement with the question of whether they could keep coming up with sufficient material and ideas to keep the actors going. The aim was to get publicity, make money from sponsors and, of course, have fun. The event was a great success. For thirty hours a permanent team of sixteen actors - plus a few visitors - acted out a stream of original scripts provided by a nucleus of nine on-the-spot writers. It made Channels 0 and 7's Sunday evening news bulletins and two editions of ABC National Radio News on the Monday morning. There were also articles in *The Sun*, *The Herald*, *The Age*, *Listener-In TV*, *Footscray Advertiser*, *Footscray Mail*, an interview with 3AW and a few other radio mentions. It was even reported in Sydney and Perth.

Both Williamstown and Footscray councils sent congratulatory messages. Footscray Council invited the theatre to stage a council-supported pantomime for local children over the Christmas period. It wasn't until sometime later that WLT realised what a unique feat it had achieved. Endeavouring to get the event registered in the Guinness Book of Records, the Theatre was told the claim could not be verified because Guinness could find no similar activity to compare it with!

Williamstown's more conventional theatrical activities in 1975 also went well. The first production was the classic British farce *Charley's Aunt* directed by Kevin Good, with a cast that included Peter Cheasely, Geoff Armstrong, Peter Crockett, Sallyann Wilson, Gail Poole, Irene Grey, Ted Smeed, Ewen Crockett, Frank Wadds and Maggie McInnes. Maggie McInnes also designed the costumes with help from Val Wilson, June Lownds and Pat Day. Inevitably, the set was designed by Grahame Murphy. The production was a hit with audiences - the Theatre had to turn away people wanting tickets.

Murphy took up the director's role once again for the next production, *A Man for All Seasons*. Les Terrill as Sir Thomas More won the Cordell Award with 'Comus' in the VDL magazine *Theatrecraft* commenting that he had 'topped many fine character studies with his account of Sir Thomas More'. It seems that he had good support. 'Comus' continued:

> Under Grahame Murphy's direction, there was a colourful array of characters in support, with Jim Fitch scoring particularly well with Norfolk, a last-

1969 - 1976

Charley's Aunt, February 1975
L to R: Frank Wadds as Bassett, Sallyann Wilson as Kitty Verdun, Geoff Armstrong as Jack Chesney, Irene Gray as Ella Delahay, Peter Cheaseley as Lord Fancourt Babberley, Gail Poole as Amy Spettigue, Peter Crockett as Charles Wyndham, Maggie McInnes as Donna Lucia Salvadore, and Ewen Crockett as Colonel Sir Francis Chesney Bart.

minute change of cast when David Bradshaw took a professional engagement.

James Shaw's Common Man had all the right comedy touches, Alison McWilliams and Sally Ann Wilson were effective as More's wife and daughter, Martin Shaw was appropriately vacillating and weak as the opportunist Rich and Gary Metcalf was monumental as Wolsley. Barry Groves was a nasty piece of work as Cromwell.

Even more successful was the Theatre's contribution to International Women's Year, a production of Aristophanes' *Lysistrata* with its cast of more than thirty. Directed by Gillian Wadds, it was an additional non-subscriber production and unusual in that it was deliberately cast and crewed entirely by women. The theme of the play was entirely appropriate to International Women's Year. As described in *Cues and News*:

'LYSISTRATA, a beautiful woman of Athens, is sick and tired of the men continually going to war and is disgusted with the submissive role forced on herself and all the women of Greece. In true Germaine Greer fashion she incites the women to stand up for their rights and force the men to end the fighting. They manage this in the only way they can - by taking a vow not to let any man near them until the war is ended. The men suffer - and so do the women (Lysistrata has great trouble keeping them all barricaded in the Acropolis!) but virtue(?) triumphs in the end and the women emerge victorious.'

A later *Cues and News* reported the success of the venture thus:

A gamble 'Lysistrata' certainly was for Gillian as well as our theatre. No one could estimate audience reaction to this bawdy classic…(but) there was rarely a night that wasn't booked out and Pat Day often had the difficult job of finding extra seats for people waiting in the foyer.

The production was a success in more ways than one, from a publicity point of view we obtained better coverage than ever before…
The confidence Gillian showed in casting so many new faces proved warranted. Their hard work … proved an inspiration to us all and came through in all their fine performances.

There was some off-stage drama for the cast of *Lysistrata*. A few days into rehearsals, Lorraine West learned that she was being considered for a leading role in a new Australian movie being shot in Sydney. No one was quite sure whether to be glad or sorry when they learned that a Sydney actor had got the part.

WLT's final production for 1975 was the American comedy *A Thousand Clowns*, a play about Murray Burns, a former writer for 'Chuckles the Chipmunk', a children's TV personality, who has given up the job in disgust. He spends most of the play trying to dodge any form of work at all despite the efforts of his young twelve-year-old nephew, Nick, to organise his life for him. Directed by Frank Wadds, the lead roles in this production were played by Carillo and Nancy Gantner, recent arrivals in Williamstown from

1969 - 1976

The Cast of *Lysistrata* July 1975
WLT's contribution to International Women's Year.

America. Both had considerable repertory experience in the United States. Carillo Gantner was runner up for the Cordell Award for his role in this play and Nancy won the Craven Award. Also in the cast was Malcolm Robertson from the Melbourne Theatre Company. As reviewer Jim Rowntree noted in *Theatrecraft*, this was 'one of the strongest casts seen in amateur theatre for some time'.

The success of several major productions in 1975 and the continued vitality of the children's and youth theatres suggests that WLT was on its way out of the trough of 1974 and 1975. Several working bees were organised in 1975, which were generally well attended and were accompanied by some amazing feats - John Fitzwater, extremely impressed by the new carpet laid in the auditorium, painted the whole of the theatre on his own, and in a single weekend! Kerry Cordell built a new flats storage rack and Pat Day embarked on a major cleaning campaign.

Records of WLT productions in 1976 are limited. There are no extant reviews, for example, only some photos. The bill of fare for the year was: 24 February to 13 March: *Ten Little Niggers* by Agatha Christie, directed by Lorna Kirwood-Jones; 27 April to May 15: *The Slaughter of Saint Teresa's Day* by Peter Kenna, directed by Doug Lindsay; 29 June to 17 July: Feydau's farce *Hotel Paradiso*, directed by Ted Smeed; 21 September to 9 October: *A Bunch of Ratbags*, a rewriting for stage by Don Battye and Peter Penne of a book by William Dick, directed by Vin Foster; and 17 November to December 4, Leonard Gorse's *Butterflies are Free*, directed by Ewen Crockett.

All of these plays except *Butterflies are Free* involved large casts, in the case of *Hotel Paradiso*, a total of nineteen. *Hotel Paradiso* was booked out before opening night and sales for *A Bunch of Ratbags* were also very good. Each of the plays had recommended it to audiences. For example, *The Slaughter of Saint Teresa's Day*, written in 1958, was one of the first plays to portray the realities of Australian life - in this case the run-down nature of the Sydney suburb of Paddington in the early 1950s, where Kenna's central character, the robust queen of Sydney's underworld, Oola Maguire, lived. Oola is modelled on the well-known Tilly Devine, described in the play's program as 'a buxom Cockney blonde with a pungent tongue and persuasive fists', who 'for more than a quarter of a century reigned unchallenged over an empire of prostitutes, thugs, thieves and sly-grog merchants'. Lyndall Heiner won the Craven Award for best performance in a supporting role in this play (as Thelma Maguire).

A Bunch of Ratbags had strong local resonances for Williamstown patrons being the story of the bodgies and the widgies who lived in Footscray (Goodway in the play) in the 1950s rock and roll era. The action of the play takes place in the well-known Oasis Milk Bar, the kitchen of the Cooke family home, and various stores and other spots around the suburb.

By way of contrast, *Butterflies are Free* was set in New York, and was the story of a young man who escapes his mother's apron strings and sets himself up in an apartment of his own. The young man, Don Baker, played in WLT's production by Peter Cheaseley, is blind, but has a sense of humour and determination as he learns to depend only on himself. His mother, played by Mary Little, is not as confident as her son, and is torn between concern, disapproval and grudging admiration. It is the young man's neighbour, Jill Tanner, who gives him confidence in himself, and he in turn learns that he can give her support in sorting out her problems. Sallyann Wilson, who played this role at WLT, comments in her theatre scrapbook that this production, the first directed at WLT by Ewen Crockett, as 'her most favourite ever'. Unusually for the time, this play got coverage in both *Footscray Mail* and *Footscray Advertiser* on 17 November 1976. Peter Cheaseley won the 1976

Cordell Award for his performance as Don Baker.

Vin Foster experienced difficulties with the casting of *A Bunch of Ratbags*. In August the production was going along quite well, but a month later there were all sorts of troubles ranging from one of the lead males having to drop out because of ill health, through conflict between the director and the choreographer, to the recurring problem of delays in set construction. Set construction was also tardy for the next production, *Butterflies are Free*. The production director warned that less and less help from members was a dangerous sign and would place the whole theatre in jeopardy.

A controversial and divisive issue at the end of 1976 was the hardy perennial of whether or not producers should be paid and, if they were, how much? Some argued that since a number of directors and producers earned their living directing and producing professionally, they should be paid for their efforts. Others categorically disagreed. The issue went off the boil but continued to simmer away in the background and relationships were strained.

Despite all the tensions, the Theatre managed to organise a celebration of its thirtieth anniversary[61] - in the form of an 'authentic Hawaiian luau 'under the palm trees' at 72 Pascoe Street on Saturday November 13. As the article advertising the event in the *Star Advertiser* of 20 October explained:

> *The focal point of a luau is the cooking of a whole pig by wrapping it in leaves and burying it in a pit of hot stones on which a great fire is built. Guests will sit on the ground to eat and the whole show will be rounded off by fresh fruit salad.*

The article further noted that:

> *The Little Theatre's Hawaiian consultants, Kinso and Florence Matsuda, will have over-all charge of the complex preparation for the event.*

There was a need, however, for considerable involvement by theatre members. As Sallyann Wilson explained in another article in the local press:

---

61   *Star Advertiser*, 20 October 1976, p.3.

WANTED - six able bodied persons to dig a pit and raise and lower a sizzling pig!

The Theatre is calling for a long list volunteers to dig the pit and lower and raise the pig, 10 reasonable cooks who will follow the recipe given by Florence Masuda for a salad, at least two strong people who are early risers who will go to the wholesale fruit market on Footscray Road at about 7.30 am on Friday, November 12 to buy bags of yams, cases of pineapples, bananas, lettuce and tomatoes; and two people who will go to the Victoria Market on the Saturday morning to buy fish and chickens.

Not done yet!

As well two or three people with an artistic flair are required to set and decorate the tables on Saturday afternoon - and two people to make paper leis prior to the function.

All in all, quite a production!

There is little doubt that the period from 1973 to 1976 was the most troubled in Williamstown Little Theatre's history. A feature of the Theatre's management team in its first twenty-five years was its stability. Individuals tended to occupy the key executive positions for significant periods of time. In the first twelve years of its existence, WLT had only three presidents, each serving for four years: Dr R J Long, Ted Cordell and Tom Craven. After Bill Ward served as the Theatre's initial treasurer, Harry Conradi was treasurer for seven years, followed from 1955 by Ivor Porter who, except for 1961, remained in that position for thirteen years. Win Stewart did the secretary's job most years from 1948 until 1958, until she was succeeded by Nell Colville for the next ten years. Most of these people moved on after the purchase of The Bakery was completed. The loss of so many of these long-term key players from the Theatre's management left a vacuum which proved difficult to fill. There were also major differences in management styles among the executive members after 1973.

In fact, the Theatre was going through a major transition, becoming less overwhelmingly local in its orientation and key personnel and beginning to draw on people from a wider area. There was also a generational changing of the guard. Families who had played major roles in building the Theatre in its first twenty-five years were seeking to play somewhat lesser parts. Yet, the new generation of leaders which would lead WLT to further success and prosperity in the 1980s and 1990s had not yet emerged.

Chapter Four

1977-1986: Recovery

At the start of 1977, there was much pessimism at Williamstown Little Theatre. Two and a half weeks before the planned opening of the first production for the year, Joe Orton's highly controversial black comedy *Loot*, director Val Lehmann hadn't managed to cast one of the central characters. Fortunately, she was rescued by the experienced Ed Bailey from Toorak Players. The choice of play also proved unfortunate: only 357 people came to see the production, including one subscriber who wrote complaining of the theatre's 'bad taste' in staging *Loot*, indicating her intention to 'sever all connection with the theatre'. No doubt the lady concerned was reacting to Orton's use in the play of 'all the apparatus of strong drama' as the Metheun edition of the play put it: 'crime and violence, pious sentiments and ironic coincidences... illicit passions and the solemn trappings of death.'

The crunch came in April when the WLT Secretary Don Joiner was forced to write to all members and subscribers advising that: 'in view of the total failure of those responsible to make proper arrangements for the next production, it has been cancelled'. On Anzac Day evening there was a frank open discussion of the state of the Theatre: no one had turned up for dodger drives; no one helped pull the set down; there was too much talking behind people's backs; people couldn't just act, they should work too, and so on, and so on.

The first half of 1977 was the nadir of the Theatre's fortunes since it had moved into the bakery. It did manage to participate in the 1977 Moomba Festival of Theatre held at the National Theatre with a re-presentation of *Butterflies are Free*. But as the WLT stalwarts had found so many times before, just when everything seemed to be going downhill rapidly, signs of a revival appeared. In his letter advising of the cancellations of the second

Loot, February 1977
Helen Jackson as Fay and
Ed Bailey as McLeavy.

planned production of 1977, Don Joiner also advised that auditions for the next planned show, *Look After Lulu,* Noël Coward's adaptation of the French author George Feybeau's comedy *Occupe-Tui d'Amelie!* would be held on 15 and 16 May. Auditions proved successful and, though Bob Karl in his review thought many aspects of the production lacking (e.g. sets, costumes and stage movement), it had attracted 'many satisfied customers'. Karl concluded his review of the 'worthy play and a massive undertaking' with the comment that *Look After Lulu* had 'proven that Williamstown Little Theatre can bounce back'.

The role of the little girl in the production was shared by Michelle Bullas and Manya West. As the local newspaper put it, Manya was 'a member of a noted family of Little Theatre performers at Williamstown', being the daughter of Lorraine West, 'the only person to have won three Cordell Awards', and the granddaughter of Jim Davey who had appeared in WLT's first production *Man of Destiny.*

Williamstown's next effort was Gillian Wadds' production of *The Philanthropist* by Christopher Hampton, a modern comedy of manners that

Gillian had wanted to direct for about six years. The cast was Bill Martin, who won the 1977 Cordell Award for his performance as Phillip, Doug Lindsay, Peter Black, Lyndall Heiner, and Robyn McNally and Janine Doherty who had both appeared in *Look After Lulu*. Gilllian's backstage crew were highly praised. The crew included her son Philip who she said 'spent a lot of time swearing and moaning and working very hard to fix my lighting and special effects'.

In his review, Bob Karl was very positive about the production. Noting the limitations of Hampton's play, written when he was only twenty-four, particularly the women's parts which tended to be characterised by long 'true confession' speeches that didn't advance the action, Karl praised Robyn McNally and Lyndall Heiner for carrying off their monologues without taxing the credibility of their characters. He continued:

> ... although the play is almost totally devoid of any action (apart from a brief moment when one of the characters blows his brains out on stage) and is heavily laden with long monologues, the finely balanced cast of Bill Martin, Doug Lindsay, Bartley McGowan, Robyn McNally, Peter Black, Lyndall Heiner and Janine Doherty, under Gillian Wadds' direction resisted all attempts to 'enliven' the play by over acting and maintained a fine restraint, playing it for real.

Another boost for Williamstown in the latter part of 1977 was the success of a one-act play, *Ritual for Dolls*. It was put together by a touring group comprised of Robyn McNally, Ian Walker, Conrad Wadds and Bartley McGowan, originally under Ian Jones' direction, but later directed by Laurie Gellon. Secretary Doug Lindsay reported to the 1978 AGM:

> *This delightful one-acter was presented at Wagga on Saturday 27th August (terrific crit from adjudicator), South Street Competition Ballarat on 8th September (honourable mention) and then Kyneton on 18th September where it gained second place, honourable mention for everyone and $75 prize money.*

WLT's final production for 1977 was *Say Who You Are*, a Waterhouse and Hill comedy. Unfortunately, Loris Blake had to withdraw from directing but Ewen Crockett stepped into the breach, and also played one of the four roles, David Lord. A further complication was that just after Ewen had chosen Sallyann Wilson to play the role of Sarah Lord, she was involved in a car accident, which meant that Sallyann, after recovering from her minor injuries, had only five weeks for rehearsal.

A particular challenge for Williamstown in staging *Say Who You Are* - as it was on so many occasions given the intimate size of the stage - was the set design. It required three big acting areas - the living room of David and Sarah Lord's upstairs flat, the lobby of a block of flats and the entrance and frontage of "The Husser", the local pub with a public telephone box outside it. The genius this time came from David and Margaret Wilson.

The production did not attract much of an audience, despite Sallyann receiving front page coverage in *Williamstown Advertiser* on 16 November. It seems, however, that the problem was the play itself. Bob Karl commented:

With the deserved success of Keith Waterhouse and Willis Hall's other theatrical works like 'Billy Liar' and 'All Things Bright and Beautiful', it come as a surprise to discover that 'Say Who You Are' is an unevenly written play that, in attempting to blend social comments and comedy, fails to achieve any depth or come to terms with the issues it raises.

During the late 1970s and early 1980s a new era of expansion and artistic development for WLT dawned. Central to the renaissance was a renewed camaraderie which had been the hallmark of the company throughout its first twenty-five years, particularly during the most difficult times. While the leadership of Laurie Gellon and Vin Foster was critical to WLT's recovery, the foundations were laid by Pat Day.

Pat joined WLT in 1968 when she was working as a dressmaker for Magg's, Zara Holt's frock shop in Toorak. She learned her trade as a junior in the workroom at Alouette's in Melbourne's Block Arcade, and later spent three years making costumes for the Australian Ballet. A friendly matron at Pat's local hospital in Footscray introduced her to WLT just as the seats were being installed at the Albert Street theatre. Ellis Ebell remembers the day Pat turned up at the theatre 'to have a look at what was going on' and recalls 'she said she could sew,' which, as we shall see, was something of an understatement. Pat's involvement started as prompt and properties person for *Barefoot in the Park*, the first production at Albert Street. Her talents were soon discovered, and she quickly became wardrobe mistress. By July 1977 she had been elected President.

At the time, the company was considering its 1978 program amid a good deal of confusion. It had been agreed that there would be four subscriber productions and one non-subscriber production that year, each with a run of thirteen performances. However, dates for only three productions had been set and the rights secured for only four. The new president called a special meeting at which it was decided that plays for 1978 would be selected on a 'bums on seats' basis, that they should have enough parts to give all members an opportunity to participate, that auditions should be widely advertised, that 'pride in the theatre be increased' and that all after-show parties be held upstairs 'to alleviate the problems of cleaning up the foyer each night'.

From the beginning of 1978, spirits at WLT lifted considerably. Continuing its tradition of celebrating every anniversary in sight, the company celebrated the tenth anniversary of the move to Albert Street with a party on the last night of *The Gingerbread Lady*. Publicity for the year also started off well. By early February, posters for the first production had been in the shops for several weeks and stories appeared in *Williamstown Advertiser*.

The year began unusually with a large-cast pantomime, *Goody Gumdrops*, directed by Peter Black presented as part of the Williamstown Summer Festival. Following advertisements in *The Herald*, *Williamstown Advertiser* and *Footscray Mail* as well as in *Cues and News*, more than thirty people auditioned for the first Albert Street production, Daphne du Maurier's classic psychological thriller *Rebecca*, directed by Peter Cheasely.

Rebecca drew large audiences with some people booking a second time. According to *Cues and News*, well-known Melbourne actor and TV personality Terry McDermott attended the show and gave the cast a sixteen-page critique that kept the cast and crew occupied until 2am. McDermott thought the cast's attitude to the job was 'commendably serious' and the results were 'a job well done and an entertaining evening'. The challenge to reproduce the 'great country mansion' in which the play is set on the small WLT stage was, in McDermott's view, managed well by designers Margaret and David

Wilson. Ewen Crockett's lighting was 'effective and helpful to the atmosphere without any tricky distractions'.

WLT entered *Rebecca* in the Moomba drama festival, but without success. *Rebecca* was followed by *The Gingerbread Lady*, directed by Loris Blake, featuring two of WLT's most reliable and much-loved actors Mary Little and Lorraine West in the lead roles. Laurie Gellon reported that set construction 'had been a most pleasant task with so much help from so many people'. John Murphy from the VDL reviewed the production for *Cues and News*. Noting that this wasn't one of Neil Simon's better plays, Murphy felt that the plot, 'was a little too predictably contrived at the expense of the characters' which provided the director and players with a few problems which weren't resolved'. In other words, a bit of a mixed bag. In detail, Murphy commented that:

> *The play was attacked with too fast a pace ... [which] detracted from the moments of pathos that each character had ... Shane Bourke as Manuel certainly had the feel of his character ... more use of gesture and a little*

The Gingerbread Lady, May1978
Lorraine West as Evy Meara and
Mary Little as Toby Landau.

more work on the accent would have made the portrayal even better. Mary Little had the challenging task in portraying the narcissistic Toby Landau, her character worked very well particularly in the monologue in Act II ... Lorraine West's Evy Meara was a tour de force performance that was a pleasure to watch ... and Linda Melville's Polly Meara was an impressive debut in a major role.'

The next production, *The Last of the Knucklemen*, directed by Ian Walker, was a bold choice for WLT. Members were warned of the play's violence and coarse language, but the caution did nothing to put them off. Originally planned as a six-night season, it was extended by three nights. Derek Richards provided the following comment for *S.T.A.G. RAG* (the newsletter of the Strathmore Theatrical Arts Group):

Williamstown must be congratulated on this production which any professional company would find hard to better. The acting was uniformly good, but I think that special praise should go to Ray Hare for his performance in the unsympathetic part of 'Pansy'. Ron Little, as Methuselah, gave a fine performance, the best that this critic has seen him give on the stage so far.

WLT's next production, the light comedy *Simon and Laura*, directed by Laurie Gellon, was the subject of a comprehensive critique by Nanette Good who came to the theatre on 7 September to deliver her comments to cast members, crew and friends. According to the summary reproduced in *Cues and News,* Good thought:

... all facets of the production were enjoyable, and the overall effect was very good. The faults which existed (such as the rather tatty looking vase of dried hydrangeas) were mostly faults of attention to detail which, while their importance should not be overlooked, did not ever detract greatly from the overall entertainment value, which was high, especially during the second act.

Good considered the acting generally good, though with room for improvement. Thus whilst 'Vin Foster and Mary Little brought the polish of experience to the title roles and were largely responsible for the pace of the production', and Derek Williams as Wilson 'showed a good sense of timing and straight-faced humour in a role it must have been very tempting to overplay', the performances of Amy Grove-Rogers as the housekeeper and Bartley McGowan as Wolfie were 'self-conscious'. On the other hand, 'The other members of the TV team were effective. It is always a pleasure to see good team work and effective playing from actors playing small parts.'

In short, it seems that WLT recovered its mojo through 1978. By the middle of the year membership had grown to 112. In July, the theatre organised another progressive dinner - 'because we haven't had one for years' as *Cues and News* put it. Forty people turned up progressing from entrée at the Wadds' household, main course at the Wests, and dessert at the Grove-Rogers. The Theatre also began a series of training sessions for backstage staff, starting with a lighting school organised by Laurie Gellon.

By 19 October 1978, the 1979 playbill had been decided and two thousand copies of the first glossy subscription brochure were produced to publicise it. This subscription brochure was an important innovation since it included descriptions of the plays to be staged. This not only meant that subscribers made a more informed choice when renewing - previously they had simply been notified that their subscriptions were renewable - but that the Theatre could be more adventurous in its programming. Subscribers were given the choice of attending three, four or five plays which meant that they could avoid plays about which they were doubtful. Simultaneously it created greater freedom for the play selection committee in that it could now choose more challenging and controversial plays, without the risk of offending more conservative subscribers.

The 1979 season included comedy with *Not Now Darling*, directed by Bob Karl; a thriller, *Trap for a Lonely Man*, directed by Loris Blake; *Wind in the Branches of Saffafras*, a send up of every American western ever made, directed by David Dare, drama with *The Anniversary*, directed by Vin Foster; and more comedy with *Hay Fever*, directed by Gillian Wadds. Each production presented particular challenges. *Not Now Darling*, a farce by Ray Cooney and John Chapman, received enthusiastic reviews when it opened at the Strand Theatre, London. Set in a fur salon in London's West End, it concerns two partners in the firm, Gilbert Bodley and Arnold Crouch, who are trying to recover a £5,000 mink coat that Gilbert has promised Janie McMichael, a professional stripper, in return for 'certain favours' (as *Cues and News* coyly put it).

Rising to the challenge that several of the female roles required the actors to strip to their bras and panties, director Bob Karl, sensitively arranged for the auditions to be 'closed' so that only he and a member of the Committee were in the room with the hopeful actors. Luckily, the play was a virtual sell-out, topped off by another first for the theatre when on the final Saturday afternoon of the season, two of the cast, Brian Jones and Sue Marshall, were married on stage! Their sixty guests attended the last performance of the play and the wedding reception held upstairs afterwards.

The following production, *Trap for a Lonely Man*, a study of the breakdown of a person trapped in a war of nerves, also enjoyed a near sell-out season, as did WLT's third production for 1979 *Wind in the Branches of Sassafras*. The latter production simultaneously generated two important 'firsts' for the theatre: David Dare made his directorial debut at WLT with this play, and it was the first WLT production to be reviewed by Diana Burleigh on *Applause Applause*, the VDL-sponsored radio program on Melbourne's community radio 3CR which was started after the demise of Laurie Landray's regular column in *Listener-In TV*.[62]

Burleigh started with the by then standard comment about Williamstown's ability to deal with its restricted stage space:[63]

> *It's amazing what they are able to achieve on a small stage, in fact they put a lot of other companies with much better facilities to shame. There's no height above the proscenium arch and wing space is minuscule, yet the level of lighting and set design was among the best I've seen ... David Dare, the director, made good use of the space available ... the positioning of the furniture and the movement of cast were excellent and that's not easy when there are eight people on a stage that's smaller than my living room!*

---

62   For the details, see my *The Victorian Drama League 1952-2002*, pp.69ff.

63   In 1968, Frank Little in *The Advocate* effectively said the same thing of Grahame Murphy's set for *Barefoot in the Park*, WLT's first production at 'The Bakery', as did Laurie Landray of Murphy's set for WLT's following production of *The Miracle Worker*.

In time, as we shall see, David became master of the WLT stage in terms of set design. David had been interested in theatre as a child[64] though he had few opportunities to see theatre in his home town of Colac. He joined his local theatre group at age seventeen playing small roles in *The Boy Friend* and *Our Town*. He trained as a primary school teacher and was offered his first position at Altona Gate Primary School. When he arrived in Melbourne, he was introduced to several theatres around Melbourne by people such as David Small and Richard Tyler. He joined Pumpkin Players as a stage manager in 1972, sharing that role with Laurie Gellon in the joint production that year by Pumpkin and WLT of *The Prime of Miss Jean Brodie*. Vin Foster directed this production. David thus had good connections with WLT before he started!

The new surge of energy and optimism at WLT during 1979 spilled over into events offstage as well as on. Members got together for theatre parties, picnics and yum cha at Chinese restaurants in the city. As long-serving member Lorraine West, production director for *Hay Fever*, the last production of 1979, reported to the December committee meeting:

The last half of this year has seen the beginning of what we all hope is the 'curtain raiser' of a new era at WLT. The high standard lately reached has been reflected by audience enthusiasm and we have a growing number of members who are proud to be part of WLT people who give their best because it is their theatre, who don't say 'That's not my job', but jump in and help because it's there to be done.

Newcomers such as Patsy and Noel Martin shared her optimism. As Patsy wrote:

I have never been made to feel so welcome anywhere before ... most groups one joins, the feeling is that you are on the outside looking in, which is perfectly understandable I suppose. It can't be all that easy to accept all newcomers with wide open arms, yet that is exactly what you people have done, everyone is so warm and friendly – and best of all, crazy.

---

64   The remainder of this paragraph is based on the article on David in *Cues and News*, July 2006 and on my own discussions with him.

In the same vein, another long-serving member Ellis Ebell wrote about his experiences during *The Anniversary*:

> As a cast member of '*The Anniversary*', I would like to thank all concerned with the production. It's a long time since I've done a show in which everything ran so smoothly. We felt really proud of our theatre. The three new members were full of admiration for the theatre's efforts and all felt like part of the family ... No 'thank you' would be complete without mentioning the backstage crew. We could not have wished for better. It certainly made our job a lot easier, knowing our props were in the right place ... The whole experience was an enjoyable one from auditions through to the final night.

The Anniversary was important for WLT in another way; it marked Barbara Hughes' debut with the company, an association which has now continued, at the time of writing, for forty-four years, involving multiple roles on and off stage.

Many members acknowledged the contribution of the new President, Laurie Gellon, to the development of this new spirit. Like Grahame Murphy, Gellon was interested in theatre as a child. He constructed theatres in a box at his Paynesville home and visits to his grandmother in Melbourne always provided opportunities to go to pantomimes. An early job at a Morwell bank landed him several roles with the Morwell Players, including in the one-actor *Joseph Wants Five Sons*, which reached the finals of the VDL one-act play festival in 1964 on the same afternoon as Williamstown were performing. There Gellon first met Vin Foster. Visiting Melbourne, he saw an advertisement for WLT's *The Boy Friend* at which production Nell Colville offered him a cup of tea and arranged for him to view the set with designer John Burrett. Gellon met Vin Foster again at an after-show party for a musical production in 1970. Vin invited him to Williamstown to stage manage their first show in 1971.

Gellon's involvement with WLT was almost exclusively backstage, not that he wasn't tempted to tread the boards on the odd occasion. In 1971 after stage managing *The Grass is Greener*, he decided to audition for *The Knack*. It was a disaster. Gellon said to himself, 'You will go backstage and you will stay there!' Even so, occasionally he played minor roles, being the one of the furniture removalists in Les Terrill's production of *Juno and the Paycock* in July 1973, a production he also stage managed. WLT has been forever grateful for Laurie's decision to concentrate on using his skills as a director, lighting designer, stage manager, set designer and theatre administrator!

Work responsibilities took Gellon away from theatre for several years in the mid 1970s. He returned to take over the stage management of *Loot* in 1977 and was elected President for the first time in July 1979. He took the opportunity to refresh and renew WLT's commitment to high quality theatre. At his suggestion, the new committee elected in 1979 adopted two aims:

1. 'That by June 1980, WLT will once again be the top non-professional 'little theatre' group in Melbourne in all respects, especially artistic standards and endeavours (keeping subscribers in mind as necessary), enthusiasm, social and internal organisation'; and

2. 'That the comforts for members and the public will be vastly improved'.

These aims provided a framework for the Committee to work within for a few years. Much effort was put into improving the theatre's facilities, such as renovating the foyer and kitchen area. After delays in getting the necessary council permits, the work was started in March 1980 and finished in time for the opening of *Don's Party* in May.

In the late 1970s and early 1980s working bees to maintain and improve the theatre's facilities became more common. Just before Christmas 1977 one such event 'to sort out and tidy up the scenery dock' was so successful that *Cues and News* bragged that 'The Council had to make two trips with their truck to take the rubbish away'. Unlike the 'presidential working bees' inaugurated by Laurie Gellon in 1993,[65] these events were organised irregularly on an ad hoc basis. Sometimes attendance was disappointing. *Cues and News* reported that 'people stayed away in droves' for one organised for the weekend of 21 and 22 June 1980, though 'another team of enthusiasts came the following weekend' and much was achieved. One major issue was the availability and organisation of storage space, especially for flats which was eventually resolved on the weekend of 25 and 26 July 1981. And there were stand out successes:

65   See page 174.

on a weekend in mid 1983 intensive work resulted in the stage being lowered and the foyer painted. In October 1984 all the 'neglected areas' of the flat and furniture bays and the theatre courtyard were tidied up.

Improving the theatre often meant grabbing opportunities as they presented themselves. An audience survey during *Journey's End* in September 1980 had revealed that the improvement patrons most wanted at Willy was better seating. Greg Bunting noticed an advertisement for eighty theatre seats available for purchase. Installing them at WLT would mean re-raking the auditorium, but once WLT's offer of $2,000 for the seats was accepted, it was immediately decided to do what was necessary during January 1981. The work entailed stripping the auditorium of seats and carpet, repairing ventilation grills in the walls, re-plastering the back wall, re-raking the auditorium, painting the auditorium walls, laying carpet in the auditorium and foyers, and fixing the new seating. The work meant that the capacity of the theatre would need to be reduced to sixty-nine seats. But there was no shortage of enthusiasm for the task. About twenty people turned up for the first working bee and it took just a couple of hours to strip the seats and carpet. In fact, the entire job was finished in time for the first 1981 production, *Equus*.

If proof is needed that a comfortable audience is a happy one, Diana Burleigh's review of Equus on *Applause, Applause* provided it:

> *The pleasure of going to Williamstown Little Theatre has been somewhat enhanced by new seating in the auditorium. Last year the company surveyed its audience and discovered regular patrons thought the seats were uncomfortable and did not give enough leg room. During the Christmas break new seats with more leg room were added, or replaced. I can attest to their comfort having sat in one for their current production.*

Funding for the renovations came from a 'buy a seat' campaign. The donors - most of them members - were listed in *Cues and News* in May 1981, with the intention that their names would also be displayed in the theatre foyer. It took a while to get around to doing it, but eventually in 1994 the benefactors could gaze at their names each time they visited the theatre! Other renovations, most of them imposed on the theatre's management by an audit which revealed some non-compliance with relevant fire regulations, plus the need to cater for disabled theatregoers, occupied a good deal of time and money between 1980 and 1983.

For the first production for 1980, WLT revisited an earlier production, *The Ballad of Angel's Alley*, first performed by the company in 1963. The new effort was, in fact, a product of Gravin productions, a joint venture between Vin Foster and Grahame Murphy, which had been staged at Pumpkin Theatre the year before, and in which ten of the fifteen-strong cast were Williamstown members and all the backstage crew, except the musicians, were also from Williamstown. A special feature of this production was that Bruce George, joint composer of 'Ballad', was the musical director.

The next production, David Williamson's *Don's Party*, directed by Ian Walker, was booked out before it opened and received a rave review from Diana Burleigh:

> *This production of Don's Party must be one of the most competently directed and performed plays that has come from any amateur company. Technically it was faultless ... the set was magnificent both in terms of visual appeal, appropriateness and technically fitting it on to the tiny Williamstown stage.*

There were accolades for the whole cast: Robert Wheeler, Don Bridges, Paul McLoughlin, Lorraine West 'who admirably sustained a character who had had little interaction with the others on stage', Margot Knight who 'put over the ultra - permissive Susan in a dress that was so revealing it had to be obscene to be believed - she certainly had the physical requirements for the part but did not let her visible assets substitute for acting talent - she has plenty of that too. A short scene between Margot and Sallyann Wilson actually brought me out in goosebumps as I watched them give each other the eye'.

Burleigh had equally positive things to say about *Journey's End*, directed by Laurie Gellon:

> *When I went to see the current production of 'Journey's End', I wondered whether it would be up to scratch. The play is exceedingly difficult in many ways ... there are many direction problems and the play calls for a set which falls down in the final moments of the play ... not only were all the obstacles surmounted admirably, but the end result was one of such excellence that*

Williamstown Little Theatre

The Cast of *Journey's End* September 1980
Sven Olsen, Frank Sullivan, Bill Martin, Alan Lee, John Chiltern, Greg Henderson,
James Fitch, Gary McConville, Ellis Ebell, Les Terrill, Chris Donelly.

'Journey's End' will rank as one of the most proficient that has been mounted by a non-professional company. Under Laurie Gellon's direction, no area seemed to have been overlooked.

Diana noted many fine performances, the most moving from Les Terrill as Osborne, the older officer who 'handled the scene before a suicide mission in which he tries to talk about anything but the war extremely well'. Terrill won the 1980 Cordell Award for this performance.

The impact of *Journey's End* extended beyond the usual Theatre community, as demonstrated by the following letter dated 16-9-80 to Laurie Gellon from Ms C Borowiecki, a teacher at Altona North High School:

Dear Mr Gellon,

Last night I attended your production of "Journey's End" with 26 students from form six at Altona North High School. Their response to the play last night was quite overpowering – a result of the brilliance and sheer power of the play. Many of the students have had little to do with theatre in any way except the plays I have taken them to this year. It was extremely important for them to see such a professional production within their own immediate vicinity.

The students had studied the Poetry of the First World War as part of their course so seeing such a play has helped them to understand further the changes wrought in men and the sheer waste of war. From my position observing the male students' responses of embarrassment it was obvious that they felt very close to Raleigh indeed.

Please pass on our congratulations to the actors and crew and especially to Garry McConville. His performance was absolutely brilliant.

There were several new initiatives in 1980 aimed at broadening and strengthening the Theatre as a community. For example, at Laurie Gellon's suggestion, Vin Foster organised a series of talks on the Sunday nights (see Table 5 p.128) by guest speakers who comprised a Who's Who of the Victorian Arts industry.

The speakers attracted variable audiences but were generally thought to be successful. Brian Crossley was reportedly so impressed by the way he was made welcome at Williamstown that he immediately expressed a wish to run a series of workshops for the Theatre and, in turn, to direct a production. Thus began Crossley's long and happy association with the company.

WLT's publicity reached new heights in 1980 under the energetic and professional management of Frank Page. *Journey's End*, for example, gained coverage in four editions of *Footscray Advertiser*, three editions each of *Footscray Mail* and *The Age Weekender* and two editions of *Sunshine Advocate*. It was covered by Ivan Hutchison on Channel 7 and three times on the John Cook show on 3LO Radio.

In September of that year, during the season of *Journey's End*, WLT conducted an audience survey, which yielded some interesting facts about the changes in the theatre community since the first survey in 1951. For example, in 1951 98% of respondents lived in Williamstown or adjacent suburbs.

Table 5: Speakers at WLT 'Sunday Night Talks', 1980

Date	Speaker
20 April	Bill Akers, Production Director of the Victorian Arts Centre Trust
25 May	Malcolm Robertson, Associate Director, Hoopla Foundation (forerunner of Playbox Theatre)
29 June	Ken MacKenzie-Forbes, General Manager, Victorian State Opera
27 July	George Fairfax, General Manager, Victorian Arts Centre Trust
24 August	Frank van Stratten, Archivist, Performing Arts Museum
24 September	Ray Lawler, Actor, Director, Playwright
23 November	Brian Crossley,* Actor, Director and Gilbert and Sullivan Expert

* Fifteen years earlier, Crossley had been the adjudicator in the first Moomba Festival of One-Act Plays in which WLT participated

Thirty years later this had been reduced to 64%. The opening of the West Gate Bridge in 1978 and increasing car ownership across Melbourne meant WLT now drew audiences from all over the metropolis. For *Journey's End*, the production during which the survey was circulated, audience members came from as far away as Springvale, Ringwood, Lower Templestowe, Heidelberg, Airport West and East Keilor.

As for their entertainment, as in 1951, patrons still wanted a mix: 'A balance ...' or 'Anything as long as it is clean'! They nominated more than eighty individual plays they'd like to see performed. David Williamson's *The Club* was the most popular, with others keen to see other Williamson plays, and also works by Noël Coward, Agatha Christie, Strindberg, Ibsen and Shaw. This gave the play selection committee a fair degree of freedom in compiling the playbill.

The following year, 1981, began on a high. *Equus*, directed by Grahame Murphy, was a great success. The fifteen-night season was sold out and it then moved to the Grant Street Theatre as part of the Moomba Festival where it played to a full house and won the award for Best Production. Then followed three nights at the Powderkeg Players theatre in Sunshine.

Steven Ritchie won a National Theatre Scholarship for his performance as the young boy at the centre of the action, and Ellis Ebell an honourable commendation from the Moomba Festival adjudicator for movement. Diana Burleigh had some reservations about the production but commented that:

Vin Foster's Martin Dysart was a masterpiece of self-control. As a psychiatrist Dysart has learnt to conceal his feelings for his patients ... I don't mind admitting that he moved me almost to the point of tears in the end. As the

Equus, March 1981
Winner Best Production Moomba Festival of Theatre: Steven Ritchie as Alan Strang supported by Paul Behan, Mark Young, Barry Hooper, Bruce Warlow, Mark Stratford and June Dodds.

boy Steven Ritchie proved a real find. He is, of course, young and lacks experience, but his performance was confident, and he communicated the confusion and anger of the psychotic boy well.

Dramatic success stayed with Williamstown throughout 1981. *The Killing of Sister George* enjoyed a successful season as did *President Wilson in Paris*. Diana Burleigh was most impressed with *President Wilson in Paris*, straining to find fault:

Surely there is something I can complain about - I mean I have a reputation to keep up ... As a play I found it enjoyable and stimulating - as a performance it was a treat for me to sit back and appreciate so skilful a piece of theatre ... Tom Travers gave a mellow performance with plenty of light and shade, Carmel Behan was probably the best I've ever seen her.

WLT wrapped up 1981 with *Only an Orphan Girl*, directed by David Dare. It played to full houses. Two extra performances were organised, one at 11pm on the final Friday night and the second on the following Sunday afternoon. Diana Burleigh again:

If all audiences were as enthusiastic as the one I was part of, Williamstown Little Theatre must be patting itself on the back for a successful conclusion for a successful year.

As indeed it was. It was a great springboard for 1982, which opened with Ian Walker's production of David Williamson's *Travelling North*. The cast included Ray Hare, Mary Little, Paula McDonald, Jennifer Price, Vesna Zovko, Brian O'Callaghan, Ron Little, Marian Hellier, and Greg Henderson. This time Diana Burleigh had many reservations, most of them about the problems of staging the play on the small Williamstown stage.

The second play presented even more staging challenges. Sir Arthur Pinero's *The Second Mrs Tanqueray* occupies a special place in British theatre history. Anticipating Noël Coward, it is an indictment of respectable society's double standard of sexual morality for men and women, an indictment which was likely to make 1890s' audiences very uncomfortable. Director Brian Crossley had difficulty casting but finally found actors for the twelve demanding roles. Laurie Gellon as lighting director was hospitalised unexpectedly a week before opening night, leaving the design in the hands of some recent 'graduates' from one of his lighting courses. Nonetheless the play was well received by the critics. Diana Burleigh, for example, thought Brian Crossley's direction had 'brought this old play to such sparkling life'. It seems that its success was due to a fine ensemble performance by the actors: Ian Walker, Christine Forsey, Barry Main, Patsy Martin, Adrienne Moodie and Marian Sinclair, the fallen woman, who as Diana put it, 'certainly looked the part in a succession of costumes which grew more magnificent with each succeeding act', congratulating Pat Day and Andrew Murphy for their work. But Marian 'was far more than a clothes horse. It was the warmest performance I have seen her give and at the same time captured many of the subtle nuances of feeling'. Marian won the Cordell Award for this performance.

The Second Mrs Tanqueray was Brian Crossley's first production at Williamstown. Before coming to Australia in 1954 to join the Union Theatre Repertory Company, Brian had had extensive experience in theatre in England, starting with Birmingham Repertory Theatre, and including performing in the chorus of the Doyly Carte Opera Company. His greatest passion and love was music - a clairvoyant he consulted early in his life saw music swirling all around him - but theatre was not far behind. As Marion Sinclair noted in her memoir of Brian in May 2020's *Cues and News*, as a director he was concerned about being true to the text and style of the play, but also tried to ensure that his actors enjoyed themselves, saying that it was much easier for an audience to have a good time if the actors were at ease and happy with what they were doing. Brian was a specialist in the theatre of the late 19th century and of the thirteen plays directed by Brian at Williamstown, three were by Oscar Wilde and six by Noël Coward. In his Coward productions, Brian formed a special partnership with Pat Day who designed and made the quality costumes which, as we shall see in Chapters 5 and 6, set those productions apart.

Williamstown's third production for 1982 was *King Lear*, that year on the Victorian HSC (Year 12) syllabus. Greg Henderson was the main force behind the staging of this play, initially directing the production and, as a teacher himself, taking responsibility for promoting it amongst schools throughout the State.

Getting *King Lear* onto the stage required something of a marathon effort. Henderson had never directed at Williamstown before and organised for a friend from Geelong to design the set. Unfortunately, however, Henderson's approach caused conflict with the cast who all threatened to walk out. Laurie Gellon, returning from a short holiday in the north of Victoria, was confronted with a major crisis.

Ian Walker, playing Lear, took over as director and Laurie as set designer while the cast helped with costumes. Two days before opening, there was concern that Walker didn't appear to know his lines and the soundtrack was incomplete. Many extra hours of effort were put in by the cast. A special system was installed to radio transmit prompts to Walker which meant that on opening night no audience member was aware of his problem and by the first Saturday night all was well, and the system removed. In the end, WLT's first production of a Shakespeare play was well directed at the student market and ran for an extra week, giving twenty performances altogether. About fifty schools saw the production, with thirty-five coming from outside Melbourne, including from Balmoral (near Hamilton), Ballarat, Cohuna, Bendigo and Wangaratta, and at least six from Geelong alone.

WLT's next production *Dusa, Fish, Stas and Vi*, directed by Laurie Gellon, was the Theatre's entry in the 1982 Waverley Festival of Theatre where it won the awards for Best Production, Best Set, and Best Actress for Patricia Watts for her playing of the anorexic Vi. Paula McDonald also received a nomination for her performance as Stas.

Festival adjudicator Malcolm Robertson thought that designer Daniel Coase had created with deft strokes the environment of the London flat and that Gellon had ensured that there was a fine sense of ensemble playing from the actors. To quote Robertson at length:

> *Patricia Watts as Vi was the waif of Pam Gem's creation. With her legs dangling in the air, to the obligatory bouts of yoga, Patricia invested her role with her own particular nuances... Alison McMichael as Dusa gave us a sense of misplaced domesticity that was palpably identifiable ... Paula McDonald as Stas is, as Pam Gems described her, magnificent to look at ... There was a wonderful sense of off-beat nonchalance in her performance*

1977 - 1986

Dusa, Fish Stas and Vi, Best Production Waverley Festival of Theatre, 1982.
L to R: Alison McMichael as Dusa, Patricia Watts (standing at rear centre) as Vi,
Helen Vorrath (seated) as Fish, and Paula McDonald as Stas.

that was altogether admirable. Helen Vorrath as Fish in perhaps the less flamboyant role in the play showed us the commitment of the character to causes and the desperate need she had to be loved.

Robertson also had high praise for the set and lighting design and concluded his assessment with the comment that 'Williamstown Little Theatre could well be the Off Broadway of Melbourne with this production'.

It is appropriate that such accolades should have been accorded a Laurie Gellon production, just a few months after he had concluded his first term as President of the Theatre. It was evidence that Williamstown Little Theatre had made considerable progress towards achieving the goal he had set immediately after becoming president - to be the best amateur theatre in Melbourne. Certainly, the spirit and standards of WLT had recovered from the somewhat dark days of the mid 1970s.

Gellon was succeeded as president by Vin Foster. Foster had been a major force at WLT for a long time, having made his debut as the clergyman in Clemence Dane's *Granite* in 1955. His talents as an actor were soon recognised. *Williamstown Chronicle* of 8 June 1956 headlined its review of his first triumph in Emlyn Williams' *Night Must Fall* 'Vin Foster's powerful performance'.

Many more triumphs followed. Les Terrill, at the time of Foster's untimely death in 1988, recalled vivid pictures of Foster 'suave in opera cape and topper' in *The Merry Widow* (for the Williamstown Light Opera Company), disreputable in a tatty dressing gown in *The Miser*, outrageous in frocked coat and plumed hat in *The Recruiting Officer*, introspective in *Equus*, and gently vague in the last role he played, Geoffrey in *The Dresser*. As a director Foster is remembered for productions which attracted the largest audiences, especially during the Theatre's difficult second decade: *Only an Orphan Girl* in 1961 and *The Ballad of Angel's Alley* in 1963. He was well connected in all Melbourne's theatrical circles as a council member of the Victorian Drama League and in 1980 was awarded the Music Theatre Guild of Victoria's Edith Harrhy Award for his services to musical theatre in Melbourne.

Foster took some time to work his way into the President's role. By October 1983, however, he had a clear set of priorities, or rather questions, about future directions for WLT. He was very concerned about the structure of the play selection committee and shared Laurie Gellon's view that so much of the success of the Theatre, in all areas, stemmed from correct play selection[66] He thought that too many plays and directors were suggested by too many people, most of whom had a vested interest of some sort and suggested that the Committee should consist of a representative of the acting members and the technical staff, a member of the general public who was a regular play goer and the current president as an ex-officio member.

The Committee considered Foster's views and at its next meeting decided that the play selection sub-committee should consist of three Committee members with the current president acting as an ex-officio member. Its duties would encompass evaluation of plays for artistic merit, casting, technical and audience appeal.

In 1983 under Foster's leadership Williamstown continued its tradition of presenting five major productions: *In for the Kill* by Derek Banfield, directed

---

66   As noted on page 5, this is a view shared by John Sumner.

by Richard Keon; David Williamson's *The Removalists*, directed by Ian Walker; Alan Lee's production of Roger Hall's popular play about the public service, *Flexitime; A Boy for Me, A Girl for You* directed by Laurie Gellon; and *Celebration*, directed by Judith Muir.

Most productions ran smoothly. *In for the Kill* gave a special performance for the Ash Wednesday 1983 bush fires appeal, and another as the Theatre's entry in the Moomba Festival of Theatre. For this Williamstown received five nominations - for Best Production, Best Director (Richard Keown), Best Actress (Louise Whiteman), Best Actor (James Fitch), and Best Set (David Dare) - but no actual awards.

The Removalists enjoyed similar success, the original fifteen-night season being extended by three nights, all of which played to full houses. This was despite the loss of Michele Levy as stage manager during the show, a job taken on by Daryl Richards, and Diana Burleigh's view that the acting in the play was 'not so much uneven as inconsistent' and that the stage design was 'not well executed and was underdressed'.

The issue of directors' fees raised its head again in 1983. It had always been a controversial subject, because many members felt the payments to anyone violated the concept of 'amateur theatre'. For years WLT's fee had been set at $250 per production. Frank Page and Ellis Ebell proposed that this be continued in 1984, but when both Grahame Murphy and Vin Foster said that they would not be able to direct for that amount, the committee agreed to raise the fee to $300. Page and Ebell were clearly upset by this decision and the matter remained something of a sore point among some members for several years.

Another recurrent problem during 1982 and 1983 was availability of set designers. The Committee investigated various solutions and finally wrote to all colleges of advanced education to see if any students would be interested in gaining practical experience in set design. Unfortunately, there was little response. The situation became desperate, prompting Vin Foster to write to all subscribers and members asking for their help.

As if a shortage of person power was not enough to worry the Theatre at this stage, its fortitude was really tested when controversy erupted over its first play in 1984. The original plan was to present Doreen Clarke's *Farewell Brisbane Ladies*, but this was abandoned when director Ian Walker was unable to cast the play, despite the fact it required only two women. In its place, the Committee chose Clem Gorman's saucy comedy *A Night in the Arms of Raelene*. It proved too much for some subscribers, who objected to the language. A member, W. E. Milner wrote:

> *My wife and I have been subscribers for many years, and it is with regret to have to tell you after only half an hour of your last production, we just couldn't stomach it anymore, and we walked out, for the first time ever. We have seen some wonderful plays put on by WLT, but I suggest that if 'A Night in the Arms of Raelene' was an experiment, please don't experiment on the subscribers, because if you do, I venture to say you won't have many for very long.*

Coral Galea wrote her letter in the foyer 'hoping that this show will soon finish':

A Night in the Arms of Raelene, February 1984
L to R: Julia Gardner as Raelene Mannion, David Scott as Rat, Ray Hare as Bronx, and Barry Main as The Kings Cross Yank.

I am very sorry that I bought tickets for the show, thinking that we were coming to see 'Goodbye (sic) Brisbane Ladies', as per the 1984 playbill. I am not a prude and feel that a risque comedy would have been fun to come to as a family. We are a church going family and we brought along our 15-year-old daughter and her boyfriend to celebrate a special family night. Instead of a fun family night, my husband is inside watching a man's show and I am filling in time out here.

The irony was that Williamstown had mounted a classy production. Diana Burleigh from *Applause, Applause*, thought it one of the most memorable and impressive amateur theatre productions of the year. She noted how well the play had been cast. The acting was good, and the production 'paced so that the climaxes built to the final moments of pathos and hope'. Ian Walker had also designed 'an attractive set' and Diana commended Pat Day for supplying a wardrobe of old rocker costumes.

Interestingly, Diana's views were shared by the adjudicator at the 1984 Moomba Festival of Theatre where the well-known Australian actor Bunney Brooke[67], gave the play five awards: Ian Walker for Direction, Julia Gardner Best Actress, David Scott Best Actor in a Supporting Role, a special adjudicator's award to David Hursthouse, and a commendation to Mark Young for Lighting Design. Ms Brooke was so impressed she wrote personally to Vin Foster congratulating the theatre on its effort. It proved the old adage, 'you can't please all of the people all of the time'. Indeed, but for a mix-up in envelopes on presentation night, apparently 'Raelene' would have won the festival.

The Theatre vindicated itself by writing to all subscribers, explaining the loss of its first choice of play and highlighting the Moomba success of the alternative. A copy of the letter was sent to all the local papers to place the Committee's position on the public record.

---

67 Brooke had started in amateur theatre in Melbourne in the early 1950s, went to England for three years working professionally in repertory theatre, radio and television, later working with the Union Theatre Repertory Company, the MTC and the Independent Theatre in Sydney, winning praise for performances as diverse as Martha in *Who's Afraid of Virginia Woolf?*, and the title role in *The Killing of Sister George*. See *Companion to Australian Theatre*, p.106.

The effects of *A Night in the Arms of Raelene* spilled over into Williamstown's next production, Jean Anouilh's *Antigone*. The cast included WLT stalwarts Les Terrill, Mary Little, Barbara Hughes and Danny Lillford as well as newcomers Steven D'Agas, Pauline Barbara, Philip Lambert, Tim Gray, Lance Patterson, Alan Mudford and Justine Nash. Diana Burleigh considered this a 'thought provoking production'. She was impressed by the acting of Les Terrill as King Creon, Mary Little who gave a 'warm performance as Antigone's nurse', and especially Barbara Hughes as Antigone who 'grew in stature from the unwilling voices of the people to a heroine of tragic proportions ... The long scene in the second act in which Antigone and Creon debate their mutually incompatible arguments was as riveting and spellbinding a piece of theatre as I have ever seen'.

Despite the quality of the production, however, audience numbers were down, partly because many felt the play was too heavy, and partly because others disappointed by their experience at the previous production would not buy tickets. Life was further complicated when at one performance a drunk patron in the front row became abusive. Again a letter of apology and explanation went out to the thirteen subscribers affected, offering them a refund or complimentary tickets to a future production.

Could there be any more crises? Unfortunately, the answer was yes. Yet another letter to members, subscribers and patrons went out in July 1984 explaining that Westgate Travel, at that time ticket agents for WLT, had been broken into and a cash box containing the tickets for *Elephant Man* - the third production for the year - stolen.

As Treasurer Amy Grove-Rogers pointed out at the time, whilst the robbery might have caused a big headache for both Westgate and herself as ticket secretary, it gave *Elephant Man* a lot of publicity. A review appeared on the front page of *Williamstown Advertiser*, complete with a large photograph of Neil Modra as John Merrick. Reviewer Sue Alexander described the play as 'brilliantly cast with outstanding performances by not only Modra, but [also] by Marian Sinclair as Mrs Kennedy, Alan Lee as F.C. Carr-Gomm and Scott Lucas as Trevis'. Diana Burleigh was more restrained, thinking Williamstown's production 'basically convincing in its presentation' although it 'was played with unrelieved intensity and at an evenly ponderous pace. Because of this it occasionally became tedious'.

There was, however, nothing ponderous about the first production for 1985, Phillip King's *See How They Run*, WLT's second presentation of this farce - the first being in 1962.[68] By the time the production got to Kew Theatre for the Moomba Festival, Burleigh thought the actors:

... had finely honed the characterisations, the timing and the pace so that the end result was fast, furious, controlled and choreographed behaviour ... Sallyann Wilson is an experienced actress who knows how to time a line, react and when to throw an anguished look at the audience. Her Penelope Toop appeared to be on the edge of desperation all night and that kept us on the edge of our seats. She was well partnered by Stephen Brown who certainly played the clean-cut British young man with a stiff upper lip to near perfection.

The production received nine nominations at Moomba, but only one award - to Derek Richards for his playing of Sir Arthur Humphrey.

The dramatic highlights of 1985 were Brian Crossley's production of Noël Coward's *Present Laughter*, and Laurie Gellon's staging of *Lamb of God*. As well as directing *Present Laughter*, Brian played the lead role of Gary Essendine. Diana Burleigh thought this resulted in some blemishes in the production 'caused by the lack of an eye out front' but conceded that she could not imagine who could have played the part half as well as Brian Crossley. Her quibbles were minor; she thought that Williamstown captured the sense of style that a Coward play required and that the period was accurately captured, the costumes superb and the mode of acting absolutely in keeping with the writing and the mental attitude suited that of the period.

Coward, however, was not *Williamstown Advertiser's* cup of tea. Critic Sue Alexander was completely unimpressed by the play, confessing to finding it hard to raise a laugh, and concluding her front-page review with the comment: 'Given the choice, I would have preferred to stay at home to be entertained by *Minder*, *Yes Minister* and Clive James on the ABC.' Others, however, could not believe that Williamstown could do something so bad and had to go to see for themselves. Ticket sales boomed in the second week! One subscriber,

---

68   See page 56.

Maurie Brearly, took up the cudgels with *Williamstown Advertiser* on the Theatre's behalf, suggesting that Alexander did not understand the intent of Coward's comedy.

Alexander was more impressed by *Lamb of God*. She saw a 'great performance from Ray Hare ... a valuable addition to Williamstown Little Theatre's group of players', and also from Enrico Luccarini in the role of the fifteen-year-old schoolboy, Jim. At the Waverley Festival of Theatre, Diana Burleigh was less impressed by Enrico but was full of praise for Mary Little as the boy's battling mother. Mary and Ray both received nominations at that Festival for their performances.

The year, WLT's fortieth, demonstrated clearly that the Theatre had recovered from the difficulties which had beset it in the mid-1970s and the numerous nominations and awards actors, directors and technicians attracted at Moomba and Waverley festivals showed considerable progress towards Laurie Gellon's goal of establishing WLT as the best amateur theatre in Melbourne.

Central to the company's success was the continuing dedication and commitment of the Committee and other key members who contributed their diverse skills. Frank Page, for example, applied his marketing training and skills to the revamping of the theatre's publicity. Frank, who had limited theatre experience, was brought to the Theatre by his partner Ellis Ebell whom he had met in 1972 – they worked for the same international trading company (Gollin and Co.) in the Melbourne CBD. When Frank suggested to Ellis that it might be fun to get involved in acting, Ellis said 'there will only ever be one actor in this relationship'. Frank decided to take on other roles!

As in many volunteer groups, however, responsibility for most of the work behind the scenes at WLT fell on a willing few as people juggled commitments to work and family life with their love of the theatre. As WLT approached its fortieth anniversary year, many people again felt stretched to their limits. As if to personify the challenges they faced, the day of the Theatre's appearance at the Waverley Festival in 1985 was extremely wet. A set of intrepid workers managed to complete setting up the stage by 7.30pm, as required, but it was what happened after the production that really made everyone's day. As Mark Young told the story in *Cues and News*:

> *We all descended on the set to demolish then start the arduous task of packing the truck amidst that wretched rain that had plagued us all since morning.*

1977 - 1986

Finally the truck was loaded and we were on our way back to WLT. The way it deluged we should have travelled a lot closer to Henry (Ismailiw) and Ray (Hare) in the Rent-A Truck in case we had to use it as an ark. The car convoy finally got to WLT to await the truck's arrival. Something obviously had to go wrong and we later received a call to say the truck had broken down somewhere in Ormond, but by some miracle it got going again and arrived at around 3.00am. What an ungodly time! By the time the truck was unloaded, I left at 4.00am

Mark's final comment: 'The things one does for ART!'

In 1986, WLT's fortieth anniversary year, there were three productions that stood out for their artistic merit. One was Julian Mitchell's play, *Another Country*, about the defection to communist Russia of Guy Burgess and Donald McLean. Directed by Vin Foster, the production required a cast of eleven young men, ten of them teenagers or teenage look-alikes. Guy Burgess was played by John Chilton and among the others were David Tredinnick,

Another Country, April 1986
L to R: Craig Hughes as Donald Devenish, Rex Callahan, John Chilton as Guy Bennet, Lance Paterson as Jim Menzies, and David Tredinnick as Tommy Judd.

141

Lance Paterson and Rex Callahan. The theatre community regarded the production as one of the most memorable for years and Cordell adjudicators Diana Burleigh, Graeme Cope and John Gunn awarded the play the Craven Award for the best production, while Chilton and Tredinnick shared the Cordell Award. Rex Callahan and Lance Patterson were shortlisted for the Win Stewart Award for best supporting actor. Diana Burleigh commented that Grahame Murphy's set deserved a standing ovation of its own.

Another highlight in 1986 was Judith Muir's production of *Stevie*, by Hugh Whitemore, a play about the poet Stevie Smith who lived in suburban London with her aging aunt. It was something of an unknown quantity for Williamstown audiences, but even though numbers were down, it was widely regarded as a charming play and beautifully presented. At the Waverley Festival it carried off the award for Best Production, Best Female Actress (Maggie McInnes) and Best Set, designed by Daniel Coase. Norah Toohey, as the aunt, was also impressive and won WLT's Win Stewart Award for Best Supporting Actor.

In between these two productions, Grahame Murphy directed Ernest Thompson's *On Golden Pond*. Diana Burleigh, reviewing the production for *Applause Applause*, commented that the play, with little plot, required a strong directorial hand to ensure it keeps moving and a cast able to sustain difficult and demanding characterisation. 'Fortunately Williamstown is well supplied in these departments', she said, adding:

> *Grahame Murphy's meticulous direction was aided by an attractive set of his own design ... Murphy selected a cast of some of the most experienced actors in Melbourne, which lent another advantage to this production. Forever battling flies, cockroaches, daddy-longlegs and other lakeside wildlife, June Lownds gave a solidly convincing performance as Ethel Theyer ... and ... Vin Foster captured excellently the crusty old man who irritates the audience as he simultaneously endears himself.*

Marian Sinclair as the daughter, Ray Hare and Ellis Ebell also did well in their roles. Diana's main criticism of the three lead actors was that 'while each gave us credible and enjoyable performances at times communication between them was lacking'. At the same time, she conceded that Williamstown had served an appreciative audience with a stylish and entertaining performance of a difficult play, which 'demonstrated why this company is considered one of Melbourne's best'.

WLT concluded 1986 with an Amy Grove-Rogers production of *The Bandwagon* which Amy herself described as 'a cockney comedy'. Reviewing it, Diana Burleigh confessed to being disappointed that the WLT production was not up to its usually high standards, because it had focused too much on the comedy, and insufficiently on the pathos underlying the play. Nonetheless, there were, Diana thought, some admirable performances:

Bryan Thomas especially managed to convince me that he could fool all of the people all of the time. As a shifty fast-talking advertising executive, I think he would be the man to sell you a used FJ Holden and make you believe it was a Cadillac.

On the other hand, Mrs Una Robinson wrote to the Secretary on behalf of her family and friends:

'I am dropping you a short note – congratulations to cast and crew etc on your latest production "Bandwagon" which was thoroughly enjoyed by all of our party (28) most of whom attend and enjoy all shows,' and enjoining the Theatre to 'keep up the good work please for our entertainment...at prices we can afford in a very friendly atmosphere.'

Another special event in the history of WLT happened far away in Queensland in July and August 1986, the Queensland Theatre Company's staging of Gillian Wadds' play *Who Cares?* The whole of Gillian's theatrical development had taken place at Williamstown. As sixteen-year-old Gillian Witt, she walked into the theatre to ask about joining and was immediately handed the book to prompt for a rehearsal of *And No Birds Sing*. The absence of the leading lady meant that she had to read in the part of the 'sophisticated older woman'. Gillian was hooked, and so began a 'life' with Williamstown Little Theatre. It was at WLT that she met Frank Wadds, her first husband, and with the addition of three sons, the Wadds became a 'WLT family'. Gillian worked as a teacher's aide at Williamstown Technical School. There she found the material for her play, the real-life problems of teenage illiteracy.

Who Cares? revolves around illiterate sixteen-year-old Brian, who, although intelligent, fails at school and leaves. Unable to cope in a world that revolves around reading and writing, Brian pretends to be fourteen and returns to a lower grade, perhaps to learn to read and write. He is befriended by a teacher, Jan Wilson who, supported by her principal, goes out of her way to help him, but at the cost of many arguments with her boyfriend.

Who Cares? was nurtured by WLT. It had an initial reading under the working title of "Brian" at Grahame Murphy and Vin Foster's home in Footscray in November 1983. The readers, coordinated by Bud Tingwell, included Neil Fitzpatrick, Vivien Davies and WLT members Doug Lindsay, Gillian's son Marcus, Danny Lillford, Christine Saunders, Barbara Hughes, Ellis Ebell and Les Terrill, as well as Grahame and Vin themselves. A produced play reading followed, directed by Gillian, stage managed by Les Terrill and lit by Mark Young, as part of Cordell Day that December. The favourable response led to a rehearsed reading in July 1984 by the Melbourne Theatre Company, as part of its Tributary Productions series of readings of new plays by Australian authors. This was followed by a radio adaptation presented by ABC FM in August 1985, and in July 1986 by a fully mounted production in Brisbane, by the Queensland Theatre Company, which subsequently toured the state. In a strange 'two degrees of separation' coincidence, this author's cousin, Kevin Hides, played the lead role in the QTC production. The play was later made into a film which had its first screening at the State Film Centre on 18 September 1993.[69]

Surrounding all these 'normal' theatre events in 1986 were several designed to celebrate WLT's fortieth anniversary, continuing a long theatre tradition of celebrating, if only modestly, every possible anniversary.[70] The WLT Committee thought something more grandiose was warranted for a fortieth birthday. So in the middle of 1985[71], a Fortieth Anniversary Committee was appointed

---

69   See front page article, *Williamstown Advertiser*, 22 September 1993.

70   Ten years up in 1956, twenty five in 1971, thirty in 1976, and in 1978 ten years at The Bakery.

71   The WLT Committee Minutes are unclear about the exact date when this happened, though the Minutes of the Committee Meeting of 3 September 1985 note that 'Frank has not yet contacted the committee to advise of his plans'.

with Frank Page in the leading role, which organised a range of activities spread throughout the year.

The first activity was a 'Back to WLT' day at the theatre on Sunday, March 16. A visitors' book, used for the first time for this day,[72] records that 144 people turned up, some of them apparently extremely eager, arriving an hour early. As it transpired, they had forgotten to adjust their clocks for the end of daylight saving. The day consisted of a technicolour repast of salads - rice salads, green salads, red, white and blue salads, the launch by Vin Foster of a book of reminiscences of early Williamstown written by Gillian's mother Haydee Witt and finally, the highlight of the day, a 'fashions across the years' parade where costumes from the 'Williamstown Collection' were modelled on stage some brave members, accompanied by a presentation characterised by both aplomb and a degree of hilarity by Gwladys Winfield. The event was voted such a success by those who managed to cram themselves into the auditorium that a repeat performance was demanded. The models, however, said once was enough!

The Theatre had invited a many of its past 'stars' and supporters to this event, and was chuffed to receive a handwritten letter from Neil Fitzpatrick who had performed in several plays at WLT in the 1950s[73] apologising for his inability to attend (because he was performing in a play in Sydney) but commenting that:

I am delighted that I was remembered as part of these early days which afforded me such valuable experience in the craft which has been my life for 30 years!

In particular he recalled working with 'Ellla Bambery, Lorraine (Davey) West, Nell and Alec Colville, Jess and Harry Conradi, Laurie McManus, and Paul Hill 'our sometimes excellent - I mean always excellent director and friend

---

72   The visitors book records attendances at subsequent 40th anniversary events - the 'Green Room' night on 13 July (55 signatures) and the 'Nostalgia Night' at the Mechanics' Institute on 13 December (90 signatures).

73   Notably in the lead role in two plays in 1953, *Young Mrs Barrington* and *Duet for Two Hands*, and in *Our Town* in 1955 – see pages 29-30 and page 33.

... to name but a few'.

Fitzpatrick's final paragraph was balm to all WLT hearts:

Though not all of us from all those years can be with you, I'm sure I can join with all in spirit to be proud of the achievements in remaining active and growing in stature over 40 years to be recognised as one of I should think Australia's finest community theatre companies, nurturing audiences with intelligent top standard drama which I'm sure is of invaluable subsidy to community and professional theatre wherever those audiences happen to travel outside good old Willy!

The second fortieth anniversary event occurred during the staging of *On Golden Pond*. On Sunday July 13, a special performance of the play was the focus of a 'Green Room Night' to which Williamstown invited members of eight other amateur companies: Heidelberg, Malvern, Powderkeg, Werribee, Altona, Pumpkin, Strathmore and the Williamstown Light Opera Company. The evening was a great success and demonstrated one of the lesser-known advances in theatre technology. Close to the end of the performance it was discovered that the sandwiches for the occasion, made ahead of time, were still frozen. As Frank Page commented in *Cues and News*: 'What a godsend to discover that the cast had a microwave oven secreted in their dressing room. In between appearing on stage, we had Marian (Sinclair), Ray (Hare) and Ellis (Ebell) ferrying frozen then thawed sandwiches to and from the Green Room.'

The year came to an end with two fortieth anniversary celebrations in December: the first a 'nostalgia night' held in conjunction with the annual presentation of the Cordell Awards, the second a joint Williamstown Little Theatre, Williamstown Light Opera Company and Altona City Theatre masquerade party on New Year's Eve.

The nostalgia night was redolent of great past achievements. MC for the evening was Les Terrill, who got the show underway with a rousing rendition of 'Comedy Tonight', accompanied by David Dare on piano. Mary Little and Grahame Murphy revisited roles from *The Importance of Being Earnest* they had first performed twenty-seven years before. Next followed June Lownds,

Gillian Wadds and Christine Saunders with *The Prime of Miss Jean Brodie*, which was almost brought undone by Gillian's glasses being left in another member's handbag. Ellis Ebell and Marian Sinclair then performed a short and very funny sketch from *Barefoot in the Park*, the first show performed in 'The Bakery'.

It was Marian Gough (Becroft) and Vin Foster who almost stole the show with a piece from *Red Peppers*, complete with costumes including the 'tightest sailor suit ever seen.'[74] They were followed by Ella Bambery, Gillian Wadds, Doug Lindsay, Marian Sinclair and Ellis Ebell in *Summer of the Seventeenth Doll* and Gwladys Winfield performing Dolly Levy's monologue from *The Matchmaker*. The evening was wrapped up by two scenes from *Equus* by Vin Foster, Marian Sinclair and Steve Ritchie, who proved to be just as chilling as when they first performed it, and the whole cast singing two songs from *The Ballad of Angel's Alley*, with a solo from Grahame Murphy.

---

74 A pun on the fact that in 1954, Ron Little, reviewing *Red Peppers*, commented that Marian had 'cut a dainty figure in a sailor's uniform' - see page 32.

Chapter Five

1987-1996: 'If Amateur Can be Termed Professional'

After a triumphant fortieth anniversary, life at WLT returned to normal in 1987. The dramatic highlights that year were Doug Bennett's production of the Eduardo Fillipo comedy *Filumena* and Grahame Murphy's staging of Ronald Harwood's *The Dresser*. Once again Filumena posed special casting problems because it required seven men. Bennett succeeded in finding the necessary septet and produced a triumph. Frances Devlin-Glass's review for *Applause, Applause* commented:

> *'Filumena' ... draws heavily for its fun on the exploitation of the cultural stereotype of the passionate, explosive hand-waving Latin temperament. The roles, to be effective, have to be overblown, expansive. Doug Bennett's casting of Marian Sinclair and Trevor Paparella as the principals was nothing short of inspired. Ms Sinclair as Filumena was a sheer delight to watch; she moved with the grace and with all the arrogance instinct in a Neapolitan schemer whose rise from the bordello to the household of Domenico Soriano, wealthy playboy, has depended on her wit and her ability to out-manoeuvre him. Trevor Paparella was also magnificent: the role demonstrated his range and flexibility as an actor. He is a superbly self-controlled and relaxed performer, who was equally convincing when the outraged, larger-than-life, expostulating tricked husband, and in a quiet reflective mode ... two cameo roles were outstanding - Rosalia, the old retainer (Barbara Hughes) and Lucia, the young maid ... played by Megan Pennicuik whose flouncing posterior must be one of the more expressive to grace the Melbourne boards.*

The Dresser was also, in Devlin-Glass' opinion 'a treat ... an elegant and

1987 - 1996

Filumena, May1987
L to R: Trevor Paparella as Domenico Soriano, Marion Sinclair as Filumena Marturamo,
Barbara Hughes as Rosalia Solimene, and Norm Steiner as Alfredo Amoroso.

intelligent production'. Again 'the principals were very strong. Les Terrill's Norman ... was ... full of energy and a pathos, which was not allowed to degenerate into sentimentalism ... Graham Fletcher and Marian Sinclair as Sir and Her Ladyship were an extraordinary duo.' Devlin-Glass continued:

Sir's role is massively demanding: we have to be convinced that he can play Lear's mad scene with authority, and he must show at the same time that after 227 performances of the play he is bored with it, and after that there is a whole gamut of his personal reactions: his lechery, his self-pity, his confusion of his role with his self. Marian Sinclair was similarly required to show both a public face, full of sweetness and self-abnegation, and a private one full of anger. She continually deflated Sir's theatrical pretensions and questioned his assumptions. Both of these actors have class, range and enormous versatility.

Filumena attracted 840 patrons, *The Dresser* 846. The next production, *Murder by Natural Causes* did even better in audience terms. 887 people saw it, the 148 empty seats through the season arising from subscribers failing to turn up on their allotted night. They missed something special. Marian Sinclair being 'as usual a delight to watch' again starred, according to *Applause*, *Applause* reviewer Frances Devlin-Glass who also thought the other actors did well. Male lead David Bergin 'looked the part' and 'was marvellous in his evocation of a man driven by the need for challenge'. Frances also thought the two cameo roles were 'handled with panache':

> *Amy Grove-Rogers was marvellous as the rather dotty maid, Marta, who is a reluctant partner in her master's tricksy games, but nonetheless a witless admirer of what in fact terrifies her. Her final appearance in a squashed hat and waving a glossy, signed autograph of her hero was delightful... Eddie, the very sleazy, drink-reclaimed private investigator was played beautifully by Derek Richards.*

The largest house for 1987 (978), however, was for the last play of the year, Alan Ayckbourn's comedy *Bedroom Farce*, directed by Amy Grove-Rogers. Frances thought the choice of the play misguided because of the difficulty of placing three double beds on the tiny Williamstown stage. Moreover, 'performances were very uneven'. The stars were Derek Richards as Ernest and Bryan Thomas as Trevor.

The following year, 1988 was the bicentenary of European settlement in Australia and WLT staged an all-Australian program as its contribution to the celebrations. The company was the only non-professional group in Melbourne to do this. The program for the year was: *In Duty Bound* by Ron Elisha, directed by Les Terrill; *On the Wallaby* by Nick Enwright, directed by Brian Crossley; *The Shifting Heart* by Richard Beynon, directed by Bryan Thomas; *A Pair of Claws*, by Michael Gurr, directed by Amy Grove-Rogers; and *The Club* by David Williamson, directed by Ray Hare.

The year got off to an excellent start with a production of *In Duty Bound*. Ron Elisha, its author, is one of the new generation of Australian playwrights which emerged in the 1970s: names such as Alex Buzo, Jack Hibberd and David Williamson come to mind. Elisha's special contribution was the exploration of his Jewish roots and the generational conflicts in Jewish immigrant families, some members of which still had vivid memories of concentration camps. Frances Devlin-Glass thought Les Terrill's interpretation of the play 'a richer, more subtle, emotional version' than the original Melbourne Theatre Company production. The acting was classy:

The three principal roles were splendidly performed. Ray Hare was brilliant as Simkeh: by comparison with the larger-than-life caricatures, his performance was very understated, and this was precisely its strength. Norman Steiner and Mary Little also put in wonderful performances (as Janko and Fania)... and as Mordecai Henry Ismailiw's gluttony and buffoonery added much to the piece.

Devlin-Glass concluded her review by saying *In Duty Bound* would be a hard act to follow, precisely the kind of challenge Brian Crossley loved.

On the Wallaby was so heavily booked its season was extended even before it opened. Devlin-Glass thought the play flawed and found it hard to believe Australians, if not drunk, would get as jingoistic in the Yankee manner about Kingsford-Smith and the death of Phar Lap as Nick Enwright suggested. Nevertheless she commended it to audiences. The star of the show was Barbara Hughes who:

... played numerous roles, and all with distinction: she belted out numbers with panache, and she played faltering vulnerable roles too. I especially enjoyed the absurdity of the song in praise of Adelaide (in which city the play is mainly set). This occurred in a cleverly staged scene where Kath, the long-suffering mother, declines to accept a prize from Myers, and the patriotic song is counterpointed with her protest at how their employment practices left her Kitty without a job. The superb soliloquy in which Barbara plays a defeated mother living in a shanty in La Perouse, by virtue of her delivery, transformed what could have been pure sentimentality into something of horror, and humour, and genuine emotion.

Four of the five plays staged by Williamstown in 1988 were written in the late 1970s and early 1980s. Richard Beynon's *The Shifting Heart*,

Williamstown's next production, by contrast, belonged to an earlier period (the late 1950s) when such classics as Ray Lawler's *Summer of the Seventeenth Doll* and Alan Seymour's *One Day of the Year*, brought Australian language, issues and images successfully to the stage. Nicky McFarlane in her review of the play on *Applause, Applause* felt the style of Beynon's play in 1988 'melodramatic and a little ponderous'. Moreover, she thought the acting in WLT's production was 'very uneven ... the accents were distracting at times'.

The last two plays for the year were arguably much better. Michael Gurr's *A Pair of Claws* deals with friendship and loyalty, the competing claims of career ambitions and morality and the tensions between parents and grown-up children. The key to the production was a strong cast, among them Shirley Cattunar, Eric Donnison and George Krupinski. Similarly, the quality of the cast was central to the success of Ray Hare's production of David Williamson's *The Club*, with Ellis Ebell, George Krupinski and David Watson performing key roles.

All in all, 1988 was a successful year for WLT, and audiences were very good. Even the smallest, that for *A Pair of Claws* at 864, was more than 80% of capacity. WLT kept up the pace in 1989 and 1990. The 1989 highlights were Brian Crossley's production of Terence Rattigan's *The Winslow Boy*, an offering completely booked out before opening night and winner of the Craven Award for best production, Laurie Gellon's July production of *The Happy Haven*, and Judi Clark's December production of *The Unvarnished Truth*.

In 1990, David Dare directed a successful production of the Dymphna Cusack play *Morning Sacrifice*, which was followed by another excellent Brian Crossley production: Noël Coward's *Noel Coward in Two Keys*. It was also the year in which WLT staged Gillian Wadds play *Who Cares?*, which the Theatre entered with considerable success in the 1990 Waverley festival. Finally, Wayne Pearn closed the year and almost scooped the pool at the annual Cordell Awards Day for his production of Tennessee Williams' *A Lovely Sunday for Creve Coeur*.

While acknowledging that *The Winslow Boy* was not her sort of play, Frances Devlin-Glass thought Williamstown did a commendable, if flawed, job. Director Brian Crossley 'was most scrupulous in conveying the period feel of the piece from casting to the minutiae of costumes and props'. The set was cleverly designed by Grahame Murphy, but the acting was 'very variable, the women being the most consistently reliable'. There was a special piquancy at one performance supplied by Etta, the theatre cat. She was a regular attender at Committee meetings, rehearsals and the occasional performance. Making her entrance in through the French windows in Act 1 of *The Winslow Boy*, she proceeded to pad her way across the stage, and made her exit as nonchalantly as she did her entrance.

Laurie Gellon's staging of John Arden's play *The Happy Haven*, about medical experimentation on old people in a decrepit home, achieved 'must-see' status as far as Devlin-Glass was concerned: 'Williamstown have a thespian triumph on their hands.' Stephen Brown was 'British charm and daily benignity itself as the public face of the home, but repressed rage surfaced when his dictatorial modes of operation surfaced'. Ray Hare whose contrasted army rhetoric and a crumbling spirit at the thought of invasive treatment and unheroic death, was also splendid. Likewise, Henry Ismailiw in the role of Mr Golightly whose 'vulnerability as both enema victim and frustrated lover was handled with comic flair'.

WLT's final production for 1989 was the farce *The Unvarnished Truth*. Frances Devlin-Glass thought it 'very well done'. The play deals with a writer who accidentally kills his wife, and as a result gets caught up in an escalating series of murders, quite unintentional, of a collection of women who subsequently visit the house. The female and male actors in this play face very different challenges. The women exist mainly as corpses, the men drive the action. Frances thought the corpse impersonations of Jacqueline Crothers, Eve Park, Vivien Spence and Amy Grove-Rogers were 'superb'. Of the men, Brad Lindsay and Bill Carlisle were very good, but some of the others variable. Nonetheless under Judi Clark's direction the production was impressive, conveying the humour effectively. The test in Frances' view was the reaction of the family of kids sitting behind her. As she put it, somewhat coyly: 'Their response to the final scene had to be heard to be believed. I was quite concerned that a mercy dash to the far-distant loos might be necessary.'

1989 was thus a good year for WLT. Members were made even happier by another birthday celebration - in this case the 21st anniversary of the opening of 'The Bakery.' Sixty theatre members sampled a special celebratory cake.

Just when things seemed to be going so well, 1990 opened with the first edition of *Cues and News* screaming in a headline: THEATRE IN CRISIS.

1989 - Williamstown Little Theatre's cake celebrating the 21st anniversary of the opening of 'The Bakery'.

It was the perennial problem: the stalwarts were feeling the strain. Editor Judi Clark pleaded:

> *Yes, we are somewhat in crisis as far as backstage crew, set designers and set construction people are concerned. We don't often have trouble finding actors (except occasionally, as we have seen, men) but getting some of the actors to expand their experience and knowledge seems to be a perennial problem. We have always survived because of the stalwarts of the group. Well, the stalwarts of the group have other things planned like overseas trips, house renovating, etc. and we are calling on help from the members to ensure that the following seasons do not see a lowering of standards as far as other aspects of the shows are concerned ... We've got the actors – let's give them the best support we can.*

A shortage of people willing to take on the 'non-glamour' roles in the theatre was a recurring theme through the late 1980s and really came to a head in the middle of 1990. There was a shortage of labour to build the set for the third production of the year, *Whose Life is it Anyway?* An SOS went out which drew a small response, but there was still two-and-a-half-days solid work ahead for such a small group.

Despite the backstage crisis, 1990 was quite a successful year for the Theatre. Bookings were heavy from the start of the year, ticket Secretary David Dare reporting to the Committee in January that, even then, the first two Saturday nights of all plays were fully booked. During the year many members were unable to get seats because they failed to book soon enough, despite regular warnings in *Cues and News*. This situation developed first for *Noel Coward in Two Keys*, but also occurred for *Whose Life Is It Anyway?*. There was a lengthy waiting list for this play in the second week. In the case of *Who Cares?* many members missed out even though an extra performance was organised.

Critical reaction was also generally favourable. Frances Devlin-Glass thought Dymphna Cusack's play *Morning Sacrifice* about staffroom politics in a Melbourne girls' high school, with a cast of nine women, 'another creditable WLT effort, lovingly put together and played with real pride'. Some of the performances were 'top-class'. Devlin-Glass thought this the best performance she had ever seen Mary give:

> *The most developed character of the piece is that of the moderately complicated deputy-headmistress who was played with real style by Mary Little. She handled the mailed fist in the velvet glove with real aplomb well earning the epithet 'spiritual vampire.*

The acting in *Noel Coward in Two Keys* also won praise with Marian Sinclair showing 'extreme professionalism', and Shirley Cattunar 'superb' as the frivolous Carlotta. Simon Killen, as the butler, was making his theatrical debut: 'A more perfect looking young man for the part it would be hard to imagine, and his dressing was very apposite. He acquitted himself admirably offering stylish, low-key service to the principals.'

Staged appropriately in the International Year of Literacy, Gillian Wadds' play *Who Cares?*, (described fully on page 143) was WLT's entry in the Waverley Festival. The cast for this production included four newcomers to WLT: Elizabeth Crockett, Matthew McConnon, Bridget Hamilton and Kathy Thomaidas, the latter two both students at the National Theatre Drama School.

At Waverley, the production received a range of nominations: for Best Actor (Ellis Ebell and Matthew McConnon), Best Supporting Actress (Bridget Hamilton and Kathy Thomaidas), Best Director (Gillian Wadds) and Best Production. The only award received, however, was the Stage Management Award given by the professional staff at Monash's Alexander Theatre for 'getting it in and taking it out as quickly as possible'.

Acting honours in this production went to Ellis Ebell, in the lead role of Colin Hunter, whom Frances Devlin-Glass thought 'gave a finely nuanced performance and was never seen to falter. His body language, business and gestures marked him off from each of the other teachers because of his naturalistic playing'. He was well supported by Mathew McConnon who 'was also superb in the role of the young vulnerable adolescent. His gait even spelt defeat. He glowered and charmed his way through a characterisation which refused to over-simplify the issues'.

The final play for the year was Wayne Pearn's production of Tennessee Williams' play, *A Lovely Sunday for Creve Coeur*, which Pearn took over at short notice. He proved a hard task master for the cast, but managed to mount an impressive production, which the Cordell judges, Pat Day, Geoff Hickey and John Gunn thought the best production for the year. Graeme Cope, reviewing the play for *Applause, Applause*, though confessing to not being particularly enamoured by the play, thought Pearn had mounted a 'taut and zesty production'. Graeme was especially impressed by the acting:

> *The four actresses - Judi Clark, Mary Little, Cathy Ryan and Paula McDonald - played the roles of the 'four lonely, unfulfilled and desperate women' whose lives provide the subject matter of the play 'with obvious relish. The fine and vital balance between these robust players was the rock on which this production stood proud and strong.' Their 'every flutter, snarl, tremble and pounce flattered their individuality at the same time as it enhanced the unity of the piece as a whole.'*

Judi Clark, Graeme thought, was 'finely drawn even when she was only back on to us, uncharacteristically silent and slaving over her hot stove. The same can be said of Mary Little's pathetic but perceptive Gluck as she cowered, seen and unseen in the kitchen' and 'As the snake/bird woman, Helena, Paula

McDonald stalked straight in from the thirties and, more importantly, didn't miss an opportunity to strike, constrict and peck anyone so foolhardy as to put so much as a shadow across her path'.

WLT's program for 1991 was a mixture of the old and the new, both in plays and directors. First was a Ron Little production of the Arthur Kopit play *Wings*, followed by Gordon Dunlop's production of *Uncle Vanya*, a Wayne Pearn production of *Bazaar and Rummage* by Sue Townsend and Grahame Murphy's staging of *Amongst Barbarians*. For the Christmas production David Dare directed Judi Clark and Barbara Hughes in the two-hander *Farewell Brisbane Ladies*, after newcomer Steve Cummins was unable to cast the scheduled play, Alan Ayckbourn's *Table Manners*, because of that old problem, a lack of men.

All were excellent productions for their own reasons. *Applause Applause* reviewer Frances Devlin-Glass thought that *Wings*, a play which deals uncompromisingly with the subject of strokes, was 'a splendid offering'. Frances praised Shirley Cattunar's performance in the central role of Emily Stilson:

Everything about her performance was professional. To have learnt this very difficult part in itself constitutes a kind of heroism as much of it is fractured language, and yet not any kind of gobbledegook will do, as the language frequently borders on poetry and has to be related to normal usage. Shirley Cattunar's voice is wonderfully dynamic, and she uses it as if it were a beautiful musical instrument. Her face too is extraordinarily expressive, and she registers often the agony of not being moored to any outside reality and of being tied to language and a body which will not serve her most vividly operational mind.

Gordon Dunlop's production of *Uncle Vanya* - his first at WLT - had a strong cast, which similarly drew admiration from Frances Devlin-Glass. She commented on Norma Milward's portrayal of Marina, 'whose every cluck and click of her complicated knitting were expressive'; Sonia played by Rhonda Papadimitriou and Veleina, played by Anaiata Gailitis, who were splendid foils for each other; Derek Richards as the parasitic Professor 'with hauteur'; Barry James as 'Uncle Vanya, who has to establish the ennui and the terrible meaningless of life on a decaying feudal estate not long before the revolution';

and Ian McMaster, who 'was always magnetic in probably the best role of the play, that of the mercurial doctor'. There was praise too for John King's set, which was 'extraordinary ... created mainly by additions of props and expressionistic doorways and archways ... and the most beautiful evocative collection of decaying artefacts - leather-bound books artfully arranged and some religious icons ...'

The dramatic highlight of 1991, however, was undoubtedly *Amongst Barbarians*, Michael Wall's satire on British society under Prime Minister Margaret Thatcher. Directed by Grahame Murphy, who also designed the set, it was in Frances Devlin-Glass's view 'of the highest technical standards: (the) set was a knockout. It is all moved by hand in the dark to the accompaniment of the most threatening gamelan music mixed with metallic sounds'. Stephen Baker's lighting also drew praise as did most of the actors, especially Jason Hopkins-Gamble who 'played the role of the more hardened but more vulnerable young man with great subtlety'. Even more disturbing and moving was the role played by Bryan Thomas: 'I found his difficulties in articulating his position heart-wrenching.'

Ihita Kesarcodi-Watson, reviewing the production for the VDL magazine, *Theatrecraft*, was also impressed, commenting that it was a superb standard of achievement, an excellent marriage of strong direction and strong acting coming together on a challenging script. *Amongst Barbarians* was Williamstown's entry in the 1991 Waverley Festival where it received nominations for Best Actor (Jason Hopkins-Gamble), Best Supporting Actor (Bryan Thomas), Best Supporting Actress (Sophie Butterfield) and Best Sset. Jason Hopkins-Gamble won the Best Actor Award and the National Theatre Drama School Scholarship. At home the production scooped the pool on Cordell Day.

1992 opened with a Grahame Murphy production of the David Pownall play *Masterclass*. It was another critical success for Murphy, according to Frances Devlin-Glass 'a theatrical treat par excellence'. Set in an anteroom in the Kremlin during the 1948 Soviet Musicians' conference in Moscow, the action revolves around a meeting between Stalin, his cultural affairs minister, Zhadonov, and the Soviet composers Prokofiev and Shostakovitch. The play placed extra demands on the casting since three of the four actors not only had to be able to play the piano but play it well. Bryan Thomas was the mercurial, manic Stalin, the peasant with a chip on his shoulder who condemned twenty

Masterclass, February 1992
L to R: Bryan Thomas as Stalin, Phillip Lambert as Dmitri Shostakovich,
David Crothers as Sergei Prokofiev, and Ken Ooi as Ardic Zhdanov.

million people to death with next to no remorse. David Crothers and Phillip Lambert contrasted as Prokofiev and Shostakovitch. The set, considered by many to be one of the finest ever at WLT,[75] was designed by Murphy and constructed by an army of members. It involved some intricate stencilling for which Mary Little was responsible, but also involved were David Dare, Graeme Cope, Ray Hare, Mark Young, Ellis Ebell, Laurie Gellon, Derek Richards, Janet Richards, Barbara Hughes, Brian Christopher, Stuart Amnos, Mark Riley, Sarah Berry, Despina Babbage, and Denise, Tara and Susan Jones.

The theatre was much pleased with this production. Audience reaction to *Masterclass* was overwhelmingly positive: Laurie Gellon reported an anonymous phone caller saying: 'I have never done this before (i.e. rung up) but had to congratulate one and all. Brilliant. We were stunned. One of the

---

75   Bryan Thomas remembers that 'everyone (audience and cast) felt they were actually in the Kremlin'.

best things ever seen at WLT.' Laurie Gellon sought audience feedback in *Cues and News*. Gail Armstrong from Essendon obliged, writing:

> *Dear Laurie, You asked in your March newsletter for feedback concerning 'Masterclass' and because I was so moved by this production...I had to put pen to paper to answer your plea. Indeed, when I left your theatre I said to my companions that I found it one of the most satisfying productions I had seen for years. We have always patronised Williamstown and this was surely theatre at its finest. You should all give yourselves heaps of pats on the back – I kept thinking about it all the next day the beautiful piano work coordination and particularly Brian (sic) Thomas as Stalin he made you feel so sorry for Russia and its peoples. Thank you again for a perfect night of theatre.*

After such a satisfying start to the year, it would be hard going to keep up the standard, but WLT went close in its next two productions, Noël Coward's *Fallen Angels*, directed by Brian Crossley, and Richard Brinsley Sheridan's late eighteenth century classic, *The Rivals*, directed by Gordon Dunlop. *Fallen Angels* was a stylish production with Paula McDonald and Marion Sinclair in the principal roles, another excellent set from Grahame Murphy, and costumes by Pat Day. With a few reservations, Frances Devlin-Glass was impressed by the acting:

> *The key women of the piece have to be very strong if the soufflé is to rise at all and both were very stylish. I have not seen Paula McDonald to such advantage before, and deeply admired the light but deft treatment she gave to the role of Jane Bradbury. She looked magnificent in her Jean Harlow wig and was insanely excitable in exact proportion to the role. I enjoyed Marian Sinclair's Julia, but her more controlled and measured performance lacked the effervescence that the role called for. One could not see her as ripe for a lapse into erotic titillation to quite the extent of her friend ... (however) These women exploited the comedy of the scene where they eat and get steadily drunker very ably. I enjoyed the moment when, with oysters poised, they exchanged orgiastic reminiscences about the former lover they are expecting, and the moment when Julia loses the final vestiges*

of propriety and spits grape seeds.

The entrance of the French lover, Maurice (Brian Christopher), was everything it should have been, and he made a wonderful contrast in his spats, cravat and light trousers with the rather more dour and unexciting Englishmen in their tartan socks, fairisle and plus fours.

The Rivals is a demanding play, vocally, technically and stylistically. Acting honours went to Mary Little who, in Frances Devlin-Glass' opinion, made a very dynamic Mrs Malaprop. Shane Luther in the role of Fag also drew praise, as did the team of Ellis Ebell - particularly well cast as Sir Anthony Absolute - and Richard Cordner as Jack Absolute.

WLT kept up the good work with the following production, Caryl Churchill's satiric comedy *Serious Money*, which centres on the wheeling and dealing amongst the leading players on the London stock exchange after its deregulation in 1986. Frances Devlin-Glass thought the high quality of the production was exemplified by the chorus at the end of act one with its precision, imaginative lighting and choreographed vocals and movement. Not everyone agreed, however: the production proved to be almost as controversial as *A Night in the Arms of Raelene* had been in 1984 - a critical and artistic if not popular triumph. Indeed, it seems that the objections centred on the confronting nature of the very chorus praised by Frances in her review.

When it first went 'all local' in the early 1950s, a key strategy used by Williamstown to build its capabilities was to import two of the best directors in Melbourne, Paul Hill and Alan Money, who between them directed half of Williamstown's productions between 1952 and 1956. In an interesting repeat of history, three directors, Brian Crossley, Gordon Dunlop and Grahame Murphy were responsible for half of WLT's productions between 1991 and 1995. Typically presentations by these three directors were the highlights of Williamstown's annual programs in the early 1990s, which is not to say that they weren't complemented by high class productions by other directors, Ray Hare with *Money and Friends* in 1994, and David Dare and Maurie Johns with the last two productions in 1995, *Oleanna* and *Cosi* respectively.

Les Terrill opened 1993 with his production of Bill C. Davis's satire about the Catholic Church, *Mass Appeal*. For its success, this play depends heavily on just two actors. In this production, Ray Hare in the leading role of Father Farley, and Andrew Doolan as the idealistic young seminarian, making his debut at WLT delivered the goods.

Gordon Dunlop's contribution to 1993, for which he won the Craven Award, was Nicholas Wright's *Mrs Klein*, an exploration of the workings of the psychoanalytic movement in 1930s London. Devlin-Glass considered this production in the 'must-see' category. Again, success in this play depends on the calibre of the three women who make up the cast. And Devlin-Glass thought highly of them:

> *Each of the three women in the piece, brilliantly cast one and all, sustained very attractive Viennese accents, at the same time that they were bent on delivering stylish nuanced performances. The pacing and timing of the playing was delicious, and so much that was effective depended on body language and subtle business. The two biggest roles were those of Melanie Kline (played by Louise Whiteman) and her daughter (Paula McDonald), and they were beautifully matched in toughness, ruthlessness and imperiousness. Louise Whiteman was the main marshall of the cast of*

Mass Appeal, February 1993
Ray Hare as Father Farley.

invisible characters who stand outside the play's three main characters, and her performance was faultless. Paula McDonald revealed how versatile an actor she is. Her easy complicitous laughter with her peer was in strong contrast to her (mainly) brutal exchanges with her mother...Colleen Ricci as the psychoanalyst in training gradually abrogated power into her own hands and grew in stature as the play evolved.

There was praise, too, for the excellent setting:

Sue McDermott's set and Mark Young and Pat Day's costumes for this production were superb – with the single exception of the turquoise curtain ... The lamp, desk, filing cabinet, books, and sherry glasses were very evocative, and the paintings, especially the one of the tortured male, were thematically appropriate. Hairstyles by Yvonne Davies were wondrous, especially Melitta's.

Brian Crossley followed with Noël Coward's *Relative Values*, in which the two outstanding performances were Marian Sinclair's Lady Felicity and Ellis Ebell's equally stylish and pointed Crestwell, the literate butler.

After such quality, Judi Clark faced a real challenge with Phillip King and Falkland Cary's *Sailor Beware*, but clearly rose to the occasion. Frances Devlin-Glass thought this was a 'heart-warming romp of a show handled very well by Director and cast...The chief virtue of this piece was its lightness of touch and its furious pace. The Willy audience risked hernias on Friday evening.' Though Frances thought the acting variable, two of the cast, Kate Llewellyn as the mother-in-law, and Maureen Phelan as the eternally 'wet' sister-in-law, received nominations from the Cordell adjudicators.

The play selection committee decided that 1994 was to be a year of comedy. The playbill was: *Same Time Next Year* by Bernard Slade, directed by Bryan Thomas; Oscar Wilde's *An Ideal Husband*, directed by Brian Crossley; *On Top of the World* by Michael Gow, directed by Gordon Dunlop; David Williamson's *Money and Friends* directed by Ray Hare; and Alan Ayckbourn's *Season's Greetings* directed by Grahame Murphy.

According to the *Applause Applause* team, Williamstown again served its audiences well. Apart from a comic theme, the common threads running

An Ideal Husband, April 1994
L to R: Mary Little as Lady Markby, Cae Rees as Mabel Chiltern, Celia Meehan as Lady Chiltern, Marian Sinclair as Mrs Cheveley, Cyndia Hillinger as Lady Basildon, Janine Evans as Mrs. Marchmont.

throughout 1994's fine productions were strong direction, good acting and the usual attention to style and detail in design and costuming. *An Ideal Husband* won the Craven Award for best production.

Artistically speaking, 1995 was a repeat of 1994 and astonishingly every production was nominated for the theatre's annual awards. Paula McDonald won the Cordell Award for her performance as Coralie in *Coralie Lansdowne Says No*, directed by Gordon Dunlop. Paula was well supported by Rhonda Papadimitriou, Anne Coleman and Trudy McLauchlan.

For Noël Coward's *Waiting in the Wings*, Brian Crossley's cast list resembled a roll call of the much admired 'grandes dames' of Melbourne's non-professional theatre: Norma Milward, Alice Bugge, Nora Toohey, Marian Sinclair, Shirley Cattunar, Judi Clark and Gillian Wadds. The cast also included Shirley Sydenham, Janet Paul, Eve Park, Alison McMichael and Celia Meehan, all of whom had long theatrical credentials, as well as a few newer faces and three excellent men, Damian Coffey, Derek Richards and Barry James. This production earned a little international acclaim as the following extract from a letter to WLT dated 1 May 1995 from Marie and Harry McAvoy demonstrates:

We had the pleasure on Saturday afternoon of visiting your delightful Little Theatre and felt we must write and congratulate you on your excellent production of 'Waiting in the Wings'. We are on holiday from Yorkshire, England, staying with our daughter in Newport, and we are members of our own local amateur dramatic society, The Keighley Playhouse which is a similar set-up similar to yours... We were very interested to see to see your production as funnily enough we have 'Waiting in the Wings' on our list of plays for next season.

The following production ran into difficulties because of director Judi Clark's encountering the perennial problem in non-professional companies of finding sufficient men (in this case only two!) who were available at the same time. The scheduled production, *Home*, had to be abandoned and Sue Townsend's play about adult literacy, *Groping for Words*, substituted. There was only a month for rehearsals, a male role had to be 'changed' to a female and to top it all *Groping for Words* required a much more complex set than *Home*. However, the company rose to the occasion and satisfied its patrons. The production also wrote itself into WLT's history thanks to a cast member called Darren. As *Cues and News* reported:

OBITUARY: It is with sadness and regret that I have to announce that Darren, our goldfish star, gave his all in the execution in his role in 'Groping for Words'. Suddenly, in the midst of a performance, he felt that it was all too much. However, he was discreet, choosing to go to sleep hidden by the foliage in his tank, so that people could continue to enjoy the action and not be distressed. The role was taken over at very short notice by Son of Darren, who wished to retain the name for perpetuity. The second dressing-room has been renamed in his honour.

The year closed with David Mamet's *Oleanna*, directed by David Dare, and Louis Nowra's *Cosi*, directed by Maurie Johns. Both had recently been performed by the Melbourne Theatre Company and were fresh in theatregoers' minds, but WLT's efforts were deemed to have compared favourably. 'Sustained, intense performances' from Brian Christopher and Tracey Mathers, for example, led to some reassessment of *Oleanna*'s qualities by Frances Devlin-Glass. She felt Williamstown's 'more intimate space and the rather more naturalistic and humanised set (compared with the very dark oppressive set used by the MTC in the George Fairfax studio) made a colossal difference to the extent to which one could identify with and feel for each of the protagonists.' Similarly, John Gunn for *Applause, Applause* thought that Williamstown's cast was a 'tightly knit ensemble' which did a creditable job of a play he thought well suited to good amateur companies.

1996 was WLT's 50th anniversary year. In keeping with its long tradition, WLT was committed to a proper celebration of the occasion. In 1995 it established a committee, chaired by Barbara Hughes, to plan the celebrations. The 50th anniversary program spread throughout the year comprised:[76]

- On 18 May: a rehearsed reading of WLT's first local production on 13 November 1948, Shaw's one act play *Man of Destiny*. (The date was chosen to be as close as possible to the anniversary of the date of the meeting (23 May 1946) which decided to set up WLT). Sixty people turned up to this event;

- On 3 August, a 50th Anniversary Dinner Dance at WLT's original 'home', the Mechanics Institute. 180 people attended this event sitting at nineteen tables each designed with a theme from a past WLT production;

- From 15 to 19 September: an exhibition of limited edition works - photographs by Christine Ramsay and prints by Mary Newsome. The suggestion for this exhibition came from Bob Glass whose wife

---

[76] The following details are taken mostly from the Report from the 50th Anniversary Committee to the Theatre's 1997 AGM.

worked with Mary's husband Bernard at Rusden State College. Forty-one of these works sold, netting the theatre $1,317; and

- On Cordell Day a special exhibition of photographs featuring the company's history, accompanied by a short presentation on WLT's evolution by Gillian Wadds.

Some of these events generated special stories:

- In the audience for *Man of Destiny* was Dorothy Porter, who as Dorothy Hughes had appeared as the 'Strange Lady' in the original production. (This time the Strange Lady was played by Jane Lindill, then a relative newcomer to WLT);

- The 50th anniversary dinner dance happened to be held on long-standing and life member Gwladys Winfield's birthday. She managed to win the lucky door prize, leading her to write the following note to the 50th Anniversary Committee:

Congratulations on a memorable 50th Anniversary Dinner Dance at the Mechanics. The catering, the band, the entertainment, the costumes and decorations all lending themselves to the wonderful air of festivity AND what a birthday party for me, one I won't forget in a hurry, in fact my door prize will be a real memento of the night.

On stage, WLT celebrated its 50th anniversary year in 1996 by entrusting its five productions to its most established and successful directors: Grahame Murphy directed Ariel Dorfman's *Death and the Maiden* in February; Laurie Gellon staged Hugh Whitemore's *Breaking the Code*, a play centred on the life of Alan Turing, in April-May; Brian Crossley did *Hay Fever* in July; Bruce Wapshott (who coincidentally had been made a WLT life member at the 1996 AGM) directed the 'Strictly Australian Ballroom Comedy' *Wallflowering* by Peta Murray in September; and David Dare directed David Williamson's *Brilliant Lies* in November - December.

The choice of Grahame Murphy and Laurie Gellon to present the first two plays in 1996 was an appropriate way to start the Theatre's Golden Jubilee Year. No two directors could better represent the history of Williamstown Little Theatre than Murphy and Gellon. Both had served the Theatre for a long time: Murphy for forty years, and Gellon for a mere twenty-six! Both provided in their distinctive ways the energy and insight, and the capacity for improvisation which the designer Kenneth Rowell once described as 'one of the key characteristics of the original theatre mind.'[77]

Murphy and Gellon each chose plays which challenged the mind. Of *Death and the Maiden*, Frances Devlin-Glass commented that the play was 'unusual in combining elements of the thriller with serious political and philosophical issues ... exploring how a society recovers from the trauma of civil war ... (in Chile) in complex and uncompromising ways'. Seeing it on opening night Frances considered the playing a little uneven, but thought newcomer Jayne Lindill as the female lead, though 'new to Williamstown and relatively inexperienced as an actor, was outstanding. She has the focus and concentration of a really class actor, moves well and has no trouble commanding the space'. Ellis Ebell as Gerardo Escobar 'was often very moving ... (but) There were occasions ... when I thought he made moves which had not been sufficiently planned'. Frances had praise for the set:

> *In typical Grahame Murphy style, the set was constructed to transform itself utterly in the final scene, where mirrors were used to incorporate the audience into the action in a very moving dumbshow in which victim and alleged torturer were required to share music they both loved, and which had been an integral and horrifying part of the sadist's repertoire of torture.*

Frances concluded her review with the comment that:

> *This is a surprising and gutsy play about important contemporary issues. It is mounted with conviction and style by Williamstown, and it invites thought and political engagement. A challenging but also entertaining play, as the players play the tension skilfully. I would advise people to book early as the word will get around.*

---

77   See Kenneth Rowell, *Stage Design*, (London, Studio Vista, 1968), p.75.

1987 - 1996

Death and the Maiden, February 1996
L to R: Ellis Ebell as Gerardo Escobar, Jayne Lindill as Paulina Silas, Grahame Murphy (Director) and Mark Robins as Roberto Miranda.

Breaking the Code, May 1996
Ian Grealy as Alan Turing and Derek Richards as Dillwyn Knox.

Death and the Maiden was followed by the Victorian premiere production of *Breaking The Code*, directed by Laurie Gellon, thus linking WLT's 50th anniversary back to its first 'all local' season of 1952 which started with the local premiere of Joan Temple's play *Deliver my Darling*. Gellon also mixed his cast between the old and the new: casting Ian Grealy in the lead role as Alan Turing, 1996 President Cecilia Meehan as Pat Green, Turing's collaborator, two newcomers Scott Mullen and Victor Gomes as Ron Miller and Nikos, and long serving members, Mary Little, Robbie McFarlane, Ian McMaster and Derek Richards in supporting roles.

Breaking The Code is concerned with the life and work of Alan Turing breaker of the German enigma code during the 1939-45 World War and the victim of contemporary attitudes to homosexuality after he stumbles into admitting his sexual preferences to a police force which believes it has no choice but to prosecute him.

Reviewing the play, Frances Devlin-Glass thought Laurie Gellon had 'assembled a cast which for depth and humanity was outstanding':

> *The portrayal of the cryptographer and inventor of the computer was played with great subtlety and complexity by Ian Grealy. To some extent the play mobilises the stereotype of the socially inept scientist caught up in his intellectual enthusiasms, but deepens it by examining a series of demanding relationships – with his childhood friend Christopher, with a prickly but increasingly reliable mother (played with passion and conviction by Mary Little), with a fellow scientist (female and played with sweet intensity by Celia Meehan) whose interest in him is as much for his intellectual energy as for himself and with a colleague whose sexual preferences and courage become palpable only after his death (Derek Richards was impressive in this role).*

Frances was also impressed by John Burrett's stunning set design 'possibly among the most inventive and challenging I have seen at Willy' which 'was atmospherically lit by Laurie Gellon'.

Brian Crossley's contribution to WLT's fiftieth anniversary year was another impressive exhibition of his love for, and capability in directing, the work of Noël Coward, in this case *Hay Fever*. Frances Devlin-Glass saw it in the second week of its season, by which time it was fully booked out. She thought the production 'worked superbly as an ensemble'. She was:

> ... especially impressed by the juvenile leads Eliot Hayes and Suzanne Daley whose realisation of the precocious eccentric siblings who feed their mother's neuroses was marked by energy and style. Indeed, the core family group, which included these figures as well as the experienced Marian Sinclair and Barry James, was wonderfully self-obsessed, and carried their roles with great assurance.

In Devlin-Glass's view, while the acting in the support roles was of mixed quality, Graeme Moore's set and especially Pat Day's costumes were of the highest quality:

> Pat Day is to be congratulated on an impressive array of period costumes which spoke to each of the characterisations very precisely, and which were the more demanding because each act, and there were three of them, entailed a completely new wardrobe. The costume-drama aspect of this production was especially rewarding for the audience at Willy to relish the superb fit and sit of luxurious fabrics, especially in the charades-like game scene of Act 2.

Hay Fever was followed by the lesser-known Australian work *Wall-Flowering* by Peta Murray, described by Frances Devlin-Glass as 'a honey of a play, seducing you into its sticky coils, inviting your laughter and a little thoughtfulness, but finally leaving one with the sense that it may have laid on the sweetness a bit heavy-handedly'. The production however, as Frances put it, 'belonged to Mary Little whose Peg was intense and focussed, and appropriately confused about the demands put on her by her oppressive feminist "girlfriends" who try to make her over against her will'.

WLT concluded its 50th anniversary year with David Williamson's *Brilliant Lies*, directed by David Dare. As Dr Greg Tillet, Director for Conflict Resolution at Macquarie University in Sydney, noted in his description of the play in the program, it 'raises many difficult and challenging issues which may appear to have been enhanced for dramatic performance, yet the play confronts situations which are very close to reality. The characters struggle

Brilliant Lies, November/December 1996
L to R Paula McDonald as Katy, Kate Dillon as Suzy, Jane Lindill as Marion,
John Hood as Vince, and Andrew Tate as Gary.

less to analyse and resolve their situation than to displace and suppress it. In so doing, they merely initiate new conflicts and reinforce old, inadequate patterns of dealing with them'. Willy's production, featuring Kate Dillon, Jayne Lindill and Paula McDonald in the lead female roles, 'specially well cast as an ensemble', forced Frances Devlin-Glass to do a 'radical reassessment of a play I don't like a lot' partly because of the 'adept handling of the dialogue between the three women'.

The joys of WLT's 50th Anniversary year were somewhat muted by the death on 30th November 1996, after a long illness, of Grahame Murphy, one of WLT's most talented actors and directors (he directed nineteen plays at WLT between 1964 and 1996), who also exhibited great ability as a set designer/builder. As noted above, Grahame had directed his last play for the Theatre as its first offering in its Golden Jubilee Year. His memory was enshrined physically at the theatre at a function on 28 March 1998 to celebrate WLT's thirty years at Albert Street, when President Celia Meehan unveiled a jarrah garden bench bearing a brass plaque worded: 'In memory of Graeme Murphy, one of WLT's leading actors and directors.'

Public acknowledgement of Grahame's contribution to the Theatre was further cemented by the decision by the Committee in 2009 to create an annual 'Grahame Murphy Award for Excellence' to recognise a WLT member for her/his excellent contribution in any field other than performance. (The winners of this award are listed in Appendix 3.)

Throughout its fifth decade the WLT engaged in continuous upgrading of its facilities, usually on its own initiative, but occasionally because of the requirements of outside regulators. The major works, and the year in which they were undertaken, included:

- 1987: the installation of a new gas heating system;
- 1988: at the behest of the Health Department, a series of major electrical works to improve safety and, at the insistence of the Theatre's insurers, major upgrades to the Theatre's fire protection equipment;
- 1989: the replacement of the stairs to the upstairs storage area, originally constructed off-site by Gary Metcalf's students at the Newport College of TAFE;
- 1991: theatre painted, new carpet laid, new male toilet, conversion of another toilet into a shower facility for the cast, acquisition of a PC;
- 1993: installation of video system including two 35cm colour monitors and three 35cm black and white monitors (following a suggestion from Paula McDonald that such a system would be a great help to both actors and the back-stage crew, as it proved to be).

The acquisition of the PC in 1991 generated eloquence from *Cues and News* editor Barbara Hughes who wrote in the February 1991 edition that:

We are very proud to announce a new arrival at the theatre. It's (sic) name is Amstrad PC6640 and it's a beautiful bouncing Portable Personal Computer complete with printer. Eventually (when we learn to drive it) it will be used for tickets, membership, minutes of meetings and Cues and News. The surrogate father is Steve Baker who has delivered our very own software package and is recovering very well from the operation.

A major organisational initiative was President Laurie Gellon's inauguration of 'Presidential Working Bees' on Tuesday nights in January and February. Laurie explained the rationale in a special message in *Cues and News* for December 1992/January 1993:

> *The Theatre needs a big clean-up/clean out. During the normal course of the year, we are so busy just getting productions on - building sets etc. - that some aspects of the theatre are a bit neglected. We will once again mount a huge assault upon the flat storage area, the furniture bay, the workshop, the green room and upstairs. We also hope to get the final coats of paint on the toilets.*

There was of course THE BRIBE!

> *Around about 9/9.30 pm each night we will finish, and the theatre then supplies a FREE BBQ – BYO NOTHING!!!*

The initiative was an immediate success. Eight people turned up on 5th January 1993 and the numbers grew in successive weeks to fourteen and sixteen. Indeed, so popular was the event that WLT members requested another one on February 1st when seventeen people turned up. The Presidential Working Bees have been held every year since, and now feature as a central 'not to be missed' event in the WLT calendar 'to start the year'.

By several criteria, including the quality and range of its productions, the sustained level of subscriber and audience support, continuing financial health, and the progressive upgrading of its facilities, Williamstown Little Theatre's fifth decade was clearly successful. If the Theatre's executive and other key players sometimes felt overly stressed, it was probably mostly because of the intrinsic difficulty of maintaining the standard which the Theatre had achieved by the early 1990s. Subscribers voted with their renewals and an occasional paean of praise such as that provided by long-time supporter Irene Gittins when she wrote with her subscription renewal early in 1995:

> *The 1994 productions were all superb - we were presented with such riches in the way of performances, direction, sets, wardrobe, just everything. If*

amateur theatre can be termed professional, then the Williamstown Little Theatre is it in every facet.

By 1996, WLT was a more financially robust organisation than it was a decade earlier. Apart from a slight dip in 1993, its total income increased continuously, its income in 1996 being 2.5 times that of a decade earlier. Reflecting the loyalty of its subscriber base, income from subscriptions typically accounted for between 40% and 50% of its total income. Every year the Theatre earned a surplus, sometimes small, but usually between 20% and 30% of total income. The upgrading of its facilities described above hence imposed little financial stress on WLT.

Chapter Six

1997-2006: Consolidating

In her tenth Annual Report as Secretary in 2008, Barbara Hughes wrote:

As I look back on the past ten years, I realise that, in essence, the theatre hasn't changed very much. And I mean that in a positive way. It is still a place where like-minded people come together to try and achieve the best they possibly can. It is still a place where audiences can be entertained and enthralled for a modest cost. And it is still a space where we can sit in the courtyard after the working bees and continue a conversation that began nearly twenty years ago. We've lost a few good friends along the way, but we've also gained some new ones.

Does the evidence support Barbara's view?

Barbara's first year as Secretary began very positively for the theatre in 1997, still on a high from the joys of its fiftieth anniversary celebrations. Perhaps the best indicator of this was its success that year in the inaugural Victorian Drama League Awards.[78] Sixteen companies had nominated twenty-eight plays for these awards. Williamstown nominated two: Gordon Dunlop's production of Athol Fugard's *The Road to Mecca* and Brian Crossley's tilt at Oscar Wilde's *A Woman of No Importance*.

'Gold' and 'Silver' awards were available in each of ten categories that year, (i.e. a total of twenty), and between them, WLT's offerings won nine: five

---

78   What follows about the VDL Awards is based on pp.93-98 of *The Victorian Drama League 1952-2002*. A full list of WLT's nominations for VDL Awards and the awards received appears in Appendix 4.

gold and four silver. *The Road to Mecca* was deemed Best Production, and secured gold for Gordon Dunlop as Best Director, and for Doug Bennett for Best Set Design. Paula McDonald and Mary Little shared gold for Best Actress in a Leading Role. Pat Day's costumes for *A Woman of No Importance* also secured a gold award.

The VDL's adjudicators' views were shared by WLT's 1997 Cordell Award adjudicators; *The Road to Mecca* won the Craven Award for best production, and Paula McDonald the Cordell Award for her role as Elsa Barlow in that play.

Frances Devlin-Glass for *Applause, Applause* was in furious agreement with the VDL and Cordell Award adjudicators about the quality of WLT's *The Road to Mecca*. The production, she thought, was 'in the must-see class'. She wrote:[79]

> *'The Road to Mecca' is stunning theatre. The piece is a rich amalgam: Gordon Dunlop's obsessive meticulousness marks every detail of the production and of the acting. The set, equally meticulous, designed by Doug Bennett and realised by David Dare and the Willy team is astonishing, with every minute and richly decorative detail strictly functional...*
>
> *The effectiveness of the set is much enhanced by the best lighting plot I've ever seen from the hand of Laurie Gellon. What was especially notable was the way the set was sometimes differentially and symbolically lit, with blue lights on the seriously depressed older woman and golden ones on her younger friend. Night and day was subtly registered, with the east being differentiated from the west.*
>
> *But the night would have been nothing without the women, Mary Little and Paula McDonald, and their well-cast support David Crothers. The two women are, of course, stalwarts of Willy and their delight in working together is palpable. Both are actors who simply grow in stature as they mature. Not only did they sustain accents which required a fair amount of attack, but they kept a fairly static script on the move by virtue of brilliant pacing of the dialogue, a very proactive use of proximity and touch to*

---

79   The review was published in *Cues and News*, July/August 1997.

indicate intimacy, and a purposeful use of domestic business. ... They gave performances which were outstanding in any league. David Crothers was wonderfully restrained as the repressed and controlling pastor, and it was to his credit and his director's that we were never at any point were invited to demonise a misguided philanthropy.

Devlin-Glass was less enthusiastic about Brian Crossley's effort at Oscar Wilde's *A Woman of No Importance*, 'a workmanlike, but not inspired production', thinking that the cast were 'handicapped by insufficient attention to the Wildean style and to orchestrating and fine-tuning the dialogue'. Devlin-Glass agreed, however, with the VDL adjudicators that Pat Day's 'array of elegant Edwardian day and evening costumes' were first class, and thought the set designed by Barry Pearce and Johnathan Benham, 'delectably detailed ... consisting of wittily painted flats in a *fin de siecle* style'.

WLT's last two productions in 1997 similarly won high praise from Devlin-Glass. Dennis Potter's *Sufficient Carbohydrate*, directed by Damien Coffey in his debut as a Director at WLT, was 'in the must-see class'. There was praise for John Burrett's set. The play is set in a Greek villa. Devlin-Glass thought Burrett had 'skimped on nothing in creating the illusion in an exhilarating assault of brilliant blue, grey and white textures and lines ... Stelios Karagiannis' lighting made the very handsome set sing.' The lead actors, Ian Grealy, Tristan Lutze and Jayne Lindill all won praise, Grealy for playing his role 'with brio', Tristan Lutze for the 'appropriate delicacy' as Clayton, and Lindill, who 'gave a classy performance as the poisonous wife and even managed to complicate the role a little'.

The concluding production for 1997 was the thriller musical *Something's Afoot*, the first play directed at WLT by Barbara Hughes. As Barb commented in an interview in *Cues and News* soon after retiring as WLT Secretary, she had always been interested in doing musicals despite her first show at Altona, *The Merry Widow*, being cancelled about three weeks before opening. She had long loved all aspects of musicals, not only being in them but also watching them. Her first effort at direction suggested a significant additional talent.

Something's Afoot is set in 1934 in an eccentric and remote country estate. The play parodies both genres with many bizarre turns requiring lots of technical wizardry and exact timing. Reviewing it for *Applause Applause*,

Frances Devlin-Glass[80] thought it a 'tight and pacy production, another Williamstown success'. Frances noted that as a musical *Something's Afoot* makes serious demands on voices which most of the actors, 'even those that weren't of musical comedy quality' met. The stand-out musical performer was Kylie Zahra whose 'previous career in musical comedy and her larger-than-life style of ingénue comedy stood out in a cast of mainly straight actors, as did Andrew Wild, Bob McKell and David Bleier'. Frances went on:

> *The real surprises in the musical department, who got away with it a lot because they are very adept actors, were Shirley Cattanur who sang a great deal ... with panache in a musical style that was half speaking voice (and) Judi Clark, as Lady Manley-Prowe, 'always one to watch when she's enjoying herself, ... (in this case by) seducing and ravishing the astonished Colonel Gillweather, Derek Richards'. That was quite a scene - a 'totally outrageous performance.'*

Judi Clark won the Win Stewart Award for that performance.

The night of Friday 13th February 1998 was a sad occasion for WLT, as after the Theatre's AGM, those gathered participated in what *Cues and News* editor Mark Young described as a 'surprise NOT' party for long-time WLT member Laurie Gellon, about to depart Melbourne for a new life in South Australia. Laurie's move had been heralded for a long time, as Barb Hughes put it in her (first) Secretary's Report to the 1998 AGM: 'Laurie keeps insisting that *Something Afoot* was his swansong, but we hope this aberration will pass.' It was no aberration. Laurie left Melbourne for South Australia later that year.

The thirtieth anniversary of WLT's occupation of 2 Albert Street in 1998 brought an unexpected financial windfall for WLT courtesy of a bequest of $27,515 from the estate of Peter Curtis, who, as previously noted,[81] had initiated in 1971 a Theatre Workshop for teenagers. The Committee decided

---

80   The review was reprinted in *Cues and News* for January 1998.
81   See page 95.

to use some of the bequest to update the front of house facilities. $7,811 was spent on this project which included carpeting of the foyers. Bryan Thomas was the heavy lifter. As well. $3,814 was spent on a new stage, and a digital camera, a new computer and CD players purchased.

In 1998, Williamstown continued its established practice of staging five diverse plays each year. The plays were: Ira Levin's *Deathtrap*; *The Sisters Rosensweig* by Wendy Wassertein; Noël Coward's *Private Lives*; Australian playwright Nick Enwright's *Good Works*; and *Steaming* by Nell Dunn.

If the views of a single reviewer (again Frances Devlin-Glass) can be believed, the highlights of the year were:

- *The Sisters Rosensweig*: 'The play...contained 'sleek and intelligent dialogue, literate, sharp, and so New York', with 'set and costumes superb';
- *Private Lives*: 'a very tight and pacey production of a delightful show';
- *Steaming*: 'It is a pity this play was not available for the VDL Awards as its production values and acting standards were very high indeed';
- *Deathtrap*: 'a creditable but not brilliant production;
- *Good Works* 'not one of Williamstown's better efforts...not incompetent, just failed to sing...not a good choice for the Willy space.'

D. William Green thought better of *Deathtrap*, suggesting that WLT's production indicated the theatre was off to a good start in 1998:[82]

Williamstown Little Theatre certainly hit the mark with their production of 'Deathtrap'. All aspects of the production were thoughtfully constructed and displayed with the effect of a suspenseful, and at times amusing, performance.

If Frances Devlin-Glass had reservations about *Deathtrap*, as noted above, she was very positive about *The Sisters Rosensweig*:

---

82   see *Theatrecraft*, April 1998, p.10.

The acting in this production was of a very high standard, and I was especially impressed by the newcomer (Oleh Kowalyk) who serves as a catalyst for the action. (There were) outstanding performances by Sallyann Wilson, Annie McBurney and Brian Christopher (though) Alison McMichael lacked some of the finer touches needing a bit more variety in body language especially in the production scene.

The set design by the director, Bryan Thomas and execution by David Dare and the Williamstown team and costumes by Pat Day (for which she received a nomination for a VDL Award[83]) were as usual superb, streamlined, classy and highly efficient as conveyors of class and taste.

Sadly for her audience, Devlin-Glass concluded, the play was already booked out.

Of *Private Lives*, 'not directed this year by Brian Crossley,'[84] but by his 'worthy successor' Mark Robins', Devlin-Glass commented that Mark:

... had assembled an excellent cast of five, with the two principals, Kerrie-Anne Baker and Stephen Brown, doing an exemplary job in the roles of Amanda and Elyot Chase. They were precisely what the script called for: refined, aestheticized, feline creatures of very volatile temperament, (who) purred erotically and scratched and fought like alley-cats.

There were, however, some problems with the set: 'the balcony scene in the hotel was too cramped' and it was 'difficult to sweep through the double doors in the kind of extravagant way the script seems to indicate'. In addition, the costumes were a 'bit of a mixed bag'.

WLT's last production for 1998 was Nell Dunn's *Steaming*, directed by Doug Bennett, which was also booked out before it started.[85] As noted, Frances

---

83   *Theatrecraft*, December 1998, p.2.

84   Crossley was WLT's resident Noël Coward 'specialist' directing five of his plays for the theatre (though never *Private Lives*) between 1985 and 1995, and winning the Craven Award for his production of *Waiting in the Wings* in 1995.

85   *Cues and News*, November 1998.

Devlin-Glass on *Applause, Applause* was highly impressed:

> *The set was magnificent: an inner London baths which had been given the modernist white tile treatment but which were mouldering to reveal a more sybaritic site with Corinthian columns and eighteenth century neoclassical murals depicting male bodies…*
>
> *The cast of six women (five of whom were making their debut at WLT) were wonderfully chosen for their bodily variations and their acting skills. … The outstanding performer in this high-class cast was Kyria (playing Josie) who, as the lower-class sexpot, combined pulsing energy with vocal intelligence and cavorted her way through the script at high octane levels.*

The Cordell adjudicators agreed with Devlin-Glass, awarding Kyria the Cordell Award; amazingly she had taken over the role at short notice.[86] Awarding *Steaming* the Craven Award for best production of 1998, the adjudicators agreed with Devlin-Glass's view that it was 'hard to imagine a production of the play with more integrity and *chutzpah*'.

Several years later, from Melbourne's Coronavirus lockdown, Maggie McInnes (who had played the role of Mrs Meadow - the only person not required to take her clothes off) contributed a special insiders' memory of *Steaming* to *Cues and News* for August 2020:

> *At the end of the last rehearsal the backstage crew, who were all men (for the sake of balance, Doug Bennett the Director told us), stripped off and joined us for the last photographs. (But) I didn't ever see the copies.*

But the photo has recently re-emerged (see p.183).

The Theatre experienced sadness in September 1998 with the death of Jim Jamieson.[87] Jim and his wife Mavis were the organisers of the 'Jamieson nights'. Both were theatre lovers, and also active members of the Williamstown

---

86 Ibid
87 See *Cues and News*, September 1998.

Little Athletics Club. They decided that they could support the theatre by buying a bulk set of tickets to on-sell them to that Club's members, friends and network. Eventually the Jamiesons booked out at least two full nights (and often more) for every show. Each year, WLT's subscription brochure identified these nights.

Williamstown's 1999 program opened with Ray Lawler's *Kid Stakes*, the first installment of a Bryan Thomas plan to stage all three of Lawler's 'Doll Trilogy' as the first production of WLT's seasons in 1999, 2000 and 2001. As is well known, this trilogy features two North Queensland cane cutters, Barney Ibott and Roo Webber who have been coming to Melbourne for seventeen years during the summer lay-off and staying at the home of Emma Leech and her daughter Olive. For sixteen of these summers Olive's best friend Nancy also shares the house but in the last, Olive has left to get married. The trilogy traces the dynamics of the relationships over those years. Whilst *The Doll* refers to the seventeenth summer, *Kid Stakes* and *Other Times*, though

Steaming 1988:
Cast and Crew: Maggie McInnes at the far left. Director Doug Bennett front centre.

written after their more famous cousin,[88] refer to the first and ninth of these summer visits respectively. Following the MTC example when it re-presented the trilogy in 1976-1977,[89] Thomas, though unaware of the precedent, decided to stage the trilogy in the order of the summers to which they refer.

A feature of Williamstown's first two efforts (*Kid Stakes* in 1999 and *Other Times* in 2000) was that four actors were able to reprise their roles - Bevan Valand as Roo, Samantha Reilly as Nancy, Amelia Davies as Olive and Moira Smith as Emma. This enabled reviewers such as John Gunn from *Applause Applause* on 3CR to note the development of these actors in their portrayal of these characters, as the characters themselves changed in light of their experiences.

Kid Stakes, John thought[90] 'a good production if not a great one, but a nice start to Williamstown's 1999 season'. The cast, according to John, acquitted themselves reasonably well:

- James Anderson as Barney and Bevan Vakland as Roo 'looked right physically and worked nicely as a team';
- Samantha Reilly as Nancy, 'with that extra dimension of an immaturity that has to grow up, effectively set the scene for the 'Doll' as to why she is not there for the seventeenth summer';
- Moira Smith's Emma was 'totally believable sharp yet good hearted'; but
- Whilst Amelia Davies' performance as Olive was 'polished', it was a little too sophisticated and lacked the vulnerability and emotional insecurity that comes to a head in 'The Doll' itself.

Kid Stakes was followed in May 1999 by Oscar Wilde's *Lady Windermere's Fan*, notable apart from anything else for its unusual program design. Again John Gunn had some reservations, commenting that the production under the direction of Brian Crossley: 'succeeded on most levels...elegant settings, superb costumes and generally a nice light touch,...though there were times, in Act

---

88   *Kid Stakes* in 1975 and *Other Times* in 1976.
89   For the details, see John Sumner, *Recollections at Play*, pp.282-286.
90   See *Cues and News*, March/April 1999.

1997 - 2006

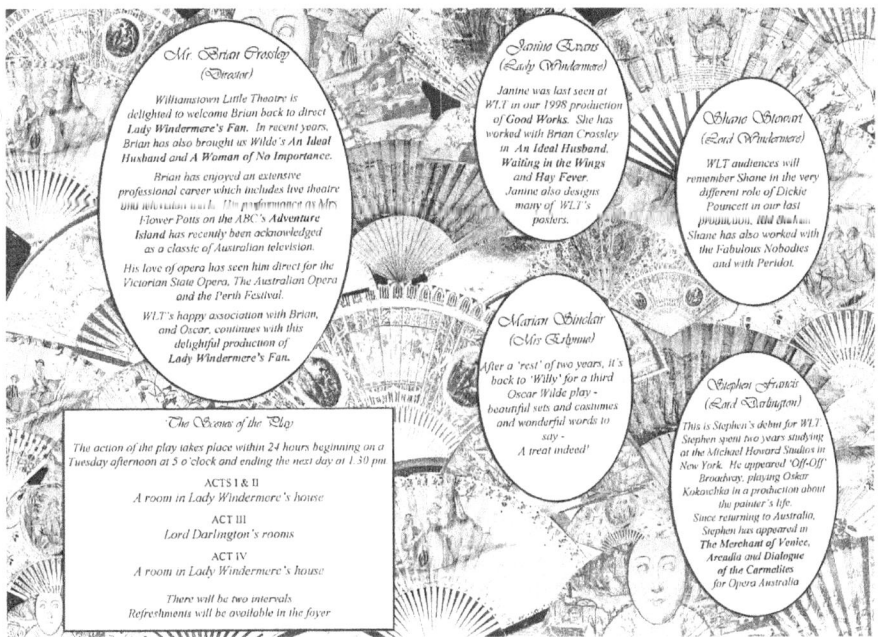

The unusual program for *Lady Windemere's Fan*, May 1999.

2 particularly, where the pace flagged and it became a little static.' Moreover, John thought, some of the male actors showed 'a lack of style, vocal skills and polished physical carriage', the exceptions being Barry James as Lord Augustus Lorton, Rex Callahan as Cecil Graham and Brian Christopher as Parker the butler. The ladies were much better: 'Janine Evans was a charming and sincere Lady Windermere and was in physical and vocal control at all times' and 'Marian Sinclair a very elegant and persuasive Mrs Erlynne'. This was Janine Evans' first lead role at WLT which she remembers as: 'A wonderful experience… I learned a lot from Brian about performing Oscar Wilde - no one could flick a fan or kick a train like Brian.'

Pat Day's costumes for *Lady Windermere's Fan* were as usual top class. To quote John Gunn:

To costume 14 actors in the upper crust elegance of the 1890's is no mean feat and congratulations to Pat Day for this theatrical achievement - at no time did we ever get the feeling of "make-shift", particularly when there were so many costume changes.

Pat won the silver medal for costume design at the 1999 VDL Awards. Simultaneously, the VDL adjudicators Special Award went to Wayne Pearn 'for WLT's programming and presentation of Australian plays'.

Nicky McFarlane reviewed two of WLT's productions in the second half of 1999. Paul King's production of *Speaking in Tongues* (for which he was declared Best Director at the 1999 VDL Awards), she thought 'would replay a second visit...It is good stuff', and Damien Coffey's effort at *Hysteria* was 'a remarkable production'.[91] In both cases the acting stood out. Of *Speaking in Tongues*, Nicky commented:

> *I could not fault the actors', each of whom played two roles: Paul Farrell as Leon and Neil, Ann Pagram as Sonja and Valerie, Christina Costigan (making her debut at WLT) as Jane and Sarah, and Brian Christopher as Pete and John.'*

Similarly, with *Hysteria*:

> *Christina Costigan as Jessica was a marvel; Chris McLean had Dali to a T; Ray Hare was 'solid as the doctor'; and George Werther 'looked right and was always believable' as Freud.*

Williamstown started 2000 (Y2K as it was widely known) with *Other Times* - the second of the Doll Trilogy. John Gunn thought 'the production under the direction of Bryan Thomas most enjoyable and at times quite moving'. *Cues and News* for March 2000 reported that 'audience reaction to the play was excellent' and that the cast managed to keep their sense of humour, despite having to wear their overcoats and greatcoats (*Other Times* is set in Melbourne in late winter) in thirty-degree-plus temperatures.[92]

---

91 Nicky's reviews are in *Cues and News* August 1999 and December 1999.

92 The weather section of *The Age* newspaper of 17 February 2000 indicated that Melbourne's maximum temperatures over the following three days would be 34, 36 and 36 degrees Celsius respectively. A week later the projected temperatures were 28, 35 and 33 degrees.

Despite thinking *Terra Nova*, a dramatization of Robert Falcon Scott's journey to the South Pole in 1912 'a bit over written and too long', Diana Burleigh felt that she had:

> ... *rarely seen a better ensemble performance than that of the cast, led by a compelling and intense Frank McCarty as Scott. Shannon Woollard, Brian Christopher, Bevan Vahland and Genarro Ferra were splendid as the men who risked all and gave all to travel with him. Peter Maver never wavered as the smug Norwegian who succeeded where Scott failed... (and) Paula McDonald turns the role of the little woman left behind into something much more. Chris Baldock, as director, demonstrates an excellent control over all aspects of the play and, with all his co-workers on and off stage, must be congratulated on a fine production, which surpasses even Williamstown's high standard.*

Terra Nova was WLT's entry in the 2000 VDL Awards and received five nominations, one each for sound, lighting and costumes, with Brian Christopher and Shannon Woollard both receiving nods for the Best Supporting Actor award. Woollard shared the gold award with Keith Norbury from Peridot Theatre.

Joan Chapman had some doubts about *The Golden Age*, mostly in relation to the acting of the minor players. But she had high praise for Mary Little's performance in the lead role of Isabel:

> *Essentially a star vehicle play, Williamstown's production featured the 'star' quality in Mary Little - every nuance was there in a carefully studied performance. She **was** Isabel, bringing a spirited dignity to the role of the daring woman of her time. This is no feminist demanding equal rights, but a feisty woman who sees men as horses which need to be broken, to dig in with the heels and control.*

Joan similarly had high praise for Paul King's production of the classic American drama *The Birthday Party*:

> *Paul King has given us a production which makes him master of the Pinteresque ... the set ... is enough to make us shudder... Lighting design*

... is effective... Costumes by Pat Day are appropriate... To the cast, my congratulations.

John Gunn also had high praise for *The Venetian Twins*, an Australian musical by Nick Enwright and Terence Clarke, first produced by Sydney's Nimrod Theatre in 1979:

What a great production this is! It abounds with energy, excellent timing, good strong singer/actors, some nifty choreography by Renee Mandancini... excellent musical direction from Chris Sluice with Jo Craven at the piano, not forgetting BevanVahland's very colourful and appropriately 'broad' style that fits neatly on Williamstown's small stage. Pat Day's costumes (as always) are an added bonus and all these quality components are drawn together by the excellent direction of Barbara Hughes, tight and imaginative...

Director Barbara Hughes has given us a show that zooms and zings along, never flagging for a minute, with lots of funny business, and smart right up to the moment quips.

John thought this reflected Barbara's extensive experience working in music theatre, concluding that 'Drama companies producing a musical should go along and see just HOW it should be done'.

The Venetian Twins scooped WLT's own awards, winning the Craven Award for best production, with Narelle Gillie as Beatrice and Shannon Woollard as Florindo sharing the Win Stewart Award, and Michael Bingham winning the Cordell Award for his performance as Tonino/Lanetto.

In his review of *Other Times*, WLT's first production in 2000, John Gunn looked forward to 'seeing this team together again with the big one, the *Summer of the Seventeenth Doll* in 2001'. Williamstown duly obliged with its first production for 2001, completing Bryan Thomas's plan. The Theatre had something of a boost when it received the following letter from Ray Lawler[93] dated 18 October 2000:

---

93   Lawler appeared in WLT's very first (imported) production, *The Barretts of Wimpole Street* – see page 9.

Dear Barbara,

This letter is to accompany the definitive script of 'The Doll', which I think your Williamstown director and cast will find more attuned and sympathetic to the evolvement of the Trilogy narrative line than the original 'Summer of the Seventeenth Doll' script. (And indeed, this is the version of the play that I want accepted as the final copy in print once stocks of the previous script has (sic) been exhausted).

You will note that a Production Note on the dolls themselves is included – you may not need this, it is intended more for the companies in the future, rather than those with links to the past. But the particulars to do with destroying the seventeenth doll should be helpful– these problems seem to recur again and again.

And of course, although timewise the play works better as a three-act work, it is possible to play it in two acts, breaking after the New Year's Eve scene, if your people can find some way of coping with the stripping of the set for the final scene that does not involve some lengthy break.

Anyway, best of luck with it – I am very touched that you should have tackled the entire Trilogy – and if I can be of any further help, do get in touch with me.

Blessings and good wishes to you and the entire Company

Ray Lawler

    Summer of the Seventeenth Doll, widely regarded as 'The most famous Australian play and one of the best loved',[94] was first performed by WLT in August 1961, directed by Gwladys Winfield, just after the amateur rights had become available. 2001 Director Bryan Thomas was aware of this and in a nice innovation included Gwlady's directors' notes, and a copy of the

---

94   *Companion to Australian Theatre*, p.564.

original cast list in his 2001 program.

Reviewing the 2001 production for *Curtain, Up* John Gunn described it as 'a good, solid and sincere production'. The acting varied in quality: Chris Baldock, making his WLT stage debut as Roo, 'worked hard and had some very good moments but could relax a little more'; Chris Perkins' Olive 'had much to enjoy but lacked (on occasion) a certain vulnerability'; and Vicki Russel as Emma was 'polished and assured ... (but) ... was a little too young for the role.' On the other hand:

> Lucy Christopher was a sparkling and fresh Bubba, getting more out of this role than I have seen previously' ... 'Bevan Vahland who played Roo in the previous productions of 'Kid Stakes' and 'Other Times' was ideally cast as Johnnie Dowd, the man who will take on the mantel of head canecutter vacated by Roo.

But:

> The performance of the night was that of Barney played by Wayne Pearn – here we see a skilled portrayal ranging from the immature and irresponsible knockabout to the sadness of betrayal of a man, always a second string, now getting older and really going nowhere, well characterised with excellent body language.

'The Doll' was followed by WLT's entry in the 2001 VDL Awards, *Amy's View*, directed by Gordon Dunlop. The production received nominations in eight of the ten categories of the Awards - including two for Best Actress in a Leading Role - Kate Bowers for her role as Amy Thomas and Louise Whiteman as Esme Allen and won two awards: a gold award to Maggie McInnes as Evelyn Thomas, and a silver award in the Best Production category.

The stand-out production at WLT in 2001, however, was *Master Class*, directed by Chris Baldock. This modern classic by Terrence McNally centres on a singing masterclass given by Maria Callas. The role of Callas is critical to its success. Reviewing the production for *Curtain Up*,[95] Joan Chapman

---

95   Reproduced in *Cues and News*, October 2001.

had high praise for Paula McDonald:

Paula McDonald as Maria Callas is electric. This is no actress playing Callas, she is Callas. From the moment she walks on stage, her by-play with the audience, the rehearsal pianist Manny, and the stagehand, she is in complete command.

And there was more:

There is immense talent in this production… Each supporting role is crucial, and the performances of Sally Kirkcaldy, Kathryn Gray, Robert Harper, David Haynes and Neil Williamson are exceptional, contributing greatly to its strength.

Technically 'Master Class' is brilliant. Williamstown's production is a master class in itself - in direction, performance, the quality of the set and technically.'

The Cordell adjudicators agreed with Joan, awarding Paula McDonald the Cordell Award for her performance as Maria Callas, and *Master Class* and director Chris Baldock the Craven Award for best production. In the program for the production, Paula McDonald provided a rare insight into her engagement with Callas, commenting that 'trying to bring her to life (had) been one of her (if not the) greatest challenges to date, and she would like to express her admiration for her favourite playwright Mr Terrence McNally … he listened to the music and the voice and then orchestrated the words'.

WLT started 2002 with a special Life Members' party on 2 February. At this event Graeme Cope was awarded Life Membership for his multiple services to the theatre - especially as chair and member of the Play Selection Committee, and as Secretary - rendering him speechless, echoing what happened to Ted Cordell when he was made WLT's first life member in 1956. Those who had enjoyed life membership status for longer than Graeme much appreciated the event. Gillian Wadds, for example, spoke for many when she wrote to the Committee thus:

Many thanks and congratulations to all the committee members who arranged the Life Members' Party ... It was a big surprise and much appreciated by all us oldies (and I'll get into trouble for that!). The old photos were a sight to see (!!) and the badges are just beautiful. They are a credit to the original designer (Grahame Murphy) and the current members who made the adaptation (Ellis Ebell organised the production of the badges). I, personally, will wear my badge with pride!

The Theatre started 2002 on stage with Liz Lipski's production of *W;t* - an unrelenting description of a woman (a Professor of Literature, Vivian Bearing) receiving experimental treatment for advanced ovarian cancer, who in her final hours finds comfort in the sonnets of John Donne. Joan Chapman for *Curtain Up*[96] thought *W;t* 'a strong play, with strong performances and a tight directorial hand'. Apart from wondering whether 'some of the literary discussion in the play (would) be dull for people who are not literary majors' and noting that 'sight lines are a problem on front stage right', Joan was impressed by the production. She thought that Jayne Lindill in the lead role was 'precise and insightful...(possessing) an obvious understanding of the terrifying and humiliating experience of a patient at her most vulnerable'. *W;t* scooped the pool at the Cordell Awards: it won the Craven Award for best production, with Jayne Lindill winning the Cordell Award for her performance as Vivian Bearing, and Judy Johnson, as E.M.Ashford, the Win Stewart Award for best performance in a supporting role.

Alarms and Excursions, by British writer Michael Frayn, had to be mounted in quick time, since WLT received advice late in the normal cycle of production that the rights for the play originally included in its 2002 playlist had been withdrawn. Nonetheless, as John Gunn noted in his review for *Curtain Up*, director Damien Coffey, had 'given us a tight production that moves well and generally bubbles along'. The actors fared well too:

With a cast of four sharing approximately 11 roles, it gives the actors plenty of opportunities to shine and show their versatility in characterization and the four actors - Rex Callahan, Celia Meehan, Mark Robins and Janet

---

96   *Cues and News*, March 2002.

1997 - 2006

Alarms and Excursions, May *2002*
Celia Meehan, Rex Callahan, Mark Robins and Janet Provan all playing multiple roles.

Provan – proved a tight and very likeable ensemble: funny, ridiculous, gormless, stupid – yet very much like us.

Willy Russell's *Blood Brothers*, directed by Chris Baldock, was so highly anticipated by WLT subscribers and patrons that *Cues and News* for May 2002, almost two months before opening night, reported that 'One week into rehearsals there are less than 100 seats left'. Joan Chapman Reviewing for *Curtain Up* thought the production 'impressive'.

One performance of WLT's production generated its own special, if rather awkward, story. At the end of the play one of the central characters, Mrs Lyons, shoots the twin brothers Eddie and Mickey who had been separated at birth and lived very different lives. Naturally the audience is somewhat stunned at the two boys laying at Mrs Lyons feet and sits in rapt silence. The silence is interrupted by an elderly voice ringing out from the back of the theatre: 'That's the end I suppose.'[97]

---

97   The story is in *Cues and News*, July 2002.

Joan was similarly impressed by Paul King's production of *Hate*, a play written by Stephen Sewel for the bicentenary of European settlement of Australia in 1988, which focuses on the fine line between love and hate in the Gleeson family where the father John is a politician, wheeling and dealing in an attempt to become Prime Minister. There is much betrayal in the family. Joan thought the actors 'well cast' - Shirley Sydenham as the mother, Chris Perkins as the daughter Celia, who is 'exceptional', Shannon Woollard the son, and Liam Creaney, the younger son Michael, playing a complex role 'with intelligence'.

WLT's final production for 2002, *Tons of Money* directed by Maggie McInnes, was in John Gunn's view,[98] a great finish to the year for WLT. There was praise for all the 'first-rate' cast (of ten) 'an excellent ensemble who played this farce for all it was worth ... and then some!'

2002 ended sadly for the Theatre's community on 26 December with the death from cancer, first diagnosed some five years earlier, of Gary Metcalf, first winner of the Cordell Award.

WLT started its 2003 season with *Quartet*, by Ronald Harwood, a very funny play with some great one-liners, set in a home for retired opera singers who each year on 10th October stage a concert celebrating Verdi's birthday. As John Gunn reported in *Curtain Up*:

> *Director Bryan Thomas has chosen a fine cast for this production a talented and experienced ensemble of four, all of whom gave classy performances. Ellis Ebell in the plum role of the lecherous Wilfred was a delight; Shirley Sydenham as Cissy a bit of a man eater in her time but now delightfully vague; Les Terrill as Reggie has the hardest role but he gave it his usual professional polish; as did Joan McGrory as Jean Horton, every inch the Diva - nicely controlled.*

The next production at WLT in 2003 was John Misto's *The Shoe-Horn Sonata*, directed by Chris Baldock, a Victorian premiere production, eight years after it was first staged in Sydney. The play is a fictional recollection of the experiences of two of sixty-five Australian nurses who were aboard

---

98   John's review is reproduced in *Cues and News*, December 2002.

the *SS Vyner* when it sank off Sumatra in 1942. They were part of a group of survivors who became prisoners of war, while others drowned or were massacred by the Japanese on Banka Island.

The Theatre took the unusual step of inviting members of the Rotary Club of Footscray to the dress rehearsal. On April 28, 2003 the President of the Club wrote to WLT President Celia Meehan expressing:

> ... *our great appreciation in letting us join you at the occasion of the dress rehearsal of 'The Shoe-Horn Sonata'. We all had a most enjoyable experience as we lived through the events of the play. Thanks to Chris Baldock, Mary Little and Shirley Cattunar. Mary and Shirley made us believe that they were in fact reliving their past, of often traumatic experiences.*
>
> *I would hope that the club could make our attendance at the Theatre a regular occasion. The night raised $800 for our club funds.*

After seeing the play, Jayne Lindill, by then a regular performer at WLT, wrote:

> *Just wanted to say congratulations on 'Shoe-Horn Sonata'. It was very moving. Shirley and Mary were perfect and it's brilliant that there's a gutsy little play like this for two women their age to get their teeth into. You could just tell they were having a great time together.*

John Gunn in his review for *Curtain Up* thought that 'This is a play that deserves to be seen by young and old', commenting:

> *The two actors in the play give outstanding performances, honest, sincere and lacking in any gimmickry and oh so moving, telling their stories in such a naturalistic way. What a pleasure to see two not so young women holding the stage and audience in the palm of their hands for two hours, leaving us all emotionally drained but quite uplifted.*
>
> *Chris Baldock has been most fortunate to have actors of their calibre bring this play to life. He has moved it at a sound pace, using slides, music and*

The Shoe-Horn Sonata, April-May *2003*:
Mary Little as Sheila and Shirley Cattunar as Bridie.

voice-overs most effectively to expand the narrative. David Dare's setting of the Motel Room and Studio complete with On-Air signs was effective as was Stelios Karagiannis' lighting design.

Sound was also obviously good; John O'Brien-Hall and Neil Williamson won the VDL gold award in 2003 for their Sound Design for *The Shoe-Horn Sonata*. In addition, Jill Claque received Libby Proctor's Adjudicator's Award for the design of the program.

WLT concluded 2003 with 'the quirky little musical' *Lucky Stiff*, based on *The Man who Broke the Bank at Monte Carlo* and directed by Barbara Hughes. John Gunn on *Curtain Up* thought it us an 'excellent and professional production' noting it was:

> ... *2 hours of mistaken identities, split second timing and some crazy fun all excellently directed by Barbara Hughes; characterisation, diction, movement, comedy style and musicality etc. All these components were fully explored with nothing wasted – definitely no dross or flat moments with Barbara Hughes at the helm...can't say more than that.* Moreover, *George Tranter's*

composite set design worked very well. The many changes of scene (with lighting to match) worked swiftly and fluidly...a very professional concept with costuming and props of similar standard. Music with Janet Provan as M.D. was spot on, music cues clearly defined, good harmonies, strong voices, colour and clear diction and well supported by two excellent pianists.

There was praise for the cast:

Andrew Wild was a beautifully naïve Harry Witherspoon, Lauren Elise, a wonderfully yet pathetic 'sad sack' type Annabelle Glick from the dog's home, Fiona Harrison was a standout as the frenetic and short-sighted Rita La Porta – they were given great support from Brett O'Meara as Vinnie, the dentist, Oleh Kowalyk (having great fun with this role) as the rather overpowering yet slightly mysterious tourist Luigi Gaudi and the superb ensemble consisting of Beryle Frees, Amy Mather, Nathan Reynolds and Dean Rogers with a beautifully 'dead-pan' performance from Brian Christopher as Uncle Anthony.

The Cordell Award judges were equally impressed, awarding *Lucky Stiff* the Craven Award for WLT's best production in 2003. Moreover, with *Lucky Stiff* almost booked out before it started, an extra performance was scheduled as a matinee on the last Saturday. The cast was rewarded for this performance with what *Cues and News* described as a 'sumptuous barbeque' at the Christopher/Hughes residence between the two performances.

Four of WLT's productions in 2004 were reviewed by the *Curtain Up* team which thought the quality varied. Based on the success of WLT's earlier staging in successive years of Ray Lawler's 'Doll' series, Bryan Thomas suggested that WLT repeat the process with the Neil Simon semi-autobiographical trilogy *Brighton Beach Memoirs*, *Biloxi Blues* and *Broadway Bound*. He started with *Brighton Beach Memoirs*, one of the most popular of Simon's plays.

John Gunn for *Curtain Up* thought the production 'pleasant if a little undistinguished' and that 'at times the pace was rather slow and energy levels tended to flag with cues not being picked up as quickly as perhaps they should have been'. Notwithstanding John's reservations, *Brighton Beach Memoirs*, WLT's entry into the 2004 VDL Awards, received six nominations including for Best Comedy Production. The other nominations were Bryan Thomas for Best Director of a Comedy, David Dare for Best Set Design, Helen Mutkins for Best Actress in a Comedy, Suzanne Daly for Best Supporting Actress in a Comedy and Paul Farrell for Best Supporting Actor in a Comedy.

Diana Burleigh had major reservations about *Three Days of Rain* as did John Gunn with WLT's presentation of Alan Ayckbourn's *How the Other Half Loves*, Shirley Sydenham's directorial debut at Williamstown. Gunn thought the production 'at times a little stodgy and obvious and lacked the subtle aspects of Ayckbourn's clever and calculated writing'. Though '... the cast worked exceptionally hard, too much so at times... The situations in this comedy should have generated much more laughter and reaction from the audience'.

Nicky McFarlane thought Shannon Woollard's production of *Macbeth*, 'bold and interesting with some flaws', which lay in the delivery of lines. To quote Nicky:

The first speech, the sergeant telling of Macbeth's victory over the Norsemen, is taken at such speed and with such poor diction that it might as well have been in a foreign language. Sadly, this was a frequent problem throughout with several of the actors. It seems that pace was asked for and achieved, but with little thought for the sense. Nonetheless there were ... *some fine performances: Brian Christopher's 'Ross', Derek Richards' 'Doctor', Nathan Butler's 'Hecat'. Yudha Pandji as 'Macduff' is excellent in his one big scene, and the witches of course. And all these actors, praise be, could be heard.*

WLT's final production for 2004 was *Daisy Pulls it Off* by Denise Deegan, set in Grangewood School for Girls in England in 1927. As part of the 25th anniversary celebrations of the school, the upper fourth form presents this two-act play, which has a cast of sixteen women and three men. The *Curtain Up* team were highly impressed, nominating WLT's effort as one of the best amateur theatre productions in Melbourne in 2004, and awarding Janet Provan and Janine Evans *Curtain Up* 'gongs' for their roles (as Daisy Meredith and Trixie Martin respectively).

WLT started 2005 with the second part of Neil Simon's semi-autobiographical trilogy *Biloxi Blues*. This John Gunn found:

... much more satisfying' than 'Brighton Beach Memoirs' due in part to the much stronger ensemble of actors and I felt that the director had a better feel for the text, plus the fact that the comedy in this play is perhaps much more universal and not quite so much the Bronx Jewish humour as in 'Brighton Beach' - consequently both director and cast had a more collective approach.

John was notably 'impressed' with the performances of Sam Lee as Eugene, Juan Modinger as the intellectual Arnold Epstein, and Oleh Kowalyk as Sergeant Merwin J. Toomey. But 'the entire ensemble worked as a team... Regina Miller as Rowena the aging 'hostess with the mostest', and Laura Brown 'who gave the character of Eugene's first love, the young Daisy Hannigan, great charm and believable innocence'. Moreover, David Dare's set 'was a masterpiece in design and construction' (and) '1940s costuming by Maggie McInnes was spot on'.

Biloxi Blues was followed by *Scenes from a Separation*, a writing collaboration between Andrew Bovell and Hannie Rayson, which in Diana Burleigh's view was not particularly successful, resulting in a long evening - close to three hours. (A positive, from the theatre's point of view, was having the play mentioned in the *The Age's 'Metro'* magazine on 28 April.)

A special event for the WLT family occurred just after the conclusion of *Scenes from a Separation*, the marriage on 23 April of two of WLT's 'leading lights', Damian Coffey and Janine Evans. A Who's Who of WLT personalities attended. Damian had started in theatre in his home-town of Creswick playing Joe in a production of *On Our Selection* in which his father played 'Dad'. After moving to Melbourne for work, Damian was doing some acting classes when his tutor got a phone call from Brian Crossley who was looking for someone to play 'Dickie' in *The Winslow Boy*. Damian got the role and, as he puts it, '31 years later I am still here'. Janine started her work in theatre doing musicals at school in New Zealand, later being cast in a one-act play written by her drama teacher which went on to win the New Zealand One-Act Play Festival. After spending some time in Brisbane, she moved to Melbourne and performed in plays with several groups including the now defunct Ravens Players in Glen Iris where in 1992 she met Damian (she played his headmistress in *The Happiest Days of Your Life*) who introduced her to WLT. While her acting ability often warranted special gongs, it was

The Glass Menagerie Cast and Crew 2005
Back Row: Alex Begg, Assistant Stage Manager, Brett Turner, Lighting Operator, Blake Testro as The Gentleman Caller, Tristan Lutz as Tom, Dominic Vinci, Stage Manager. Front Row: Maggie McInnes, Costumes, Sophie King as Laura, Ellis Ebell, Director, and Christine Andrew as Amanda.

her skills as a program and poster designer which led to her being the first recipient of the Grahame Murphy Award in 2009.

After this happy event, Ellis Ebell made his directorial debut at WLT with a highly acclaimed production of Tennessee William's *The Glass Menagerie*. This was WLT's entry in the VDL Awards for 2005. It secured eight nominations: for Lighting Design (Maureen White), Sound Design (Neil Williamson), Costume Design (Maggie McInnes), Set Design (David Dare), Best Supporting Actress in a Drama (Sophie King as Laura Wingfield), Best Supporting Actor in a Drama (Blake Testro as Jim O'Connor), Best Director of a Drama (Ellis Ebell) and Best Drama Production. David Dare and Neil Williamson won silver awards in their respective categories.

This time John Gunn was most impressed.[99] Noting that he 'had lost

---

99   *Cues and News,* August 2005.

count of the number of the number of productions of this play' he had seen, he commented that:

> *Director Ellis Ebell has given us a very fine production of this classic, bringing out the humour as well as the sad and at times pathetic and despairing aspects of the characters, their life and their environment - a carefully crafted mood piece; David Dare's set design is, as always, just right, very atmospheric with carefully selected nondescript furniture and sombre colourings (so appropriate for a poor family in the 1930s); Maureen White took a risk in the lighting design in that it was deliberately gloomy, but it was one that paid off creating excellent moods and a feeling of entrapment and hopelessness...; Neil Williamson's sound design ... enhanced the moods of the play... ;All in all, quality production values we expect and get from a Williamstown show.*

According to John Gunn, the actors did very well:

> *I enjoyed very much the portrayal of Tom by Tristan Lutze, a difficult role but he showed us the complex nature of this young man... Christine Andrew as the mother Amanda was a delight... Sophie King as the withdrawn Laura walked the fine line between physical frailty and delicate emotions beautifully.* Finally, as to the role of Jim, the gentleman-caller: *Blake Testro, with very good vocal delivery, gave it great meaning, credibility and compassion. I honestly think that this is the best I have seen this role played and as I said earlier, I have seen this play a number of times - both amateur and professional.*

Ellis Ebell's efforts as Director won him the 2005 Craven Award for best production.

WLT concluded 2005 with two more high quality productions: Patrick Marber's *Dealer's Choice* (about a poker game), and Joe Dipietro's *I Love You, You're Perfect, Now Change* which, according to John Gunn, reviewing for *Curtain Up*, had just become 'the longest running Musical Revue of all time'.

Frances Devlin-Glass was highly impressed with Chris Baldock's production of *Dealer's Choice*, a play which was 'a sizzling little confection' requiring pacy delivery of dialogue, 'which we certainly got at Willy'. Ellis Ebell was 'the stand-out actor' of a strong cast. Devlin-Glass praised 'his presence: his timing was excellent and much of what he achieved, he did non-verbally. His eyes work very hard, and one is never in any doubt that he is fully immersed in the role'. The balance of the cast also won praise: Tim Constantine as Mugsy 'was as over the top as his boss was held back', Paul Dineen playing Frankie was 'another intelligent and subtle actor', and Peter Prenga as Ash 'was terrifying... His body language was that of a menace' with the lesser roles of Sweeney and Carl being 'played competently by Daniel O'Connell and Jonathan Oldham'. And of course, 'David Dare's set was terrific, especially the dining room/kitchen'.

During the production of *Dealer's Choice*, the theatre conducted another audience survey. One of the respondents confirmed that Frances' review was 'spot-on'. The respondent wrote:

> *I'd like to add more and more praise for 'Dealer's Choice'. Such a strong cast with exceptional performances. I had one of those pretty rare moments in the theatre where I was totally absorbed in the story to the exclusion of all surroundings. The actor playing Mugsy was terrific in a great role, but it was Ellis Ebell who moved me (though) it seems unfair to single anyone out when there wasn't a weak link.*[100]

The audience survey revealed several other dimensions of the workings of the theatre, for example, the reasons why casual patrons came - everything from 'a friend in the cast', to 'came with family who are subscribers', 'Theatrecraft', 'friend of member', and 'nanna is the ticket seller'. Moreover, only one third of patrons lived in Melbourne's western suburbs - patrons came from everywhere including one from London UK and one from Toowoomba in Queensland. Nearly 16% ranked their experience as 'excellent' and only 5% 'poor'.

Noting that *I Love You, You're Perfect, Now Change* was a 'clever, funny and sophisticated' piece, John Gunn commented that with a cast of just four

---

100   This respondent had had lots of good experiences at WLT, noting that *Biloxi Blues* also achieved the heights of *Dealer's Choice*. And "Going back some years I saw *Serious Money* at the MTC and hated it. Same play at WLT knocked me out".

(Michael Bingham, Catherine Kohlen, Melanie Paroz and Andrew Wild), 'under the sharply focused and excellent direction of Janet Provan, the show sings along at a fine pace and without any frills to stand in the way of the clever lyrics and oh, so smart sketches, simply an open stage with basic furniture/props etc. and some clever scenic work from Oleh Kowalyk'. John said of the cast that they:

> ... embraced the many characters with skill and panache, working as a great ensemble and so very talented; body language, movement, vocal projection and diction, the many character changes, the singing and the well-paced lyrics are all first class.

The Theatre put considerable effort into planning an appropriate celebration of WLT's sixtieth anniversary in 2006. *Cues and News* in October 2005 announced the formation of a 60@WLT team comprising Brian Christopher, Ness Harwood, Frank Page, Ivor Porter, Trish and Greg Stowe, and Bernadette Wheatley. Already the team had determined that there would be different displays in the foyer for each production, focusing on revealing some of the 'backstage mysteries' - light and sound, costumes, props, set design and stage management.

The same *Cues and News* requested WLT members to nominate the theatre's 'Unsung Heroes', those people who beaver away doing lots of stuff - usually hard work - without any fuss or desire for recognition...(doing) 'front-of-house, working bees, cleaning out the furniture bays, vacuuming the theatre or cutting back the ivy'. On Cordell Day 2005, Dot and Ivor Porter, well-sung heroes of the early days of WLT, agreed to be matron and patron of the 60th anniversary celebrations.

Apart from the regular displays in the foyer, the celebration of WLT's golden jubilee comprised three major events:
- A 'celebrate 60 years day' on Sunday 5th March;
- A reprise rehearsed reading of WLT's first 'all local production', George Bernard Shaw's Man of Destiny on Saturday 18 May; and
- A 'Black Tie Gala Evening (à la dinner dance) on 21st October at the Williamstown Mechanics' Institute, the theatre's 'home' from 1946 until 1965.

The Celebrate 60 Years Day on Sunday 5 March commenced with a Presentation '60 Years in 60 Minutes', where the theatre's 'sixty years of theatrical endeavour' was presented as a series of short talks, poems and songs covering each decade. After a two-minute introduction by Brian Christopher, where he assured those present that every one of the Theatre's 270 productions got a mention, Brian, Ellis Ebell, Janine Evans, Bernadette Wheatley, and Barbara Hughes took turns in making presentations and introducing songs. Most of it was original script, including an imagined conversation between Noël Coward and Oscar Wilde. There followed:

1. A presentation by Ellis Ebell about the Theatre's thirty-two life members, after which all the Life Members present were invited onto the stage for appropriate acknowledgement;
2. A similar presentation (this time by life member Mary Little, and Paula McDonald) about the careers and achievement of the 69 people, 24 of whom were present, who had directed for the Company. They noted that the most prolific director had been Graeme Murphy with twenty-three productions, over thirty-three years, followed by Vin Foster with eighteen over twenty-eight years and Brian Crossley (WLT's resident Noël Coward specialist) with thirteen over eighteen years; and
3. A celebration of the theatre's 'unsung heroes'. Through three editions of *Cues and News* in 2005, the Committee called for nominations from members for people they identified as unsung heroes, 'those people who over the years quietly contribute to all and every aspect of the theatre's operation and yet are never publicly recognised'. Over forty such people were identified; their names are listed in Table 6.

The 60 Years Day event triggered appreciative letters from several significant players in the theatre's history, for example Joan and Doug Lindsay (the latter had been President on three occasions between 1968/69 and 1976/77) and Dot and Ivor Porter.[101]

The longest and most fulsome came from Gillian Senior (Wadds). It is worth quoting in full:

---

101   *Cues and News*, June 2006.

1997 - 2006

Table 6: WLT's Unsung Heroes 1946-2006

Sarah Berry	Harry Conradi	The Williamson Family
Mark Riley	Doug Lownds	Paul King
Trevor McKay	Alan Stewart	Maureen White
Wal Philpot	Jack Cochran	Judi Clark
Tom Parkinson	Harry Press	Oleh Kowalyk
Bruce Mc Calister	Bill Ward	Maggie McInnes
Alice Cordell	Eddie Marr	Phillip Wadds
Kerry Cordell	Harry Barclay	Geoff Dougall
Becroft Family	Felicity Buckley	John Fitzwater
Alf Davidson	Euleen Darcy	Derek Richards
Cr Keith White	Ross Duffy	Ness Harwood
Alec Doig	Janine Evans	Brett Turner
M McChesney Mathews	Mavis Jamieson	Dominic Vinci
Jock Gravel	David Carne	Frank Page

Words cannot express how much I enjoyed the 60@WLT celebrations on Sunday. Not only enjoyed but admired the concept – the research – the preparation – the organisation and the plain hard work behind all that made the day go with such flair and efficiency.

I could rave on for hours – and have done so already to long-suffering friends and relatives – about all the elements: the magnificent Honour Board, the PowerPoint Presentation for the Life Members, the thoughtfulness of remembering and honouring the Unsung Heroes, the very impressive statistics about plays, directors, awards etc. But nothing could have ended the formal entertainment with a greater or more successful climax than

Williamstown Little Theatre

Sixty Years in Sixty Minutes.

Who said you need six weeks rehearsal? Give a bunch of talented people some words, some music and an appreciative audience and watch them go! Of course, not only did they perform but they wrote the material as well. Fantastic! We even had our own sing-song as a finale.

This letter is to thank each and every one of the 60@WLT Committee and the Management Committee of the theatre for putting together a truly 'Major Event'.

No wonder Frank Page had a big smile all over his face as the evening drew to a close. And so should every one of you!

Cheers and Thanks

Gillian Senior (Wadds)

The Black-Tie Gala at the Mechanics' Institute on 21 October attracted more than 100 people. The major reference to the anniversary during the evening was a Salute to the Music of WLT, devised and performed by Barbara Hughes, with support from Bernadette Wheatley, Michael Bingham and Ellis Ebell.

Though enjoying WLT's first 'normal' production in its sixtieth anniversary year, John O'Donoghue's *A Happy and Holy Occasion*, directed by Vicki Smith, Frances Devlin-Glass had many reservations. She thought the play dated, though it gave 'some insight into the ways of thinking of a much less secular society, and in particular into that odd version of class and upward mobility that the clergy represented to Catholics in Ireland and Australia'. The production she thought 'competent but flawed'.

Of Bryan Thomas' production of Neil Simon's *Broadway Bound*, John Gunn of Curtain Up wrote:
> *Director Bryan Thomas obviously has a passion for the work of Simon and this production is a loving testimony to this. John's first comment on the production was that: David Dare has, as usual, done wonders on the small*

stage at Williamstown, with a beautifully detailed set of living room, boys' bedroom, corridors and part of the kitchen and bathroom.

Of the actors, John commented:

I was impressed by the strength, control, warmth and at times serenity of Helen Mutkins as the mother and wife Kate. Derek Richards as the grandfather was also a delight - wise, crusty. Two excellent performances here, warm yet so well crafted. Bernadette Wheatley as the wealthy yet caring sister Blanche and Ray Hare as the up until now blinkered husband Jack rounded out this strong quartet.

The supporting actors John thought had room for improvement:

Dan Brothy has an engaging personality but was a little too laid back and his diction was not always as sharp and clear as it could have been, whereas Alex Christopolous as Stanley had fine clear delivery but could perhaps a little in his energetic characterisation thereby getting more light and shade in the persona of his performance.

John Marans' *Old Wicked Song*s was a Pulitzer Prize finalist for drama in 1996 and winner of the New York and Los Angeles Drama Awards that year. Its reputation had obviously filtered through to WLT's subscribers and casual patrons since bookings were so heavy that, before the season even started, an extra performance was scheduled on the last day of the season.[102] The play was WLT's entry for the VDL's 2006 Awards.

Reviewing the play for *Curtain Up*, Joan Chapman thought it 'one of the finest all-round productions (she had) seen in a long time'. She started by praising David Dare's set as 'a beautifully detailed realisation of the music studio of Professor Josef Mashkan' where clever changes in angles and levels adds an interesting and workable dimension to the small stage'. Joan then provided the detail:

---

102   See *Cues and News*, June 2006.

> *On the upper level is a grand piano stacked with music and on the lower a hallway leading to unseen kitchen area ... The set is furnished with couch, coffee table, busts of composers, flyers for operas, bookcase, music stand, piles of books and a grandfather clock to recreate a rehearsal studio.*

Lighting and sound were also good:

> *From the perfectly positioned piano comes the beautifully produced sound of Schumann's music, a feat by sound operator Ness Harwood which deserves the highest praise. Adding to the finesses of this production was the sound design and musical direction, another role taken by David Dare.*

Cues and News reported that many people thought that the actors were playing the piano, but the music had in fact been pre-recorded by Tom Buchanan, described as 'a young up and coming musician'. Joan was most impressed by the acting:

> *The performances of two actors are exceptional. As the brash Stephen Hoffman, Tim Constantine handles the gradual respect for his tutor with skill. In his characterisation of Professor Mashkan, Ellis Ebell gives a faultless performance. His body language, intonation and depth of characterisation are outstanding. Both actors handle their respective accents as if native-born and work perfectly together to convince the audience that they are their character.*

Joan also had praise for the director:

> *The story is handled meticulously by director Chris Baldock. He focuses on the power of the script and balances the drama with moments of humour and poignancy. His direction and control is evident throughout and no detail is overlooked.*

WLT's 2006 Cordell Award adjudicators agreed with Joan; Ellis Ebell won the Cordell Award for his performance as Professor Mashkan, and Chris Baldock the Craven Award for best production.

Another 'first' for WLT came out of *Old Wicked Songs*. As *Cues and News* for July 2006 reported:

> On the night before the full-house dress rehearsal director Chris Baldock rustled up a bunch of friends and colleagues in addition to about 30 budding adjudicators. These folk were on a field trip from their two-week VDL adjudicators' course. They will use our production as part of their course … The reaction of this rehearsal audience was fantastic with sustained applause getting Ellis and Tim back on stage for an extra curtain call. The adjudicating tutor was so impressed he was going to be encouraging the MTC to schedule this play in its program.

In her review for *Curtain Up* Frances Devlin-Glass advised that Paul King's production of Michael Frayn's *Copenhagen*, a play about the uncertainty principle involving Heisenberg, Neil Bohr and Margethe, was 'pure delight' for a self-confessed 'intellectual substance junkie'. The special quality of the play and the production was perhaps best captured by subscriber Irene Gittens who wrote to the editor of *Cues and News*[103] that:

> I felt I must write to say how deeply impressed I was with the performance of 'Copenhagen' last night. The three principals were outstanding, so completely did they absorb their characters of Heisenberg, Bohr and Margrethe. At times I had difficulty in remembering I was in a theatre and not a reluctant but avid eavesdropper to a private conversation between three people whose emotions were so tightly pulled that they threatened to snap at any moment. I had not previously known of this extraordinary situation of which the playwright wrote before last night, and the premise that fate will decree the outcome, no matter how minor the catalyst might be. The set design was also perfect – in no way would it detract from what was being presented. Paul King should be lauded to the skies for his magnificent direction…
> The play depicted a very moving situation in which these three brilliant minds found themselves. Yes, I include Margrethe as a brilliant mind too – her way of presenting facts lucidly was just so powerful as the minds of

---

103   *Cues and News*, October 2006.

the two scientists. I encourage your selection committee to keep choosing dramas that make the theatre-goer think, and mull over aspects of the play for days later.

Forgive me for this long-winded appraisal, but I really wanted to say thanks!

Some people in the audience compared *Copenhagen* with *Breaking the Code* - the play about Alan Turing which WLT performed at the start of its 50th anniversary year.

2006 ended with an entirely different concoction - *'Allo 'Allo* - Jeremy Lloyd and David Croft's adaptation of the very successful BBC comedy series, a 'piece of theatrical floss' to use John Gunn's words. This was Peter Newling's first involvement in a Williamstown production, though he had been an audience member for a long time. Peter had moved to Melbourne in the late 1980s and joined the Peridot Theatre Company in Mount Waverley, starting as a stage manager, but eventually taking acting roles. From 1993 to 1996 he did a B.Ed degree at Rusden State College, with a double major in Drama and Psychology, despite an audition process 'which scared the shit out of me'.[104] The Rusden degree exposed him to most aspects of staging theatre, including as Judith Buckrich recalls, being part of a 'fledgling absurdist theatre company Rampant Inc. creator of fine live radio plays and improvised nonsense five-minute dramas'.[105] The training at Rusden was supposed to lead him into teaching, but the teaching rounds 'really put me off teaching'.

According to John Gunn, Peter started on the front foot at WLT, 'giving us a really fun evening at the theatre' which was 'a great way for Williamstown to wind up this, their 60th anniversary year'. The cast (which included long-time WLT stalwarts such as Chris Baldock, Ellis Ebell, Janine Evans, Melanie Rowe and Ray Hare, as well as relative newcomers Juliet Hayday and Paul Dineen), 'were uniformly good…all perfectly in character with excellent pace, timing and especially diction, so important in a difficult farce with a range of French, Italian and German accents'. In conclusion John wondered 'how

---

104 This material on Peter's time at Rusden is taken from Peter's 'own words' in Judith Buckrich, *The Making of Us: Rusden Drama, Media and Dance 1966-2002*, pp186-187. He was exposed to most aspects of theatre production during that time.

105 Ibid, p.89

many other presentations of this play we will see in the future but must say that Williamstown Little Theatre's production will be the benchmark for others to come'.

Such an accolade from John Gunn, someone who had been around Melbourne's amateur theatre scene for almost forty years, was evidence of Williamstown's high standing amongst its peers.

This standing was reaffirmed (and in a way gave WLT a last sixtieth birthday present) when the Theatre achieved one of its best outcomes in the VDL Awards. Its entry *Old Wicked Songs* was nominated for eight awards, including Pat Day for Costumes, and Tim Constantine as Best Actor in a Drama for his role as Stephen Hoffman.

The other six nominations won gold awards: the Company for Best Drama Production, (see certificate on p.212), and David Dare for Best Set Design, Stelios Karagiannias for Lighting Design, David Dare and Chris Baldock jointly for Sound Design, Ellis Ebell for Best Actor (as Professor Josef Mashkan) and Chris Baldock as Best Director of a Drama Production.

Careful readers will note from the first page of this chapter that in 1997, the first year of the VDL Awards, WLT won nine out of a possible twenty awards for its two nominated productions. The VDL changed its rules in 2001, so that companies could only nominate one production for awards in any year so that six out of ten gold awards in 2006 represented a 60% 'success rate' compared with 1997's 45%!

The final theatrical event at WLT in 2006 was a new initiative to introduce fresh new talent to the company – 'Play Six', a season of short plays, held at the theatre from 14-16 December. The initiative was driven by Shannon Woollard, who had arrived in Melbourne in 1998 to further his own theatrical career. He made acclaimed appearances in several WLT productions, for example as Lieutenant Henry Bowers in *Terra Nova* for which he shared the Gold Award for Best Supporting Actor in the 2000 VDL Awards.

In this first year, WLT received no fewer than thirty-six entries for their new venture. The six chosen plays, their authors and directors, which featured in the first season of Play Six are listed in Table 7 on page 213.

Records of Play Six are a little sparse in the WLT archives but successive presidents expressed satisfaction with the venture in their Annual Reports, as illustrated by the views expressed in the 2008, 2010 and 2012 reports

Victorian Drama League Award
for Best Drama Production
2006: *Old Wicked Song*

summarised in Table 8 on page 213.

The reality was, however, that Play Six was placing enormous strain on WLT's human and physical resources. As Ellis Ebell put it his President's 2013 Annual Report:

The Committee has been reviewing Play Six and have decided to not continue with this event in future. The reason for this decision was that we felt it was not meeting the objectives that we had originally identified. This was about securing new young members into the mainstream of WLT by their participation in Play Six.

The Theatre agreed to support Woollard financially to continue Play Six elsewhere in 2014. It has since operated at several different theatres around Melbourne, without WLT support, the best known being the Gasworks Studio in Albert Park (in 2017 and 2018). As Woollard puts it:

1997 - 2006

Table 7: Plays, Authors and Directors in First Season of Play Six, 2006

Play	Author	Director
A Dog's Life	Michael Olsen	Cameron South
Singular	Christina Costigan	Kelly Somes
The Gift of the Gun	Alex Broun	Josie Scott
Cocky Two	Cerise de Gelder	Tania Le Page
Flowers	Michael Olsen	Shannon Woollard
See	Mark Andrew	Mark Andrew

Table 8: Presidential Views of Play Six, 2008, 2010 and 2012

Year	President	The View of Play Six
2008	Bryan Thomas	Play Six was a Great success even improving on last year. It was a very slick operation with an excellent front of house display, quality plays, productions and performances, thanks to the 2006 crew plus Bob Harsley and his front of house team
2010	Bryan Thomas	Play Six was even better this year and we are very pleased with the quality of plays and performances. Sharon Woollard, Maureen White and Ness Harwood are getting quite a following, which is well deserved.
2012	Ellis Ebell	WLT also hosted Play Six giving playwrights the opportunity to present their work to an audience ... in the capable hands of Shannon Woollard, with assistance from Maureen White and Ness Harwood

213

Play Six has progressively emerged into 'a fully-fledged, independent short play festival'. Many of the works first produced here have gone on, in various guises, to great success at other local and even international events.

In a sense, therefore, WLT's support for Play Six bore fruit. Some of that fruit came to WLT itself in 2019.[106]

In its sixth decade, one of sustained growth and success, WLT generally continued to stage productions of sufficient quality to maintain its position as one of the leading non-professional theatres in Melbourne. One indicator of this is that in the decade leading to its sixtieth anniversary (in 2002), each year WLT received at least five nominations for a VDL award, the exception being in 1998 when it received only one (for Pat Day's costumes for *The Sisters Rosensweig*). Perhaps as a consequence, the theatre's patrons continued to support it enthusiastically, but that created its own problems. As Secretary Barbara Hughes commented in her report to the AGM in February 2002:

Our subscriber base continues to grow which is a two-edged sword. Most of our productions are sold out well before opening, making it difficult for family and friends of the cast to obtain tickets. This has been covered in some shows by allowing family and friends to attend the dress rehearsal, which can also be useful for the cast and crew, or staging an extra show and giving preference to the cast. It is an embarrassment of riches.

This embarrassment of riches continued. By mid-January 2004 68% of all 2004 seats had been sold, including those guaranteed from the 'Jamieson Nights', and in 2006, the comparable figure was 78%.[107]

Whilst a high level of repeat annual subscriptions and near sell-out general sales are major indicators of a successful theatre company presenting good quality productions, all theatre managers are aware that for that to happen on an ongoing basis requires willing and capable people (the 'unsung heroes'), doing all sorts of tasks, a comfortable well-appointed theatre, and effective

---

106   See page 276.

107   It is worth noting here how Mrs Jamieson - our 'most valued customer' though 'not a member' - has been selling tickets to our shows for more than 25 years!

management of resources. WLT has always recognised these efforts, but in its sixth decade the Theatre's executive broadened the range of individuals publicly applauded for their efforts. Celia Meehan in her President's Report to the 2001 AGM, for example, said about the set builders:

> ... *the strong cohort of "blokes" who seem to like nothing better than spending their Saturdays at WLT hammering, sawing, nail gunning and building our sets. Thank you Ray Hare, Bryan Thomas, Brian Christopher, Derek Richards, Neil Williamson, David Dare, Oleh Kowalyk and Ross Duffy for donating all that spare time and ensuring that WLT's reputation for spectacular sets is maintained.*

The following year it was the turn of the Play Selection Committee which Celia described as 'the backbone of the work we do at WLT'.

Sometimes, despite all this effort, the Theatre struggled over the course of the sixth decade to attract people with specific skills. In 1997 it was seeking help with set building.[108] In 2001 there was a shortage of production coordinators.[109] At the 2003 AGM, Secretary Barbara Hughes confessed that she felt 'a bit like a cracked record talking about lack of production personnel' noting the need for assistance in the area of 'costumes, stage management, lighting and sound'. The following year Barbara reported that 'our set construction team is very stretched' and that there was shortage of lighting operators. At the 2007 AGM, reflecting the challenges faced in the theatre's golden jubilee year, President Bryan Thomas was still pleading for more help with set building.

Over the decade to 2006, the Committee made continuing efforts to improve facilities at the theatre. In 1998, for example, there were two major improvements to the Theatre's infrastructure: the painting of the foyer by David Dare, and the construction by Mark O'Connell and a bunch of WLT members of a new stage, described by Barbara Hughes in her Report to the 1999 AGM as 'stunning'. In 2002, the auditorium was air conditioned.

Occasionally, opportunities for improvements arose unexpectedly.[110] Early

---

108   *Cues and News*, February 1997.
109   *Cues and News*, January 2001.
110   The balance of this paragraph is based on information provided by Bryan Thomas.

in 2000, the Theatre received a phone call from a relative of the original owner of Cliff's Bakery who was now associated with the Dendy Cinema in Brighton. She reported the Cinema's intention to replace its seats and carpet. Would WLT like them? Some very fast renovating work ensued. Later, someone from the Altona West Primary School reported the availability of kitchen cupboards and a sink after some renovations at the school. There were more quick renovations at WLT.

The Theatre's capacity to undertake these improvements was greatly enhanced by almost continuous growth in its income from subscriptions and ticket sales. Such income increased by 50% between 1997 and 2006, and every year from 1999, income from subscriptions exceeded 50% of its total revenue. 2006 was a bumper year in this regard when subscriptions accounted for 70% of total income. Most years produced a surplus; only once between 1997 and 2006 did the theatre suffer an overall loss. That year (2005) the Theatre spent nearly $30,000 on repairs and maintenance to deal with some structural problems in an aging building - see below. Even in leaner years, when income from subscriptions and ticket sales did not increase, Treasurer Brian Christopher was able to advise the AGM that 'the Committee is pleased to report that the Group is in good financial health'.

The building WLT has occupied since 1968 was constructed before the 1920s. Peter Cliff's autobiography *Dare to Dream* (launched at the theatre in November 2015), talks about his father buying 'a rundown bakery in a dilapidated building in Williamstown' in 1928. Unsurprisingly, by the start of the twenty-first century the building began to show its age. Cracks began to appear in the wall of the building in the early 2000s, some of which were quickly repaired. But there were more problems requiring, as the President told the 2004 AGM, 'some minor structural work on the east wall of the foyer and some major structural work on the north wall of the furniture bay'. The work continued through 2004 and 2005 necessitating expenditure of $47,000 over two years. As Brian Christopher noted in his Treasurer's Report for 2005: 'Expenditure on fixed assets has been relatively high over the last few years.'

I need to end this chapter by answering the question posed at the beginning: Does the evidence support Barb Hughes' view that the theatre didn't change very much between 1997 and 2006? The answer is largely yes, though by 2006 WLT was even more secure in its standing as one of the leading non-professional theatres in Melbourne compared with 1997 and was also in even more robust financial health. And if some of the old - some might say perennial - challenges of running a high-quality theatre almost entirely on volunteer labour remained, the Theatre's executive could take comfort from the ongoing vigorous support of its subscribers.

Chapter Seven

2007-2016: The Loyalty of Subscribers

Strong subscriber support continued throughout WLT's seventh decade. At the time of the Theatre's 2007 AGM, 67% of all seats available at WLT shows in 2007 had been sold. This pattern continued for most of the following decade, sometimes at the cost of not being able to accommodate the requests of casts and crews, let alone casual bookers.

The first production in 2007 was Robert Harling's *Steel Magnolias*. This play focuses on the interaction between six very different women in a hair dressing salon and is a great vehicle for six very different female actors to strut their stuff. Casting is hence critical and as John Gunn put it in his *Curtain Up* review:

> *Director Bryan Thomas has assembled a fine cast, perhaps the best I have seen for this play and has directed it and them with warmth, humour and compassion.*

John thought 'Janine Evans showed her versatility and range as the mother M'Lynn, her big dramatic scene at the end of Act 2 was a winner'. Forwarding the review to Bryan, Carolyn Gunn commented that she '... had to get a Kleenex at the end of Janine's scene - so well done'. As well, John thought that 'Nicola Wright was a dazzling Shelby - a well-crafted and appealing performance'. He also saw some excellent work from Regina Miller as the caring Trudy, Laura Brown as the 'born again' Annelle, Barbara Hughes as the crusty Ouiser and Robyn Legge as the more sophisticated Clairee'. David Dare's set, and costumes and props 'were all plus factors to the production and the music was well chosen'. Nicola Wright won the 2007 Cordell Award for her performance in the role of Shelby in this play. *Steel Magnolias* became

Beyond Therapy, May 2007
Christina Kyriakou as Deborah and Ben Starick as Bruce.

so heavily booked that there was an extra performance on the last Saturday of the initial program.[111]

WLT's second 2007 production was *Beyond Therapy* by Christopher Durang. This play traces the fortunes/misfortunes of Deborah and Bruce over the long period they have known each other. It received mixed reviews. In *Theatrecraft*, June 2007, Deborah Fabbro wrote:

> *Ben Starick and Christina Kyriakou as the hapless couple worked so well together, each bringing the right approach to their respective characters, but also bringing a real sense of ensemble to their performance. As always, I was impressed with what can be incorporated into a set on Williamstown's smallish stage. This time the set, designed by Kerry Cordell, and dressed by David Dare, gave us the two psychiatrists' offices upstage on a raised area.*
>
> *This was an enjoyable evening, well presented by a cast and director who grasped the meaning of the play and presented it accordingly.*

---

111   See *Cues and News*, April 2007, p.7.

Frances Devlin-Glass on *Curtain Up* was not quite so fulsome:[112] 'not the best show I've seen at Willy, but solid and enjoyable.' Though she thought Christina Kyriakou in the lead role was 'brittle, subtle and always good to watch', Ben Starick, a newcomer to Williamston, 'was not as effective as her leading man'. The production, she wrote, was 'not as slick and pacy as it needed to be, to be really funny.' Moreover, 'set construction was unusually sloppy by Willy standards with Struan McGregor's lighting showing up defects in construction'.

Bruce Cochrane in *Theatrecraft* described some of the directorial challenges facing Ellis Ebell, and his effective responses, in his July 2007 production of Joanna Murray-Smith's *Honour*, 'a cracking piece of contemporary theatre' thus:

Challenge 1: Like other plays written in episodic short scenes, and calling for frequent costume changes, this format does have its problems, primarily how to manage the gaps between scenes and the constant interruptions to the flow...

Response 1: Director Ebell chose unobtrusive link music to go with 'brownout' lighting and kept costume changes to a minimum.

Challenge 2: With a considerable amount of intense, intellectual conversation the challenge is to make the people and their ideas accessible and interesting...

Response 2: Ellis had clearly put a lot into achieving this through movement that made full use of the space and sensitive interpretation of the text.

Cochrane also noted that 'notwithstanding the depth of emotion inherent in the script, the potential exists to tip over into melodrama if characters are not truthfully realized in the acting'. Fortunately, 'pace and variety of speech was naturalistic and spontaneous with each of the four cast (Susan Stafford

---

112   Frances' review was reprinted in *Cues and News*, May/June 2007, pp.8-9.

as Honour, Chris McLean as Gus her husband, Tanya Rich as Claudia, the object of Gus's affections, and Vicki Doak, Susan and Chris's teenage daughter) creating realistic people with a personal perspective on what is happening in their life'. Coupled with 'David Dare's brilliantly designed split-level set, and effective lighting and sound, Cochrane concluded that the production 'further enhances Williamstown's reputation for producing work of the highest standard'.

Honour was followed by *Gross Indecency*, Moises Kaufman's play about the three trials of Oscar Wilde, directed by Peter Newling. *Theatrecraft* reviewer Graeme McCoubrie thought this a 'must-see production'. The VDL Award adjudicators agreed, nominating *Gross Indecency* for seven awards: Set Design (David Dare); Lighting Design (Stelios Karagiannis); Costume Design (Pat Day); Best Actor in a Minor Role (Brad Lowry as the Narrator Alan Wood); Best Actor in a Supporting Role (Ellis Ebell as Sir Edward Clarke); Best Actor in a Leading Role (Chris Baldock as Oscar Wilde); Best Director of a Drama Production (Peter Newling).

McCoubrie praised the set as 'another work of art created by David Dare' and the 'accuracy and delicacy of the lighting', designed by Stelios Karagiannis, and operated by Brett Turner and Adrian Valenta. Of the direction he said 'This is a powerful piece of work, brilliantly brought to stage by director Peter Newling with the crème de la crème of actors'.

The set for *Honour* July *2007*, 'brilliantly designed' by David Dare.

The acting was clearly of high quality. Tim Constantine as Bosie 'gave a performance of great heights'. Performances by Ellis Ebell as Sir Edward Clarke and Brian Christopher as Lord Queensberry 'were hard to split', 'Bruce Akers as Edward Carson, the prosecutor was heartless and relentless', and 'Brad Lowry, Justin Royce and Shane Ryan played Narrators as well as two or three other roles and by adept direction were able to change characters and costumes before our very eyes'. The Cordell Award adjudicators agreed: Tim Constantine and Brian Christopher shared the Win Stewart Award for their performances. It also won the gong for best production for 2007.

After Chris Baldock had impressed the VDL adjudicators sufficiently to secure a nomination for best actor in a leading role, he contacted Peter Newling[113] on the Friday of week two of the production to advise him that he (Baldock) was in hospital with suspected pancreatitis. Peter telephoned the other cast members to see what they thought should happen. There was general agreement that if the play could continue, it should. Assistant Director Sandy Green and Newling discussed the options – do we bring in another actor to fill in? Do we cancel the run until Chris could return? Over that weekend it became apparent that Chris would not be able to continue in the role over the run of the season. WLT cancelled the Friday show, as well as the Saturday matinee and evening performances. On the Saturday, the cast gathered at the theatre, and did a run with Newling filling in for Chris. Sandy was in the unenviable position of being asked to make the call as to whether the show still worked. It was decided that having Newling fill in for Baldock was a preferable option to cancelling the show. According to Newling, Chris was released from hospital in time to attend the final performance of the play as an audience member.

WLT's last production in 2007 was *Bullshot Crummond* directed by Janet Provan. Janet stepped into the director role when Chris Baldock had to withdraw for health reasons. Reviewing it for *Theatrecraft*, Ken Barnes wrote:

Williamstown ended its 2007 season with a riotous send-up of that British super-hero 'Bulldog Drummond'. Farce is never easy to do (so I'm told) and

---

113   The rest of this paragraph is an (only slightly) edited version of the story as provided to me by Peter Newling.

surely to parody a fictional figure can't be a pushover either. However, the team of American writers did it successfully, and so did Williamstown on the night…for three reasons…The casting (originally by Chris Baldock), the brilliant direction of Janet Provan, and 'the quality of the performance by all five actors, each of whom seemed to be finely tuned to the quirky characters they played…' Supporting and adding to the on-stage performance, the Williamstown team created some of the most innovative (and hilarious) sets and props I have seen in ages.

In 2008 WLT had the rare experience of having all their productions reviewed in *Theatrecraft*. First was Phyll Freeman's review of Michael Healy's *The Drawer Boy*, directed by Chris Baldock. Freeman thought the support actors Andrew Mayes and Paul Freeman gave reasonable performances in their roles, the latter being a 'strong foil for Bruce Akers, who was the stand-out performer' in the role of Angus. Freeman added that she had 'always admired Bruce Akers' character interpretations over the years but this one as Angus, showed him at this peak. He WAS Angus.' Akers won the Cordell Award for his performance.

The Drawer Boy was followed by A.R. Gurney's play *Another Antigone*, directed by Juan Modinga. Jill Watson in *Theatrecraft* found the production 'quite good', praising the actors thus:

I really enjoyed Geoff Arnold's portrayal of Henry – an impressive performance. He gave him integrity mixed with obsessiveness, arrogance and intolerance, but also a certain dryness of with.

Laura Brown as the aggravating student did extremely well too, Adam Cemerlengo 'ably played' Laura's student friend David, and Annie Bieniek gave us 'a very wise Diana…a steady elegant performance'. Unusually for Williamstown, Jill was critical of the simple set: 'an office with a desk, filing cabinet, chair and bookcase' which 'doubles for Henry and Diana's':

I would question why the top drawer of the of the cabinet was virtually empty – surely both people would have had plenty of files in there? The in-tray appeared empty. The bookcase needed more used looking books rather than the obvious sets of books which appeared too neat.

Williamstown's reputation for good sets was restored in Bernadette Wheatley's production of *The Cemetery Club* by Ivan Menchell - this was Bernadette's directorial debut at WLT. Ken Barnes commented in *Theatrecraft*:

> *Despite Williamstown's space limitations, David Dare's set was entirely adequate and appropriate, including some well-chosen touches of Jewish culture arranged by Regina Miller... Maggie McInnes, Jenny Koch and Janet Provan combined some interesting (and in Lucille's case, outrageously flamboyant) costumes. The whole performance moved along with a swing thanks to Bernadette's tight and imaginative direction coupled with efficient stage management by Alex Begg and Sam D'Amato.*
>
> *In attempting to describe the performances, I'm likely to run out of superlatives - Carol Shelbourne as Ida... Annie Bieniek as Lucille ... 'an absolute knockout in this role',... Shirley Sydenham was beautifully cast as Doris... Trevor Hanna 'fitted the role of Sam perfectly ... (and) Robyn Legge who played Mildred so well that I thought it a pity she had a relatively small part in the story.*

Williamstown's next play, its entry in the 2008 VDL Drama Awards, was Brian Friel's modern Irish classic *Dancing at Lughnasa* which tells the story of five sisters and their brother living in Ballybeg, County Donegal in 1936. The production secured seven nominations for the VDL Awards: David Dare for Set Design, Ellis Ebell for Sound Design, Pat Day for Costume Design, Gail Bradley for Best Actress in a Leading Role in a Drama, Blake Testro for Best Actor in a Leading Role, and Ellis Ebell for Best Director of a Drama. WLT's seventh nomination Katherine Hubbard won the Gold Award for Best Actress in a Supporting Role in a Drama, thus vindicating Bruce Cochrane's view in his review for *Theatrecraft* that 'she excelled in everything she did'. Cochrane was especially impressed by the acting of the women:

> *There were several outstanding performances in this production... As Chris, one of the younger and more sophisticated sisters, Vicki Doak was a joy*

Dancing at Lughnasa, 2008
L to R Vicki Doak as Chris, Gail Bradley as Kate, Katherine Hubbard as Maggie,
Melanie Rowe as Rose, and Laurie Rothmanand as Agnes.

to watch whether speaking, listening, dancing or brooding... Katherine Hubbard as Maggie excelled in everything she did... Gail Bradley impressed as the strait-laced elder sister Kate... Director Ellis Ebell succeeded in creating five different female characters and the ebb and flow of their interaction fitted visually and verbally with impeccable accents in perfectly authentic costumes (by Pat Day).

David Dare's set design, Craig Pearcey's lighting and Neil Williamson's sound work also scored highly with Cochrane whose overall conclusion was that:

This was a production which achieved at all levels largely because of attention to detail in performance and visuals and is a worthy addition to the Williamstown tradition of top-class theatre.

2008 ended on an artistic high note at Williamstown with Barbara Hughes' production of *Honk!*, a musical comedy based on the story of the Ugly Duckling. Richard Burman from *Theatrecraft* had a joyous night at the theatre because:

> *Barbara Hughes had selected an excellent cast for this musical...led by Damian Calvert as Ugly and here was a skilled performance... Strong of voice he clearly portrayed all the different emotions and the innocence of the little swan... Clarissa Leach played Ida, his mother, and again here was a consistent performance of the mother standing up for and searching for her child against all the aggression of the world.*

Burman also praised all the other actors playing multiple roles, but he thought:

> *...the show was stolen by Robbie Carmelotti as Cat (and a French cat at that) - the villain of the piece who wants to eat Ugly. Robbie, who is a professional dancer, moved, pranced and slunk around the stage and gave a wonderfully comic performance which made him a favourite with the audience.* Moreover: *The costumes and the additional touches (e.g. as the ducks grew older) deserve full marks to Pat Day and Maggie McInnes, while the set, designed by David Dare, was a storybook delight.*

Burman continued his positive experience at Williamstown in February 2009 when he saw *LifeX3* by Yasmine Reza, directed by David Dare, who also designed the set which, in Burman's view, 'set the scene perfectly for the play to follow'. Burman commented favourably on the performances of all the actors (Vanessa Alpins and Jason Rionfi as the hosts, and Penny Salazar and Adam Taylor as the guests) but commented that:

> *The performance which stole the show was that of Penny Salazar as Hubert's put-upon wife Inez, who has been consuming alcohol on an empty stomach. Penny gave us delightful comedy acting and cleverly played her different levels of intoxication in the scenarios.*

The second play for the year in April, *A Few Good Men* by Aaron Sorkin, directed by Shane Ryan, earned largely positive reviews from both Bruce Cochrane in *Theatrecraft* and Carolyn Gunn for *Curtain Up*.[114] Cochrane thought WLT's effort was 'a high standard production which at three hours

---

114   Carolyn's review was reprinted in *Cues and News*, April 2009, pp.2-3.

was always absorbing' noting that 'Williamstown continues to do wonders with their limited stage space and innovative approach to set design (in this case brilliantly executed by John Shelbourne)'. Of the acting, Cochrane wrote that 'the dialogue is a gift to actors (and) Director Shane Ryan had ensured the performances were fully developed'. Production standards were high:

> *The production made demands on lighting designer Craig Pearcey and operator Ken Wilson who both did a fine job. All too often plays with constant transitions and numerous scenes are badly handled, so it was pleasing to see blackouts and furniture movement done swiftly without stage crew.*

Rough Crossing by Tom Stoppard was WLT's next production, directed by Peter Newling with musical direction by Janet Provan. It is set aboard a luxury ocean liner crossing from England to New York in the 1930s where a theatrical troupe are about to present a new musical comedy starring the darlings of the London stage Ivor Fish and Natasha Navratilova, who have been lovers. Ken Barnes, writing in August 2009's *Theatrecraft* was impressed:

> *'Rough Crossing' has a delightfully whimsical storyline laced with sophisticated dialogue calling for talented actors, and all six fitted the bill. (The actors were Brian Christopher, Robert Harsley, Andrew Wild, Ian Grealey, (who won the 2009 Win Stewart Award for his role as Dvovnichek), John Cheshire, and Janet Provan.)*

> *The two actors who played actors (John Cheshire, and Janet Provan) were sublime.*

In summary Barnes thought:

> *Rough Crossing is surely one of Tom Stoppard's best plays, brought to the stage by the experienced Peter Newling and the Williamstown team in great style. This reviewer enjoyed every minute of it.*

The Program for *Rough Crossing* contained an obituary for Pat Day (complete with her photograph and a page illustrating a selection of her

The cast of *Rough Crossing*, July *2009, in full voice*.
L to R: Brian Christopher as Sandor Tarai, John Cheshire as Ivor Fish,
Janet Provan as Natasha Navratilova, Andrew Wild as Adam,
Ian Grealey as Dvornichek, and Robert Harsley as Alex Gal.

'magnificent creations', i.e. costumes, for WLT). Pat had died suddenly on 31 May 2009. The obituary recalled that Pat had walked into WLT just before the opening of 'the bakery' saying she could sew.[115] The program recalled:

> ...her talents reached their full flower when Brian Crossley began his series of Oscar Wilde and Noël Cowards productions. Their collaborations resulted in some of the most beautiful and historically accurate clothing ever seen on the Williamstown Little Theatre stage. Pat even taught herself to cut authentic Edwardian patterns.

WLT's next production was Diane Samuel's *Kindertransport*, directed by Chris Baldock. The play focuses on the experience of a Jewish child, Eva, living in Germany at the time of the rise of Hitler whose parents arrange for her to be evacuated to England for the period of the war in the belief

---

115   See page 115.

that she will be able to return home in due course. *Curtain Up's* John Gunn thought the production 'a stunner, atmospheric, sad and a sense of wanting to belong, (with) a superb cast who don't put a foot wrong'.[116] Moreover, 'David Dare's necessarily cluttered but versatile attic set and Jason Bovaird's subtle yet clever lighting make us feel that we are there in this space watching the story unfold unobserved'. John continued:

> *This superb cast comprises Rebecca Jones as the young Eva, Katherine Hubbard as Helga (Eva's mother), Paula McDonald as the older Eva/ Evelyn, Eileen Nelson as the elder Lil and Jenny Young as Faith, Evelyn's daughter, with Ellis Ebell excellently playing all the varying male roles with the different accents required.* He concluded: *I, like Tuesday night's audience, was totally absorbed and moved by this play, so much so that the audience continued to remain seated when it was over, still lost in the story we had just witnessed.*

Kindertransport was WLT's entry in the 2009 VDL Awards and secured nominations for ten of the eleven gongs available - including for Best Drama Production. Both Rebecca Jones and Paula McDonald were nominated for the award of Best Actress in a Drama. In the event, only two awards came WLT's way: Neil Williamson and Chris Baldock won the Gold Award for Sound Design, and Shirley Sydenham the Silver Award for Costume Design.

WLT started its 2010 season with Alan Ayckbourn's *Role Play*, part of his *Damsels in Distress* trilogy, directed by Gaetano Santo, in his directing debut at Williamstown.[117] Both John Gunn for *Curtain Up* and Phyllis Freeman in *Theatrecraft* were impressed, John thinking WLT's production was 'one with style and gave the audience plenty of laughs'. Both John and Phyllis thought that the show belonged to Janine Evans in one of her favourite roles as Justin's drunken mother Arabella Lazenby. To quote Freeman:

> *Just when the pace had started to pall, in lurched Justin's alcoholic Mum …beautifully acted by Janine Evans. What a fillip to the proceedings!*

---

116   John's review was reprinted in *Cues and News*, September/October 2009, pp.4-5.
117   This is based on information in *Cues and News*, May 2013.

She brought the pace up quite a few notches. Her carefully timed drunken utterances had the audience in stitches.

Janine sold to Gaetano her idea of staying face down on the sofa during interval after her 'faceplant' at the end of act one which she remembers was 'great, except I got to hear all of the audience chatting about what they thought of the play'.

Next was David Hare's *Skylight* directed by Bernadette Wheatley. As Bruce Cochrane commented in his *Theatrecraft* review:

Ultimately the play revolved around Kyra, in whose London flat the play is set, who is never offstage, making considerable demands on Rachel's (Dewar) energy, focus and credibility. From the outset, Rachel created Kyra as a real person; her speech, delivery and facial expressions were all consistently convincing and her stagecraft was always natural and spontaneous.

George Tranter received a nomination for best set design at the VDL Awards for his work on this play and Craig Pearcey one for Lighting Design.

In his review of *Glorious* by Peter Quilter, a potted biography of the would-be operatic soprano Florence Foster Jenkins, directed by Doug Bennett, Richard Burman[118] started by commenting on the set:

When audiences moved into the auditorium...they were immediately transported into the right frame of mind by the excellent set David Dare had designed. It was decorated in a way to epitomise the wealth and opulence in which Jenkins lived. With changes of furniture and dressing it took us effortlessly from the Hotel Seymour to the Ballroom of the Ritz Carlton Hotel to Carnegie Hall.

The key performer in such a play must be the one who plays the person whose story is being presented and Bennett made a wise choice in selecting Patricia McCracken. The role is a large one, and Patricia played it for all it is worth... She used the full range of her theatrical experience to give the audience a warm-hearted, generous, but untalented performer.

---

118   *Theatrecraft*, August 2010.

2007 - 2016

Glorious, July 2010
Patricia McCracken
as Florence Foster-Jenkin.

Ellis Ebell's fascination with family stories led him to direct *Hotel Sorrento*, one of Hannie Rayson's early success stories. Well-known Melbourne theatre personality Nicky McFarlane[119] noted the effectiveness of David Dare's set design which enabled 'Williamstown (to show) us how to produce a play with a bakers' dozen of scenes and make it look easy.' Ellis took the unusual step of dedicating this production to an individual, in this case Dorothy 'Dot' Porter who had died in June 2010, '... a dedicated loyal member of WLT for 64 years' as Ellis's note in the program for *Hotel Sorrento* records.

WLT's last production for 2010 was Alan Bennett's popular comedy *Habeas Corpus*. Following Ellis's initiative, Director Lois Collinder dedicated this production to Lorraine West, one of WLT's leading actors in the 1960s and 1970s[120] 'who was my friend and agent for twenty-seven years'. (Lorraine had died on 15 March 2010 after a long battle with cancer). Deborah Fabbro commented in *Theatrecraft*, December 2010:

As with any play of this genre (a comedy bordering on farce), there is a fine line between nicely exaggerated performance and slapstick. Having chosen such a talented cast, director Lois Collinder was able to extract just the right balance and not miss any opportunities to raise a laugh.

---

119   In her review for *Theatrecraft*, October 2010, pp.16-17.

120   Readers may recall that Lorraine won the Cordell Award on five occasions - in 1963, 1964, 1971, 1978 and 1979, and remains the actor who has won the most Cordell Awards.

Deborah also thought that 'lighting and sound enhanced this (polished) production' and that 'Maggie McInnes did an accomplished job with costumes'.

WLT's first production in 2011 was *Two Weeks with the Queen*, co-directed by Shirley Sydenham and Robert Harsley, and the recipient of a special 'in-house' review from former President Celia Meehan, home briefly from a teaching job she had taken in America in August 2003. Noting that the play was based on Morris Gleitzman's novel about childhood cancer, unusual for a comedy, Celia thought that 'directors Shirley Sydenham and Robert Harsley ensured that Colin Mulford's story was told with the kind of love and humour that helps us get through such times'. In Celia's view:

The cast 'brought the love and enthusiasm to the stage, balancing the fun with great poignancy'. The production 'was blessed with an astoundingly brilliant central performance from Tim Walker as the likeable Colin... Dylan Boyd's performance as Colin's supposedly sickly but more spoilt English cousin Alistair was engaging and believable ... there was never any doubt that these two young men were twelve-year olds.

Celia thought that Barbara Hughes' witty and whimsical set design solved many of script's demands for multiple locations without being too overwhelming, a view endorsed by Phyllis Freeman in *Theatrecraft* who observed that Barbara 'had excelled herself with set design and construction'.

WLT's next production *Not About Heroes* is a play about two British poets, Siegfried Sassoon and Wilfred Owen, who meet by chance in Craiglockart War Hospital in Scotland towards the end of the First World War. Success in this two-hander depends on the performance of both actors. Jill Watson in *Theatrecraft*[121] thought that Alec Gilbert and Andrew Mayes had succeeded:

Both actors were totally immersed in their roles. Alec Gilbert gave us a dapper, disciplined, uptight Sassoon, with occasional glimpses of emotion; a beautifully controlled and touching performance. Andrew Mayes as a fresh faced, initially unsophisticated Owen, was fabulous; so many telling facial expressions. He also successfully showed the more mature Owen in later scenes.

---

121   June 2011, pp.16-17.

Not About Heroes was WLT's entry in the VDL Awards for 2011 and received nominations for all four technical awards, with John Shelbourne and Shane Ryan winning the Silver Award for Set Design and Costume Design respectively. Jennifer Paragreen suggested that *Not About Heroes* was a play which was challenging for audiences perhaps unfamiliar with Wilfred Owen's poetry, reporting[122] that 'seven women sitting along the row from me announced volubly that they were bored and did not return for the second act'.

This was Jennifer Paragreen's first review for WLT. Shortly after, Jennifer was appointed WLT's in-house reviewer, which she has done ever since, sometimes providing the only critique of a specific production. Jennifer's association with theatre started in the 1960s, especially after she (then Jennifer Holland) went to South Gippsland as a young teacher in 1968[123]. On arriving she joined FAMDA - the Foster Film, Art Music and Drama Association. Soon after joining she was cast alongside then FAMDA president Brian Paragreen in Salad Days. Soon it was romance, and they married early in 1970. The Paragreen family has been central to the growth and development of FAMDA - warranting a chapter to themselves in the Association's initial history, *Famda's Frolics 1953-2003*.[124] Jennifer's first contact with Albert Street was attending a production of *Old Wicked Songs* in 2006.

Not About Heroes was also the first to use WLT's newly installed audio loop. A patron, Janet Howie, wrote to Shirley Sydenham:

Dear Shirley,

Congratulations to WLT for a wonderful performance of 'Not about Heroes' last Friday night. Such strong and clear voices, such a powerful story.

Congratulations too, on the audio loop. It's on and it's WORKING. I was able to hear nearly all of the play, rather than some of the play. This makes

---

122   *Cues and News,* May 2011.

123   This and the next three sentences are taken from Cheryl Threadgold's already cited work *In the Name of Theatre*, p.157.

124   See Kate Crowl, Famda's Frolics, *A Potted History of Foster Amateur Music and Drama Association*, 1953-2003, pp. 22-24.

a huge difference to understanding and morale. I took a friend with hearing aids in the front row. It worked for her as well.

WLT's willingness to meet the needs of hearing impaired has encouraged me in my efforts to establish audio loops in public places.

Three cheers for the WLT committee,

*Janet Howie,
Williamstown.*

Come Back to the Five and Dime Jimmy Dean, Jimmy Dean by Ed Graczyk, WLT's next production, directed by Peter Newling, probably generated more 'it could only happen in theatre' stories - positive and negative - than any other WLT production. Before it started, Shirley Sydenham received the following letter from the playwright: [125]

Dear Shirley,

I received a Google Alert[126] of your upcoming production of "Come Back to the Five and Dime, Jimmy Dean, Jimmy Dean" and am struck by the stunning artwork that is being used for it. I think it's probably the best the play has had. It has the wonderful look of an old movie poster from the 50's found in somebody's attic with torn edges and faded once bright colours and captures the level of the play perfectly. Is this truly a poster you are using to promote the production or just a logo?

If it is a poster I would really love to have one. My office walls are covered with posters from productions from around the world: London, Paris, Sweden, Poland , Germany etc., but although there have been many productions there, none from Australia. Let me know if this is possible.

---

125   Reproduced in *Cues and News*, May 2011.
126   Made possible by the major upgrade to WLT's website which occurred in 2011.

I wish everyone connected with the production all my best and please congratulate the artist behind the creation of the artwork for me. If the production's as good as the poster, you've got a winner.

Many thanks
Ed Graczyk

Shirley of course sent him a copy of the poster, and advised that its creator, Janine Evans, was playing the role of Joanne in the production. This created a special moment with Grazyck replying:

Shirley, I'm thrilled!! Tell Janine I will hang it in a very prominent spot. Keep in touch and let me know how it goes. If I can be of any assistance in any way, please don't hesitate to call on me.

Thanks, and my best to all.
Ed

But there were more 'only in theatre' stories. The first, that during the rehearsal period, the Theatre's heating system broke down and could not be replaced before the production started. Small heaters were purchased and installed to keep cast, crew and patrons warm. There followed two more dramatic stories rolled into one in *Cues and News*:

Was there a bit of a techno jinx hanging over 'Five and Dime' we wonder? Just before the scheduled time to hang and focus lights and run a tech, Craig Pearcey had an accident with boiling water, and his foot got in the way. Roger 'Angel of Mercy' Forsey took him to hospital, where Craig's foot was diagnosed with second degree burns and bandaged up. He may need a skin graft. (He didn't). So, pale and in pain, he was hopping about directing Peter Newling who was on the ladder fiddling with lights. Meanwhile, no sign of Kieran Hanrahan, our lighting/sound operator, and we couldn't contact him. Turns out Kieran was at that moment being involved in a car accident, in which he luckily escaped in better condition than his car, which was towed away with his phone inside, so communications were impossible.

Williamstown Little Theatre

Come Back to the Five and Dime, Jimmy Dean, Jimmy Dean, July *2011*
Sitting at the Front - Janet Provan as Edna, Katherine Hubbard as Mona.
Standing L to R: Kris Weber as Stella, Chris Perkins as Juanita, Janine Evans as Joanne and Helen Ellis as Sissy.

Next day was tech/dress rehearsal. The sound system played up. Roger to the rescue again, and finally everything came together despite the delays.

And then the Question arose 'WHO LOCKED THE LADIES IN?'

There was a delayed start to last Friday night's performance, because half the cast were locked into the alternate dressing room, affectionately known as the 'Old Man's Dunny'! It appears that the door latch seized up and, try as they might, they couldn't get out for Act 1 of Jimmy Dean!!!!

Yikes - what to do? Pass a screwdriver under the door, that's what. These multi-skilled actors set about dismantling the lock and managed to free themselves ready for their performance.

There is no truth to the rumour that this was a bad case of stage fright detaining these actors from another night in their Texas Five and Dime.

Despite all the dramas, the show went on, providing, according to Jennifer Paragreen's review, 'an excellent evening's entertainment with just the right amount of laughter to contrast with the sad aspects of the characters' lives.'[127] All the actors, according to Paragreen, did well: 'Kathryn Hubbard's performance was exceptional as Mona… Melissa New (making her debut at Williamstown) was pert as Mona's younger self so that the contrast stood out. Helen Ellis and Petra Elliot both made the most of the opportunity in their exuberant interpretations of the older and younger Sissy' and Kris Weber and Janet Provan completed the excellent cast which also included Janine Evans, she of international fame for her poster, who 'brought a quiet dignity to the role' of Joanne'.

The History Boys, directed by Bruce Akers, was a joint effort with Heidelberg Theatre Company coming to Williamstown after its Heidelberg season. The collaboration produced a nomination for Best Director of a Comedy Production in the 2011 VDL Awards. The 'jointness' of the production was reflected in David Dare's set. He designed and built it at Williamstown, being mindful of the need to use it on two quite different stages and the need to move it from one venue to the other as smoothly as possible.

With a large cast of eleven, *The History Boys* requires not only capable individual actors, but also good teamwork. Jennifer Paragreen was positive about all the performances, noting that 'The chemistry between the actors really worked with excellent teamwork. Each performer really inhabited the skin of his individual character while sticking to the tone, timing and rhythm of the piece'.

Once again WLT concluded the year with something of a triumph. Introducing her review[128] of Woody Allen's *Play It Again Sam*, directed by Gaetano Santo, Jennifer Paragreen commented:

What a great way to end the theatrical year with a delightfully staged

---

127   *Cues and News*, July 2011.
128   Reproduced in *Cues and News*, December 2011.

clever comedy! With 'Play It Again Sam', WLT chose a quality vehicle and then equipped it with an Excellent production team and cast to ensure its audience an hilarious evening's entertainment, an ideal Christmas present for Williamstown's theatre-goers. Jennifer concluded this review with the hope that: *May there be many more, like me, looking forward to enjoying Williamstown Little Theatre's largesse again in 2012.*

Alan Burrows, well known around Melbourne's amateur theatre network, made his directorial debut at Williamstown in their first production for 2012, *Moonlight and Magnolias*. Bruce Cochrane, reviewing the play for *Theatrecraft*, was impressed by all the actors, and David Dare's 'practical and immaculate set design'. Cochrane concluded that 'yet again WLT maintained the professional standards for which they have been known for many years'.

Moonlight and Magnolias was followed by Jeffrey Hatcher's *Compleat Female Stage Beauty*, directed by Chris Baldock. Joan McGrory, writing in June 2012's *Theatrecraft*, was impressed: 'Chris Baldock has once again gathered a wonderful cast and crew and the audience was given the type of performance that one has come to expect from this director.' *Compleat Female Stage Beauty* won the Craven Award for best production on Cordell Day.

Ben Mitchell, a newcomer to WLT, was so impressed with his experience that he wrote for *Cues and News* that 'for an amateur theatre, the WLT is one of the most professional companies I've ever worked for... All aspects of the backstage crew blew me away as well...the set created by David Dare was amazing'.

The quality of the acting was also highlighted by Phyll Freeman in her *Theatrecraft* review of Jasmine Reza's *God of Carnage*, directed by Bruce Akers. *God of Carnage* is a play about two sets of parents coming together to discuss their sons' misbehaviour. What starts out as an ultra-polite meeting degenerates into a physical farce. Freeman commented:

Although a small cast of only four (Chris Baldock, Kellie Bray, Janine Evans and Stephen Shrinkfield) they were talented and mature enough to make the most of the writing... Good use was made of facial grimaces by the two mothers.

John Patrick Shanley's *Doubt, A Parable* is set in 1964, a time of great civil unrest in the US. It tells the story of how Sister Aloysius, principal of a Bronx parish school, investigates a priest she suspects of abusing the only African-American pupil at her school. We are fortunate to have the reviews of two experienced thespians of Ellis Ebell's production of this play. Both were fulsome in their praise. Jennifer Paragreen, by then well-established as WLT's internal reviewer, thought that 'Every element…had been carefully thought through for maximum emotional impact in this beautifully designed production.'[129] Nicky McFarlane, writing in *Theatrecraft*, thought it a 'brilliant production'. Paragreen's comments on the staging elements were all positive:

> David Dare's impressively cohesive set bred our confidence from the moment we entered the theatre. (Nicky: 'David Dare's set design was beautiful and practical… Perfect); Craig Peacey's lighting design was really sensitively handled; Sound design by Neil Williamson and Ellis Ebell was 'evocative and just at the right volume down to the last bird call'.

On the acting, Paragreen commented that Director, Ellis Ebell, 'established an excellent cast' (Tim Constantine as Father Flynn, Marianne Collopy as Sister Aloysius, Emily Davison as Sister James and Shelia Allen as Mrs. Muller) all of whom 'conveyed their characters' motives compellingly in accents appropriate to the locale. A special feature of the production was that the play selection committee told Ellis Ebell that, as required by the script, he had to get an African-America woman to play the role of Mrs. Muller. Ellis was blessed to have found Shelia Allen, a former Texan who had come to Melbourne to marry an Australian she had met on the Internet - they exchanged 500 emails in six weeks.[130]

Nicky McFarlane was also impressed with the acting: 'As a team the four actors make the story come alive in a most emotional way, very moving, and vocally they were all spot on.' At the conclusion of her review, Nicky wrote that she was 'tempted to stick my neck out and think it might be in for an

---

129   Jennifer's review is published in *Cues and News*.

130   This information is derived from a profile of Allen which appeared in the *Hobsons Bay Weekly*, September 10th, 2012.

award or two this year'.

Nicky proved right: WLT received nominations in ten categories in the VDL 2012 Awards. It not only won the Gold Award for Best Production, but also for seven individual efforts viz: David Dare for Set Design, Craig Pearcey for Lighting Design, Emily Davison for Best Actress in a Supporting Role, Marian Collopy for Best Actress in a Leading Role, Tim Constantine for Best Actor in a Leading Role and Ellis Ebell for Best Director. Ellis Ebell recalled in his 2013 President's Report that he 'often overheard patrons in the foyer (during *Doubt*) saying that they enjoy WLT more than attending the MTC'.

2012 brought two moments of sadness for the WLT community with the deaths of Gwladys Winfield, aged eighty-eight, in May, and Brian Crossley, aged eighty-five, in September. Gillian Wadds wrote a tribute to Gwladys Winfield in *Cues and News* for June 2012. She remembered Gwladys 'as a very energetic, cheerful and dedicated actor and director' recalling in particular her roles as Dolly Levi in *The Matchmaker* and as one of 'The Molls' in *The Ballad of Angel's Alley*. Gwladys directed Williamstown's first production of the iconic Australian play *Summer of the Seventeenth Doll* in 1961, and famously hosted a fashion parade as part of the Theatre's fiftieth anniversary in 1996. Gillian concluded her tribute with the well-known injunction 'Don't ever spell her name incorrectly for fear of your life'![131]

Ellis Ebell wrote a memorial of Brian for *Cues and News*, noting how he had 'known of Brian long before he actually met him. His reputation preceded him, as he was the over the top "Mrs Flower Potts" in the ABC children's television show *Adventure Island*. Ellis recalled the many plays Brian had directed at WLT - he started with *The Second Mrs Tanqueray* in 1982. As Ellis noted, Brian is remembered especially for his stylish accounts of plays by Noël Coward and Oscar Wilde such as *Lady Windermere's Fan*, *A Woman of No Importance* and *Relative Values*. Four productions directed by Crossley - *On the Wallaby* in 1988, *The Winslow Boy* in 1989, *An Ideal Husband* in 1994 and *Waiting in the Wings* in 1995 won the Craven Award for

---

131   I wish to add a personal note and an apology. In my first effort at WLT's history (p.28) I described Gwladys as 'newly arrived from Scotland', an error she pointed to out to the WLT Committee many times!

best production. At a farewell to Crossley held in the foyer of the Malthouse Theatre, Barbara Hughes remembered Crossley's comment to her at Grahame Murphy's funeral in 1996 that 'he (Crossley) wanted a standing ovation at my funeral'. Barbara promised him that she would make sure it happened. At the end of the Malthouse farewell, at Barb's instigation and with the support of Marian Sinclair, Crossley's long-time friend, and lead actor in many of his WLT productions, the gathering stood and applauded.

In audience terms, 2013 was one of WLT's biggest ever, with 98% of available seats being sold for the year. The year began with Lois Collinder directing *The Dixie Swim Club* (by Jessie Jones, Nicholas Hope and Jamie Wooten). This play involves five female characters, played by Helena Chanya, Janet Provan, Bernadette Wheatley, Georgette Oakley and Janine Evans, who all impressed *Theatrecraft's* Bruce Cochrane who commented:[132]

Each of the actresses gave a spirited and energetic performance, although during the first act there was a tendency to emphasise pace, giving an impression of rattling off lines when they might have occasionally paused to reflect on what they were saying. The second act appropriately slowed the delivery of dialogue and allowed for more emotion and expression.

Shirley Sydenham then directed another All-female cast in Alan Bennett's *Talking Heads*, each delivering separate monologues: Pauline Snell playing Miss Ruddock, Marianne Collopy as Susan/Mrs Vicar, and Mary Little as Muriel. Deborah Fabbro in the March *Theatrecraft* had praise for all of them:

Mary Little (as Muriel) gave a beautifully gentle performance. Her command of every little nuance in the dialogue was superb; Marian Collopy used wonderful timing and facial expressions to bring out the pathos of (her) piece; Pauline's performance was well balanced and she portrayed the enthusiasm of Miss Ruddock's vitriolic meddling so well; Director Shirley Sydenham elicited beautiful performances from each of her actors; each of them gave eloquent and expressive renditions that drew the audience into their story.

---

132   *Theatrecraft*, February 2013.

33 Variations, July 2013
George Werther as Beethoven and Brian Christopher as Anton Schindler.

Long-term member Norah Toohey sent an email[133]

Thoroughly enjoyed 'Talking Heads' last night. I was already a fan of Alan Bennett and, of course, Mary Little. During my earlier life at 3RPH I had done the monologue "A Lady of Letters" with Maggie Steven as my technical director and loved doing it.

A sold-out Australian premiere production of Moises Kaufman's *33 Variations* directed by Chris Baldock followed. This play combines a chapter of musical history: Beethoven in failing health wrestling with a commissioned piece with the story of a musicologist Dr Katherine Brandt, suffering from ALS or motor neurone disease, who is running out of time on a project which will throw new light on Beethoven's work.

33 Variations was WLT's entry in the 2013 VDL Awards and won twelve nominations[134] for Set Design (David Dare), Lighting Design (Jason Bovard), Sound Design (Chris Baldock), Costume Design (Tony Tartaro), Best Actress in a Leading Role (Julie Arnold), Best Actor in a Leading

---

133 reprinted in *Cues and News*, March 2013.
134 See *Theatrecraft*, December 2013, pp.2-5.

Role (George Werther), Best Director of a Drama (Chris Baldock) and Best Drama Production, AND, in a very rare occurrence at the awards, two each for Best Actress in a Supporting Role (Kellie Bray and Ella Harvey) for Best Male Actor in a Supporting Role (Brian Christopher as Anton Schindler and Ellis Ebell as Anton Diabelli). Ella Harvey, Brian Christopher and Tony Tartaro took home the Gold Award in their respective categories, and Jason Bovaird the Silver Award.

The Beauty Queen of Leenane was the first play written by now well-known Irish playwright Martin McDonagh. Set in the interior of an old bluestone cottage in a small Irish village in the late 1980s, the plot centres on the manipulations and machinations that begin to occur between a seventy-year-old woman Mag Folan and her forty-year-old spinster daughter Maureen, when two men enter the scene. Director Ellis Ebell reported that he personally was 'more intrigued by the psychological penetration of the play than by its violence,' and that 'both he and the actors were interested to find motivations for the extreme behaviours that both generations engaged in. For example, what were the costs of staying in a claustrophobic community where there was little to sustain hope and interest? Why did they so torment each other? What pleasure did each character derive from mutual torment?' Jennifer Paragreen[135] thought these concerns came through loud and clear:

> *The Williamstown teamwork magic was once again in action with everyone combining their considerable talents to present a gripping tale which kept the audience enthralled with the plot's twists and turns…(They) really captured the aura of the play as well as its story.*

That tradition was well maintained in WLT's last presentation for 2013, its second production of the Stephen Sondheim musical comedy *A Funny Thing Happened on the Way to the Forum* directed by Barbara Hughes, with musical direction by Janet Provan. WLT had staged 'Forum' as a joint production with Pumpkin players in 1974, directed by Grahame Murphy. Barbara had performed in the play (as a courtesan) in an Altona City Theatre production 'last century' (in 1988 in fact). Whether one considers that it was

---

135 In her review in *Cues and News*, July 2013.

forty or twenty-five years between drinks for *A Funny Thing Happened on the Way to the Forum*, it was clearly time for another one, as Barbara asserted. As early as September 2013, tickets for this production were reported to be 'selling like hot cakes', and indeed it was a sell-out.

One particular challenge posed by 'Forum' was the making of multiple costumes for the cast of seventeen. To do the job, Tony Tartaro organised a special 'Saturday sewing circle' of WLT members and friends - which would later become known as "WLT's Ancient Roman Sewers". The results were spectacular. To quote from Jennifer Paragreen's review:

Tony Tartaro's costumes were excellently tuned to the stereotypes of the characters with, for example, Philia and Hero both in virginal white, Hero with a precariously short tunic. Touches like Vibrata's leopard skin knickers, the phallic tassels on Senex's red and gold outfit and Miles Gloriosus' impressive breastplate augmented their attributes and amplified the humour... The sandals were also notable.

It seems that WLT delivered a stellar production of this old favourite, though Graham Cope says that he and others thought it not as good as the Murphy effort. David Collins in *Theatrecraft* thought the effort 'simply incredible', adding: 'To be honest, I wish that could be the review, but unfortunately the editor of *Theatrecraft* requires a slightly more substantial word count.' Jennifer Paragreen agreed with Collins. She introduced her review by saying that the production 'was a wonderful early Christmas present for anyone fortunate enough to secure a seat'. She thought that the show:

...was magnificently cast and far funnier than the professional production staged at this time last year in Melbourne. EVERYONE on stage, and those creative people pulling the strings behind the scenes, was not only talented but also fully committed to making this production a hoot. And they did!

WLT's internal adjudicators agreed; *A Funny Thing Happened on the Way to the Forum* won the Craven Award for WLT's best production in 2013. In addition, on Cordell Day, Marian Sinclair conferred her Adjudicator's Award to Loraine Callow and Barbara Hughes for the set which 'was clever, colourful

and so vibrant that its impact was felt as soon as people entered the theatre'.
WLT's first production for 2014, John Cariani's *Almost, Maine*, directed
by Kris Weber was a sell-out almost before it started. The front page of
Cues and News for March recorded the many positive comments about
the production posted on WLT's Facebook page: Wonderful production,
beautifully performed, ... it was delightful ... ABSOLUTELY STUNNING.
Ewen Crockett in the March *Theatrecraft* wholeheartedly agreed:

I have 600 words to describe what I felt about this play and I can only find one suitable: WOW.

From the moment I entered the theatre, stunning scenic art by Janine Evans, clever lighting (including snowfall and Aurora Borealis) by Craig Pearcey, Kris Weber's audio and an evocative set by George Tranter transported me instantly to the mythical town of Almost, Maine.

I watched spellbound as four actors (Rowan Howard, Samantha Ellen Bound, Janis Coffey and Ben Mitchell) donned various characterisations and moved seamlessly from vignette to vignette. Their stagecraft, use of body language, facial expression and voice were a delight to see. Movement around the stage was beautifully choreographed, at times almost balletic.

Janis Coffey won the Win Stewart Award for her performances in multiple roles in *Almost, Maine*.

Next on WLT's 2014 playlist was American playwright David Auburn's 2000 play *Proof*, directed by Jeff Saliba. *Proof* centres on the relationship between Catherine and her deceased mathematician father Robert. The action takes place on the day before Catherine's 25th birthday, the day of her father's funeral.

Jennifer Paragreen thought the lead roles were very well played: 'In the central role of Catherine, Melissa New is luminous... The scenes with her father, sensitively and believably played by Ian Grealy, were pivotal to the play.' There was praise also for the other two actors - Robert Bender as Hal, a former student of Catherine's father and Melanie Rowe as Claire, Catherine's estranged sister. Noting that whilst '*Proof* is most definitely a drama, Auburn's script contains plenty of laugh lines which poses a challenge for the Director', Paragreen wrote:

> *Director Jeff Saliba has admirably succeeded in securing finely nuanced performances from his cast so that the serious aspects of the drama are never trivialised. (Moreover) his thoughtful musical selections helped sustain the momentum of the piece during the costume changes between scenes.*

Proof was Jeff Saliba's directorial debut at Williamstown. And he clearly enjoyed the experience writing in the March *Cues and News*, that: 'Coming to direct at Williamstown was like coming to a large extended family, except with less arguing.'

Six Dance Lessons in Six Weeks by Richard Alfie was directed by Alan Burrows, and featured Christine Andrew and Colin Morley in the lead roles of Lily and Michael. Deborah Fabbro, in her *Theatrecraft* review wrote:

> *Christine Andrew is a consummate performer who brought charm, grace and feistiness to the role of Lily. Her ability to produce just the right amount of emotion tugs at the heartstrings of the audience and invokes our compassion for the character even when she is not so likeable.*

> *Colin Morley's Michael prances around the stage and is a wonderful foil for Lily's archness without making the character too over the top. He too had the ability to extract from the audience exactly the right feelings for the character.*

David Dare's set design and Tony Tartaro's costumes also 'excelled'. These 'lessons' earned a grade of A+.

Thespians from Mount Waverley's Peridot Theatre came to see this WLT production and, in what was and still is an unusual arrangement among non-professional theatres, arranged for it to be their first offering in 2015: 'We would move over their production to the Unicorn so that another audience could see it.'

Beau Willimon's play *Farragut North* takes its name from a metro station on the red line servicing Farragut Square in Washington D.C. - a noted

Farragut North, 2014
Madeleine McKinlay as Molly and Tim Constantine as Stephen.

gathering place for political hacks and washed-up wannabes. David Collins, reviewing Peter Newling's production in *Theatrecraft*,[136] noted that the play's impact depends heavily on the skill of the two lead actors, in this case Tim Constantine as Stephen and Madeleine McKinlay as Molly. Collins commented:

Tim Constantine gives Stephen the drive of Malcolm Tucker, but none of the charm. As much as there is a kind of lightness to him at the beginning, there's also an ugly smugness that sows the seed for his eventual downfall, all portrayed brilliantly.

McKinlay's bio in the programme mentioned that she danced with the Australian Ballet. On Williamstown's tiny stage close to the audience, she used this training to great effect, not in her movements, but in her stillness. By making Molly not someone overly physical, we concentrate more on her

---

136   November 2014, pp.14-15.

voice and her reactions. It makes for some effective moments, especially in scenes opposite an increasingly frantic and upset Stephen.

The rest of the cast were pitched just right, including an excellent performance from Rowan Howard as the waiter.

Farragut North was WLT's entry in the VDL Awards for 2014 and received ten nominations. The VDL adjudicators awarded Gold Awards to Rowan Howard for Best Actor in a Minor role in a Drama, Stephen Shinkfield for Best Actor in a Supporting Role, Peter Newling for Best Director, and a Silver Award to Bruce Parr and Jeff Saliba for Sound Design. At home, *Farragut North* won the Craven Award for best production, and Tim Constantine the Cordell Award for best actor in a principal role.

Sharr White's *The Other Place* directed by Kris Weber was WLT's first production for 2015. Describing the piece as a 'taut 90-minute play first staged on Broadway in 2011 and by the MTC in 2013', Jennifer Paragreen thought that WLT's production 'proved to be another fine example of talent and teamwork combining seamlessly to provide WLT's audience with engrossing contemporary theatre.' Bruce Cochrane in *Theatrecraft*[137] agreed.

Visiting Mr Green, Jeff Baron's play about reconciliation, youth and age, was directed by Brett Turner. Success in this two-hander of course depends on the actors. Reviewed by David Small for *Theatrecraft*, Small thought that:

The two award-winning actors were at their best with Trevor Hanna calling on his experience when playing two different New York seniors (in two different plays) in recent years, yet here his character was more subdued and his innocent, impromptu remarks timed to amuse.

Kieran Tracey has been making his mark in even more recent years, winning awards and nominations in a variety of roles and several acclaimed productions. As a director, Brett Turner - another award winner - has contributed to the ever-improving quality of non-professional theatre in Victoria.

---

137 March 2015, p.6.

Visiting Mr Green, 2015
Kieran Tracey as Ross and Trevor Hanna as Mr Green.

Visiting Mr Green was WLT's entry in the 2015 VDL awards and received four nominations: for Set Design, Stage and Hand Props Design, Best Actor in a Drama (Kieran Tracey as Ross) and for Best Production. Barbara Hughes and Maria Haughey won a Gold Award for Stage and Hand Props Design, and WLT shared with Sunshine Community Theatre the Gold Award for Best Production.

Of WLT's production of Donald Marguiles' *Time Stands Still*, directed by Ellis Ebell, David Collins wrote in the August 2015 *Theatrecraft*:

> When 'Time Stands Still' opens, we segue from the sounds of conflict, gunfire and screaming to sounds of city traffic, car horns and more screaming. It's the only intrusion of the outside world on the play, which takes place entirely in a loft. It's a nice piece of set design by David Dare, making the most of the smallish Williamstown stage.
>
> While the set is a physical diorama of a Brooklyn apartment, the story soon turns it into a kind of psychological diorama of a difficult relationship. All

the performers do well in drawing from Donald Marguiles' script ideas about youth, ego, passion, and how people prioritise their life, i.e. what is most important.

Both Tim and Pauline Constantine give wonderful performances, communicating clearly that these characters carry a heavier burden than just their physical bruises Rowan Howard ... was nothing but terrific in playing Richard ... Howard plays Richard throughout with a good mix of patience, empathy and pragmatism.

The 'play file' for *Time Stands Still* in the WLT archives records these audience comments about the production: 'Such an intelligent script, well handled'; 'The set is well designed and well used'. Audience member, Lorna McLeod, posted the following comment on WLT's website:

What a joy to view such a talented performance. Each production leaves me in awe of every aspect, scenery, lighting, sound, direction, professionalism and the intensity of the performance. Last night's performance of Time Stands Still was a standout in all aspects. Truly worthy of top awards. Each character appears to give their all and we appreciate every effort. I have inadequate words to express how much I applaud you all. Thank you and I look forward to the next performance.

Of George Werther's production of *Buffalo Gal* by A.R.Gurney, Ken Barnes wrote in October 2015's *Theatrecraft*:

The director and Williamstown's proficient crew drew on an impressive array of creative talent in staging this play. The foyer was dressed as "Buffalo Theatre"; the accompanying music (including "The Buffalo Gals", some well-chosen Tchaikovsky and a Cole Porter song) was just perfect; the lighting was delicate and imaginative; the sound totally appropriate.

Barnes thought all the minor actors were ably cast and brought credibility to their roles. The principals did particularly well:

Amanda, the star herself, was played with distinction by Venetia Macken. Venetia swept onto the stage in grand style and held our attention with her engaging personality, perfect diction and clear delivery of some very complex lines and delicate moments. Hers was a riveting performance from start to finish.

The two ex-boyfriends were played by Wem Etuknwa (as James) and Ken McLeish (as Dan) and both performed well in these roles.

2015 saw the death of Ian Grealy. Speaking at Grealy's funeral, Peter Newling remembered Ian as 'a damn fine actor' recalling his performance as Alan Turing (a 'complex, emotional and multi-dimensional character' in *Breaking the Code*). Others remembered Ian as an 'absolute gentleman' with a great and wicked sense of humour. Ian won the Cordell Award for his portrayal of Alan Turing in 1996 and the Win Stewart Award in 2009 for his memorable performance as Dvornichek in *Rough Crossing*.

WLT celebrated its seventieth anniversary in 2016 with a program of events spread throughout the year. The events were:

- On Sunday 17 January the unveiling of a 'birthday wall mural' (organised by Kerry Drumm) by indefatigable life member, ninety-eight-year-old Ella Bambery, at the 2016 AGM on 5 February.

- The presentation of a collage of many photos organised by Barbara Hughes and a talk by Peter Cliff - descendant of the original owner of Cliff's Family Bakery;

- A series of three 'pleasant Sunday afternoon entertainments', each of which shone a spotlight on a specific era of WLT's history, specifically:
  - On 28 February, *Down Memory Lane the period 1946-1967*, featuring players from that era: Ella Bambery, Marion Gough (nee Becroft), Mary Little, Doug Lindsay and Graeme West;
  - On 8 *May A Bakery doth a Theatre Make, the years 1968-1990* starting with extracts from *Barefoot in the Park* - and a range

of performances featuring Ray and Rosemary Hare, Maggie McInnes, Marian Sinclair, Les Terrill and Bryan Thomas ;
- On 25 September, *Onwards, Upwards and Many Awards 1991-2015*, reprising parts of production from those years.

- A Gala Dinner at the Williamstown Town Hall on 20 August; and

- A 'Back to Willy' event on Sunday 21 August.

One of the people who attended that first 'Sunday afternoon entertainment' was June Lownds, star of many a WLT (and Williamstown Light Opera Company) production in the 1960s and 1970s. June and her husband Doug had moved from their home in Newport to Tasmania many years previously to be close to their son John and his wife Sue and their grandchildren. She had been suffering from deteriorating health for many years, but still managed to sing from her wheelchair in the Theatre's courtyard at the event. In his email to the Theatre advising of her death later the same year, her son John wrote:

Those who lovingly looked after June at Glenview commented that she had been so much brighter since her return from Melbourne and Sue and I had noticed it too. We will be forever grateful that we took Mum to the WLT 70th anniversary celebrations, Down Memory Lane 1946-1967. Even though she couldn't remember having attended or whom she had seen, I believe it triggered something in her subconscious memory, perhaps taking her back to the stage where she belonged and gave so much to others over so many years. It took her to a joyous place over the last three months of her life.

Mary Little was also highly appreciative of the first event. She sent the following handwritten note to Shirley Sydenham:

Dear Shirley,

Please thank everyone who organised everything so well on Sunday.
Thanks
-for making a few oldies feel special for a day

-for the costumes
- for stage management and lighting
- for the guys who helped us up the little step backstage
- for the champagne.

I am well aware that some of you who were there at 10am had been involved with the last night of 'Sweet Road'. Believe me I don't take anything for granted. I love WLT and am proud to be a member.

Love,
Mary

The WLT community experienced a moment of sadness two days before the gala dinner at the Williamstown Town Hall with the death of Bruce Wapshot. Ellis Ebell recalled in *Cues and News* for September 2016 that Bruce had joined WLT at the age of fifteen when the Theatre performed at the Mechanics Institute. There he was tutored in 'all things technical' by Alec Colville, which was 'where Bruce obviously picked up his stage management skills', for which he was particularly remembered.

If the reviews by Jennifer Paragreen and different *Theatrecraft* reviewers are any indication, WLT audience were treated to much quality theatre in WLT's 70th year, thus fulfilling subscribers' expectations - *Cues and News* for February 2016 reported that, even then, 85% of seats available for the year had already been sold. Jennifer's review of *Sweet Road*, for example, suggests that WLT started 2016 very well:

This dark comedy written by Debra Oswald in 2000 is episodic with several story strands which manage to interweave in various quirky and sometimes quite unexpected ways - easy to do with film and television editing facilities but takes a lot of forward planning to achieve on stage. Director, Peter Newling, with his very talented cast and support crew strategically created an engrossing production with scene changes flashing before our eyes in almost no time at all.

The Nance by Douglas Carter Beane, directed by Chris Baldock, was

The Nance, May 2016
Cat Jardine as Sylvie, Kate Lewis as Joan, and Dianne Algate as Carmen.

WLT's second offering in 2016. Jennifer Paragreen thought WLT's decision to stage this in its seventieth anniversary year was indeed fortuitous. The fact that it was an Australian premiere showed WLT's (continuing) propensity for innovation. Jennifer was highly impressed with the staging on Williamstown's tiny space; with the casting 'which was superb'; with Janet Provan's musical direction -'the music was a joy'- and with the costumes designed by Tony Tartaro.

In a rare occurrence, *The Nance* scored a review by Coral Drouyn in the national theatre magazine *Stage Whispers*. She noted that WLT was 'a charming company which consistently punches above its weight'! She had praise for all the lead actors in the production: Kirk Alexander 'brings just the right amount of Yiddish chutzpah and humour to the sketches', and Phil Lambert, the Nance of the piece, 'matches him blow for blow'; Cat Jardine 'brings her usual forceful presence and skills to Silvee', Ziv Gordon 'is wonderfully focused throughout and Dianne Algate 'is a firecracker as Carmen'. Drouyn thought 'Janet Provan's music was terrific', and Tony Tartaro 'did a terrific job with costume design'.

Williamstown was also in pioneer mode with its third production in 2016, staging the premiere non-professional production of Rebecca Lister's *If I*

Should Die Before I Wake, directed by Ellis Ebell. Ken Barnes in Theatrecraft thought the production 'an outstanding example of the best that community theatre has to offer.'

If I Should Die Before I Wake centres around a mother's care of her intellectually disabled daughter Gillian, assisted to some extent by her other daughter Isabelle. When she becomes gravely ill, Gillian's future is in doubt, and some difficult choices confront the family. Barnes noted that: 'For a poignant story of this kind to succeed, each of the actors must engage with the audience with realistic interpretations of their roles and maintain the emotional connection throughout the performance.'

In this Barnes thought Ellis Ebell made inspired choices as his cast and that Shirley Sydenham 'played Joan with considerable skill, projecting a stoic determination to see it through as Gillian's patient, loving mother and taking us on the downward path as her health declined'.

He further commented that Rosalin Shafik-Eid played the role of the daughter:

... so well we often felt like giving her a hug or (even more often) yelling in despair or telling her off. Her portrayal of Gillian was nothing short of brilliant; Equally impressive was Sass Pinci as Judy's second daughter Isabelle, her fractured life demonstrated by tortured facial expressions and attitudes of frustration as her character wrestled with conflicting demands of her emotional stability.

In addition, Barnes thought that:

David Dare's set design was first rate, and facilitated the several seamless scene changes, entrances and exits called for in the plot ... Lighting by Craig Pearcey was excellent and the director and Neil Williamson had paid great attention to the sound, including realistic music which was integral to the plot and even the chirping of crickets at night.

A special feature of WLT's presentation *If I Should Die Before I Wake* was that one night during the season, the playwright Rebecca Lister, who was a friend of the Director Ellis Ebell, came down from Sydney to participate

If I Should Die Before I Wake, July 2016
Shirley Sydenham as Joan, Sass Pinci as Isabelle, and Rosalin Shafik-Eid as Gillian.

in a Q&A with the audience about the play. This was a special night for Ellis since the play's subject overlapped with his day job as a welfare officer with Scope Victoria, working with adults with disabilities and their parents to encourage independence. Many at WLT remember the Q&A as a very memorable event.

Williamstown's final production in 2016 was Neil Simon's *London Suite*, directed by Gaetano Santo, a series of playlets about very contrasting subjects set in a hotel in London, the ambience of which, in Jennifer Paragreen's view, was well captured by David Dare's set. Jennifer thought that the director had obviously worked hard with his talented cast to ensure that the audience was kept happily engrossed and richly entertained with a tightly paced production. Her conclusion:

> *What a delightfully uproarious way to end Williamstown Little Theatre's 70th year! The combination of Neil Simon's comedic script and the production's phenomenal cast and crew should send audience members scurrying now to book their subscriptions for what promises to be another wonderful year*

of theatre in 2017.

It is clear from the foregoing that WLT staged many quality productions over the decade 2007-2016, reflecting a continuing ability to attract talented directors, actors and crew to work with the company. The result was that patrons continued to vote with their feet (and money) so that the organisation became increasingly financially robust. Revenue from productions increased by 36% between 2006 and 2016. Underpinning this prosperity was a continuing very high level of support from subscribers: in most years 70% or more of all tickets available for the year (including the 'Jamieson' nights) had been sold before the first production in February. Treasurer Brian Christopher has been able to tell every AGM since 1996 that the Theatre is in robust health financially.

Brian's own contribution to the effective management of WLT's finances should not be underestimated, a fact recognised late in 2016 when he won, from 1,500 nominations Australia-wide, the 2016 Commonwealth Bank's Not for Profit Treasurer's Award for his significant and long service as Treasurer of the Theatre.

It does well to recognise, however, that presenting a successful 'visible' product on stage requires effective ongoing management by the people responsible for running the theatre i.e. the President, Secretary, Treasurer and other members of the Committee, and a host of other folk providing specialised skills such as set design and construction, costume design and dressmaking, program design and printing, and publicity.

In its seventh decade, WLT has further developed what has long been its broadly systematic approach to management which can be traced back at least to 1968. At their first meeting after the AGM each year, individual Committee members now take responsibility for oversight of a specific aspect of the Theatre's operation; there are sixteen of them. Most Committee members assume responsibility for one, but some take on two or more. For example, in 2011 Bob Harsley accepted responsibility for Front of House and Awards, and Ellis Ebell for Archives and Grounds, but several of the responsibilities (for example for Wardrobe and Props) are commonly shared.

The Committee has progressively addressed a number of policy areas relevant to the ongoing work of any organisation in the twenty-first century, such as occupational health and safety and working with children. In addition, the Committee prepared a number of written protocols such as a Stage Manager's information booklet, an evacuation procedure (which included securing permission from the owners of the Prince Albert Hotel for the Theatre to designate their car park as the emergency evacuation area) and a production coordination checklist.

At one level it is banal, though no less true, that all this success depends on people, and Willy has done all sorts of things since 1996 to recognise and enhance the capabilities of its people. Starting 'at the front', in February 2010, just before the AGM, the Theatre inaugurated a special 'thank you' evening for front of house volunteers, who as Shirley Sydenham put it, echoing the quote from Anthony Parker cited in my Introduction,[138] 'present the welcoming face of the theatre to our audience'. The event was repeated in 2011. Recognising one special challenge for front of house, the theatre organised in March 2011 a one day first aid training session 'using scenarios relevant to our situation' for regular front of house staff and Committee members. Similarly with regard to the Responsible Service of Alcohol accreditation. Such programs are repeated on an 'as-needs' basis.

Bob Harsley took over as Front of House Coordinator in 2011, developing a checklist to assist people in their work. Those working front of house soon started to take responsibility for the work themselves, organising a meeting early in 2013 to discuss how to improve their performance. Out of this came the radical suggestion that the theatre purchase a coffee urn so that patrons could be served 'real' coffee rather than Nescafe, a move received with real satisfaction by patrons.[139]

To counter the recurring, not to say perennial worker shortages required to keep the theatre operating, and to reduce pressure on individuals, the Theatre has also made efforts to develop more people with the specific skills required, primarily by having the relevant local 'experts' run programs to train other interested people in those skills. Thus, in 2014, Alex Begg and Neil Williamson ran a Technical Workshop on backstage work on 29 January, repeating it in September that year. In 2015 Tony Tartaro started conducting

---

138   See page 1.
139   See *Cues and News*, Feb 2013.

Costuming Workshops. One aim, as Shirley Sydenham's Secretary's Report for 2015 indicated, was to be able to designate in one swoop the production coordinators, stage managers, and costume coordinators for all productions in the next year, an aim achieved for the first time in 2018.

Other approaches have been used to embed processes that ensure that fresh ideas and new ways of doing things are sought and encouraged. In 2016, for example, the Committee decided to structure the membership of the theatre's in-house adjudication team (for the Cordell Awards) around a three-yearly cycle, with each member being on the panel for three years, with one retiring at the end of each year. At the same time, it was determined to change the membership of the Play Selection Committee (PSC) regularly to ensure constant renewal and to reduce the pressure on individuals. There has been a more or less 'permanent' PSC coordinator role (at the time of writing occupied by Damian Coffey) who carries the responsibility for ensuring that the work of the PSC is completed in a timely manner.

The Theatre has made increasingly effective use of modern information and communications technology to increase the efficiency of its operations. At the 2012 AGM, for example, Secretary Shirley Sydenham reported that in 2011 there had been a successful transition to an electronic *Cues and News* organised and supervised by Frank Page. The electronic newsletter broke new grounds on many fronts, not the least of which was its absolute adherence to being issued on the 15th of every month, requiring that all contributors have their material to the editor by the 7th of same month. This proved a great success; the database of recipients increased to almost 400 within a year, to 575 a year later, and 'almost 1000' at the end of 2014. Early in 2022, the *Cues and News* mailing list numbered 1,042.

At roughly the same time there had been a revamp and simplification of the theatre's website, *wlt.org.au*, with fewer headings and more information that is easier to find. In April 2012 the Theatre made online bookings to all WLT productions available to both subscribers and casual patrons.

One particular use of the website has been to streamline the Theatre's audition process. A formal auditions policy was adopted in 2012, whereby auditionees would be asked to download a standard audition form from the website, and bring it to the audition already filled in, together with a non-returnable head shot. This is a huge time saver for everyone because, as Shirley

Sydenham noted in her 2013 Annual Report:

> *We no longer require two people in attendance to photograph and print off forms, instead only having only one person to welcome people as they arrive. We no longer have a foyer full of people filling in copious bios on their forms, trying to remember details. Filling in the forms at their leisure beforehand also results in easier to read information.*

Shirley further informed the 2012 AGM that the theatre was becoming 'tech-savvy' in other areas:

> *A new laptop computer and photocopier were purchased during the year, to increase and streamline our operations, and a wi-fi router has been installed so that the laptop now can access the internet and send documents to the office from anywhere on the premises. Barb Hughes has a laptop and printer installed upstairs so that photographs and descriptions of costumes and props will be electronically catalogued and loans tracked. Our volumes of audition forms and pictures will gradually be scanned and will be stored electronically.*

Upgraded facilities were also installed backstage. Ellis Ebell's President's Report 2012, for example, noted that an aging lighting desk had been replaced by 'a whiz-bang new computerised system', which 'means that one operator can work both sound and lights'.

Since occupying 'The Bakery', the company has progressively accumulated a vast stock of costumes and properties stored in the space above the stage, which became increasingly cluttered and difficult to manage. Barbara Hughes started a process of reorganisation in 2011, at first being assisted by newcomer Linda Smart, later joined by Maggie McInnes. By the time of the 2013 AGM, President Ellis Ebell reported that 'one can almost see the floor'. Later Tony Tartaro joined the team. Two years later the President was able to report that 'wardrobe continues its awesome progress towards being a vast ordered, catalogued, barcoded collection that includes hats, wigs and accessories,' another instance of the effective use of technology to increase the efficiency of the theatre's operations.

Along the way the theatre community had some fun, organising a 'retro sale' of garments modelled by a 'Who's Who' of WLT's long-serving members - including Judi Clark, Maria Haughey, Shirley Sydenham and Bernadette Wheatley, with Tony Tartaro stealing the show by appearing in a wedding gown! Later the props collection was similarly 'attacked', largely by Judi Clark. In 2016 the Secretary was able to report that: 'Huge progress has also been made this year in the props bay, with ruthless culling, organising and labelling of the collection.'

The decade from 2007 to 2016 saw continuing work on the physical infrastructure of the theatre. Some of this was driven by necessity - as President Ellis Ebell put it to the 2013 AGM 'our building is old and continuing maintenance costs are a fact of life'. Successive Annual Reports from the President record that:

- In 2008, the main sliding gate into the theatre was replaced with an exact replica which slid a little easier;
- 2009 saw the setting up of a food preparation area (kitchen) in the office;
- In 2011, a new front gate, affectionately known as the Cordell Gate (courtesy of Kerry Cordell) was installed.

In 2011, some maintenance and upgrading work was also thrust upon the theatre. As the President reported to the 2012 AGM:

With the heavy rains earlier in the year, we experienced flooding on stage. A plumber was engaged to install baffles on our external air vents and plug any existing leaks. Our heating system broke down (which necessitated us hiring temporary heating for our winter productions). Unfortunately, the old system could not be repaired, and we have had to install a new and hopefully more efficient system.

2012 saw several projects, including plumbing work in the toilets and external dressing room (the old men's dunny), fine tuning the audio loop, a new heating system and reconditioned seats.

Chapter Eight

2017-2021: Making Covid an Opportunity for Renewal

Jennifer Paragreen observed at the end of her review of WLT's last production for 2016, *London Suite*, that its quality 'should send audience members scurrying now to book their subscriptions for what promises to be another wonderful year of theatre in 2017'.

WLT subscribers took Paragreen's advice. Robert Harsley, Ticket Secretary, reported to the Committee early in the year that 'Subscribers for 2017 got their forms in with record speed; not so much a trickle but a rush, so much so that late subscribers were not able to be fitted in.'[140] This subscriber enthusiasm has continued since, as the quotes from various sources relating to subscription renewals in 2018, 2019 and 2020, collected in Table 9 on page 263, demonstrate.

Subscriber's enthusiasm usually reflects a belief that they will be seeing quality theatre. In-house reviewer Jennifer Paragreen, and a range of experienced *Theatrecraft* critics, indicate that the subscribers were on the money. For example:

- In her review of Tess Maurici Ryan's account of *Bad Jews*, Paragreen put it very succinctly: 'The production is so good because every aspect is so good'.[141]
- Andrew Gemmel, in *Theatrecraft* said of Shirley Sydenham's production of *Vincent in Brixton* that 'Measured by any yardstick, Williamstown's production, with its active attention to detail, is sheer quality'.
- He continued this theme in his March 2019 review of *Body Awareness*

---

140   *Cues and News* April 2017.
141   *Cues and News*, April 2017.

Table 9: WLT Subscribers' Enthusiasm for Renewals 2018, 2019, 2020

Year	Quote	Source
2018	Ticket Secretary reported on 22 January that 'there were only 18 tickets left for WLT productions in 2018 with a waiting list of 52 for Play 2, Stones in his Pockets'	Minutes WLT Committee Meeting 22 Jan 2018
2019	'Subscriptions for 2019 are flooding in'	Robert Harsley in *Cues and News*, November 2018
2020	'Some plays in 2020 (already) have nil tickets available).	Robert Harsley in *Cues and News*, December 2019

concluding that 'The Williamstown organisation continues to challenge its audience with plays of contemporary relevance and always respects their patrons' ability to form their own conclusions.'

Ken Barnes' *Theatrecraft* review of *Bad Jews* focused on the principal protagonists who 'were perfectly cast and produced outstanding performances'. Julia Lambert as Daphna 'delivered her extremely complicated lines with great verve' whilst Charlie Collopy-White 'was equally proficient as Liam … The scenes in which he and Julia traded barbs, often with overlapping and multiplexed lines resulted in gasps of astonishment (or knowing chuckles) from the audience'.

David Small in *Theatrecraft*, June 2017, was similarly impressed with Brett Turner's production of *When I Was Five* by Jeff Baron writing that:

Well written and well directed, this play tells of the encounter between a woman therapist and a young man who is struggling with relationships. It can be said that the author makes us explore our own past, our stored-up pictures and forgotten world, but much of this would not have been so clearly understood without the excellent portrayal of Will by newcomer Seth Kannof.

Although Ellen (Janine Evans) sits with her notepad and pencil for most of the time, she too becomes animated at times, probing and prying, and there are one or two surprises.

Designed by the Director, the WIWF set is beautiful. Minimal furniture and complementing pastel colours make it easy on the eye and not competing with the characters. Thank you WLT for WIWF.

When I Was Five was so heavily booked that an extra performance was scheduled.

Vincent in Brixton, directed by Shirley Sydenham, was WLT's entry in the 2017 VDL Awards. The play focuses on the early life of Vincent van Gogh, especially the time he spent in London. As Jennifer Paragreen pointed out in her review:

… the stars really aligned for WLT's staging, as it coincided with an exhibition of Van Gogh's works at The National Gallery of Victoria, one of their 'Winter Masterpieces' series'.

Paragreen saw quality acting in the play, for example noting that 'Jonathan Best portrayed Vincent's emotional journey vividly. As Ursula, Cat Jardine balanced melancholy sadness with a desperate determination to get on with the mechanics of life… (and) Ella Hill-Cotter brought vigour to her role as Vincent's younger sister, Anna.' Production qualities were also high:

Part of the charm of WLT's production lies in the meticulous research lavished on the authenticity of the settings, props, costumes and artistic allusions which serve to create the ambience of the era.

The VDL adjudicators agreed with this latter point. *Vincent in Brixton* received nominations in seven Award categories, winning the gold awards for Set Design (for Kerry Drumm - this was a major achievement, given that this was her first effort at set design!), Properties Design (Barbara Hughes and Maria Haughey) and Costume Design (Tony Tartaro, who in a post to WLT's Facebook page graciously acknowledged 'the wonderful sewing team at WLT who bring the costumes from page to stage'.)

Of WLT's next production, *The Seafarer* by Irish Playwright Conor McPherson, directed by Bruce Akers, Ken Barnes in *Theatrecraft* wrote:

All five actors performed extremely well, each one with believable Irish accents, mannerisms and voice inflection that suited their roles. The director had ensured that the whole stage was used effectively and each of the actors projected well to the audience.

A feature of the show was the way the director and all five actors were able to convey the interaction between the players in a realistic way, partly by what I call multiplexing, allowing the actors to interrupt and sometimes speak over other actors without destroying the dialogue or losing the plot. This meant that the audience became engaged and felt absorbed in the ever-changing relationships.

Vincent in Brixton, July 2017
L to R: Marion Griffin as Eugene Layer, Cat Jardine as Ursula, and Jonathan Best as Vincent van Gogh.

The fine acting was accompanied by a first-rate set designed by George Tranter… The lighting by Deryk Hartwick and sound by Neil Williamson were also well designed.

The director, technical gurus, and production coordinator Peter Newling and each of the cast would have known that 'The Seafarer' audience was well pleased with this outstanding performance.

WLT's last play in 2017 was Patrick Barlow's theatrical adaption of John Buchan's literary masterpiece *The Thirty-Nine Steps*, directed by Barbra Hughes, the first and only time Barbara has directed a 'straight play' rather than a musical. In summary, Bruce Cochrane writing in *Theatrecraft*, thought that:

There was considerable inventiveness in both staging and acting and successive fast overlaps of scenes handled with great dexterity; Ultimately this was a show that achieved its resulting entertainment due to a concerted effort by a lot of people on and off stage.

In her usual style Jennifer Paragreen provided more detail, though she didn't explicitly mention that the play involves thirty-three scenes and seventy-eight costume changes for its four actors! Noting that the emphasis in the play was on comedy, she commented that the director, Barbara Hughes 'had the herculean task of coordinating all the supporting elements which assist the four onstage actors in the theatrical shenanigans required for their quest'. In this, Paragreen thought Barbara had succeeded. Elaborating on Cochrane's theme of inventiveness, she commented that:

Creativity, pace and timing are crucial and Barbara Hughes' direction wrangles these well with original elements introduced ranging from the spitting and guttural sounds associated with pronouncing names such as Schmidt and Alt-na-Shellach to the Christmas flavoured ending.

The acting also impressed Paragreen who thought Mark Briggs 'turned in a pivotal performance as Richard Hannay, suave, staid and well intentioned', Claire Abagia 'made her characters distinctive in accent, posture and motivation', (and) 'the two clowns … Liam O'Kane and Brad Lowry combined excellently in some hilarious routines … O'Kane's scenes as a singing angel and the recitation of formula were among the show's many highlights'.

The Thirty-Nine Steps scooped the pool on Cordell Day, winning the Craven Award for best production, Liam O'Kane the Win Stewart Award, and Mark Briggs the Cordell.

The BIG change at WLT during 2017 was David Dare's retirement from the position of Ticket Secretary after a mere thirty-five years in the role. In recognition of this long service, and his contribution to many other aspects of WLT's work (especially set design), he was awarded the Grahame Murphy Award for excellence.

WLT made 2018 its own special year, commemorating the fiftieth anniversary of its occupation of 'The Bakery'. Ellis Ebell got the ball rolling when in *Cues and News* for March 2018 he reflected on the first production at WLT's new home *Barefoot in the Park*, in which he performed along

The Thirty-Nine Steps, November 2017
L to R: Brad Lowry and Liam O'Kane as the Clowns,
Clair Abagia in multiple roles, and Mark Briggs as Richard Hannay.

with Helen Koefed, June Lownds, Bill Stevenson, Mick Ashman and Barry Chandler. He recalled standing in the wings waiting for his cue, 'my stomach in knots and nerves causing my body to shake, thinking would I rather be at the dentist'. The pain was overcome when the cast received a standing ovation for their performances.

The focus of the 2018 'fifty-year anniversary' was, in many ways, fundraising for the future. In April's *Cues and News*, then President Peter Newling reported that the WLT Committee had been putting in place a ten-year plan to develop the theatre and had formed two sub-committees, one looking at physical refurbishment, and the other fundraising. For the former, at that early stage, the Committee was looking for people with specific skills or knowledge (eg in town planning and structural engineering). The fundraising committee, led by Maria Haughey, however, was already at work.

The biggest effort was a 'monster mystery raffle' to be drawn on Cordell Day. The Committee successfully approached a long list of potential donors for prizes which ranged through an original Laraine Williamson quilt, dinner for two at the Prince Albert and Stag's Head Hotels, and seasons' double passes at both Heidelberg and Essendon theatre companies, and Altona City Theatre. The major prize was an all-inclusive Yarra Valley Winery Tour for ten people, provided by Yarra Valley A2B.[142] Within the WLT community, Tony Tartaro donated some gift-boxed wine and Emma Hunt some BP vouchers. A signed Collingwood football jumper was obtained for a silent auction. The raffle alone raised $3,971, and total fund raising amounted to $6,436[143]. The Theatre's 2019 subscription brochure provided a special opportunity for subscribers to make a special donation to the fund-raising effort and more than $5,000 was raised.

According to *Theatrecraft* reviewers, WLT maintained its reputation for quality gigs in 2018. Bruce Cochrane was upbeat about the first production of the year, *Mr Bailey's Minder*, commenting that director Deborah Fabbro 'has a record of putting together plays which are off the beaten track', praising the performances of all the actors - Damian Jones as the artist Leo Bailey, now an alcoholic and suffering from dementia, Clare Hayes as Margo, Leo's daughter 'with the impossible task of making her likeable…succeeded in

---

142   See: https://www.yarravalleya2b.com.au
143   *Cues and News*, Feb 2019.

revealing the vulnerability under the steely protective exterior which she had developed' and Emily Renalson O'Kane 'totally believable … (with) the body language, the speech rhythms and expressiveness to hold our attention and manage the mood swings the character displays'. In a Facebook post on February 18, audience member Helen Taylor agreed, thinking O'Kane 'outstanding…with a very big future'.

David Collins reckoned that in its staging of *Stones in His Pockets*, directed by Travis Handcock, 'WLT continues its fine pedigree of making tricky shows look easy, entertaining and exceptional'. Brian Edmond and Roger Bak played the respective heroes of the piece, Charlie Conlon and Jake Quinn. Collins thought Brian and Roger gave excellent performances:

The most effective moments remained those simply staged conversations amid the hijinks between Charlie and Jack.

It is a play which requires its two actors to switch characters repeatedly, yet the largest risk in Maris Jones' script is placing a suicide right in the middle of the larks and comedy. What is a short description of Sean's death on the page is made mythic here: the video camera allowing the audience to join Sean in the last moments in the water – seeing the stones in his hands, then putting those in his pockets. A sudden dramatic turn like this can pack more of an emotional wallop, but it can also be confusing because it is so unexpected to an audience who up to now have been happy chuckling along. Thankfully, Director Travis Handcock and his cast do splendidly in navigating from comedy to tragedy and back up again in a way that feels coherent and truthful.

Moreover, Collins thought that 'Les Hart's set was lovely… There was a strong sense of place'. Two Facebook posts supported Collin's views. Mary Pszczolkowski said simply: 'Great play!! Actors were amazing - very clever with character changes.' An earlier post on 22 April by Marti Ibrahim is worth quoting at length:

Together with his cast and crew, director Travis Handcock has put on a beautiful and touching piece of theatre, and he is to be congratulated on another great production. In spite of the overwhelming sadness I felt at interval, I found myself unable to stop myself from laughing at the witticisms and humorous interludes that are dotted throughout the second half of the play (as well as the first half). The message of this play is ably communicated by actors Brian Edmonds and Roger Bak who fill the theatre with their versatility and energy as they each inhabit multiple characters with precision and aplomb. This is an important play for our times. Get along and see it if you can.

Ewen Crockett in *Theatrecraft*, August 2018, reckoned that director Sandy Green 'should be very proud' of her production of Dylan Thomas' classic *Under Milk Wood*, 'the most entertaining I have seen for quite some time'. Reserving special mention for David Runnalls as the narrator of the piece 'a massive role which was handled expertly', Ewen noted that the cast of eight 'held his attention to the end'. Jennifer Paragreen in her review noted that:

> The playwright's instructions dictate that the actors must play multiple roles without leaving the stage and issued the actors with just one stage direction, 'Love the words, love the words'. WLT's production followed this to the letter of the law with eight extremely talented actors playing well over forty different characters and each giving full weight to the poetic beauty of Thomas' writing with its inventive imagery, word play and lilting rhythms.

Jennifer also had praise for Patrick Slee 'who operated sound and lighting with great precision from the confines of the onstage sound booth. Evocative sound effects including music, a cat, baby, bells, cock crow intensified the atmosphere at just the right volume.' The Cordell judges agreed with the reviewers, awarding *Under Milk Wood* the Craven Award for best production of the year.

Reviewing for *Theatrecraft* what was an Australian premiere production of *Silent Sky* by Lauren Gunderson, directed by Ellis Ebell, Cate Dowling-Trask wrote that.

> The play is based on the adult life and work of Henrietta Swan Leavitt, born 1868, who worked at Harvard College Observatory between 1904

and 1921. Each of the technical aspects of this production, with set by David Dare, lighting by Jason Bovaird, audio by Ellis Ebell and Neil Williamson, and costuming by Tony Tartaro, was outstanding in both design and execution. Seldom does a play come along in which there is no discernible weak link among the performances, but in this production each of the performers was confident, clear and authentic.

Dowling-Trask praised the acting of Paula McDonald as Williamina Fleming, Melanie Rowe as Annie Jump Cannon (who classified over 350,0000 stars without any technological aid except a glass comparator slide known as a spanker), Richard Mealey as Peter Shaw, Lee McClenaghan as Margaret Leavitt, and Ruby Duncan as Henrietta Swan Leavitt 'who gave her character a full emotional range from determined and assertive to fragile and defeated by illness'. She concluded:

Ellis Ebell, the director, was actively involved in every aspect of his production. His attention to detail was evident in the work. Congratulations to all at WLT ... for a play that was fresh, entertaining, thought provoking and beautifully produced.

Jennifer Paragreen agreed. The VDL adjudicators were also impressed, nominating *Silent Sky* for five awards, and awarding the Gold Award to Paula McDonald for Best Actress in a Supporting Role in a Drama and the Silver Award to Jason Bovaird for his Lighting Design.

The theatre scored at least two new subscribers from this production. In a Facebook post Ronel Burger enthused:

'Wonderful play... Our first taste of WLT, and we are hooked. When will you be taking 2019 subscriptions expressions of interest?'

Ewen Crockett, reviewing for *Theatrecraft* in December 2018, was also very impressed with WLT's last production of 2018, *The Complete Works of William Shakespeare (Abridged)* directed by Peter Newling. Ewen had special praise for the three actors Liam O'Kane, Rik Brown and Travis Handcock, whose performances 'were brilliantly enhanced with lighting by Craig Pearcey

Williamstown Little Theatre

Silent Sky, September 2018
L to R: Richard Mealey as Peter Shaw, Paula McDonald as Williamina Fleming,
Ruby Duncan as Henrietta Swan Leavitt, Lee McClenaghan as Margaret Leavitt,
and Melanie Rowe as Annie Jump Cannon.

and sound by Jasmine Tolentino. Without their expertise, given the simplicity of the set, the scenario could have been a bit two-dimensional.' Crocket was also impressed by George Tranter's set design (which gave ample space for the three actors ... to own and use to best advantage), the backstage crew and the costuming: 'How difficult it must have been to design costumes that could be changed in a matter of seconds is beyond belief. Congratulations Shirley Sydenham.'

WLT's first production for 2019, directed by Kris Weber, was American teacher and playwright Annie Baker's *Body Awareness,* an exploration of the lesbian relationship between two psychologists: Phyllis, played by Janis Coffey and Joyce, played by Jeanne Snider:

> *They live together in Joyce's home with her adult son, Jared (Robert Ruscitti), who is clearly on the Asperger's spectrum but refuses to acknowledge his*

position. This unconventional household has been expanded with the presence of houseguest, Frank Bonitatibus (Brian Edmond), in town to exhibit his photos during Body Awareness Week. His arrival exacerbates some of the existing tensions in the household but also provides some impetus for a change of perspective, particularly for Joyce and perhaps Jared. Baker claims that her 'goal for the play is to not judge anyone, to get at that point where everyone is equally right and equally wrong, so the humour comes from that ... I wanted to write a play about issues that wasn't an issue play.

Director, Kris Weber, and her well-chosen cast have clearly taken Baker's brief to heart, creating vivid characterisations with sustained emotional trajectories. The production makes the most of the inherent humour in some of the contradictions within the characters but also keeps them grounded in their perceptions so that we can see their viewpoint.

Paragreen saw high production qualities:

Set design by Gaetano Santo was a joy to behold with honey toned timber providing a unifying effect across two rooms. Sound design by Patrick Slee utilised wistful solo guitar music to good effect. Body Awareness proved to be another example of WLT's amazing ability to engage and entertain its audience with skilled interpretations of unusual and intriguing material.

A week after the conclusion of this play, on 2 March 2019, another marriage took place on the WLT stage – that of Brett Turner and Adrian Valenta – only the second time the space has been used for such an event. The ability of these two men to formalise their long-standing relationship reflected the amendment of the Australia Marriage Act on 9 December 2017 to give same sex couples the same rights to marry as heterosexual couples. Turner's association with the theatre has been the most visible. He directed *Beyond Therapy* in 2007, *Visiting Mr Green* in 2015 (which shared the VDL Gold Award for Best Production that year), and *When I Was Five* in 2017. Valenta has appeared on our stage in a number of productions, and was frequently listed as Assistant Director on Turner's shows.

After this rather unique event, WLT staged *The Exorcism* by Don Taylor.

Jennifer Paragreen introduced her review of this play by noting that:

> Williamstown Little Theatre is certainly providing its patrons with an amazing variety of plays this year. The opening gambit was a twenty-first century American comedy, 'Body Awareness', and now we go back in time nearly 50 years with a spooky drama, 'The Exorcism' by Don Taylor, laced with Gothic horror set in a remote cottage in England in the 1970s.

She concluded her review with the observation that:

> Being a play from the 1970s 'The Exorcism' seems to be more verbose and to move at a slower pace than we encounter in more contemporary material, but it contains enough of the macabre and sinister to make for a spine-chilling experience plus some food for thought.

In between, Paragreen commented on the set and the 'acting skills aplenty':

> The set, designed by Dion Sexton and Les Hart, shows the results of Edmund's lavish expenditure on the renovations with a neat and spacious living room featuring a paned door and window looking out onto a garden. A huge stone fireplace dominates one wall while passage doors open on either side to a kitchen and a staircase leading to a bedroom. It all looks quaint and cosy.

Paragreen was impressed by all the actors: Brian Christopher as Dan, Wayne Gleeson as Edmund, Ella Harvey as Rachel and Venetia Macken as Margaret. They were greatly enabled by: 'the powerful ingenuity and teamwork involved in the lighting design by Craig Pearcey and sound design by Jasmine Tolentino, in combination with Dion Sexton's set, to create a really chilling effect as the cottage becomes an impenetrable fortress which entombs its four inhabitant.'

Cate Dowling-Trask, in *Theatrecraft* agreed, commenting at the end of her review that:

> Whilst the play itself may have been anachronistic, the production was meticulously directed, well-acted, beautifully designed and technically adept.

Each aspect worked in harmony with the whole definitely being greater than the sum of the parts.

Moreover, said this reviewer: 'At the performance I attended, the audience were discussing it enthusiastically as they departed.' The ghost that features in *The Exorcism*, Sarah Jane, has been regularly blamed ever since for any mysterious occurrences that occur at the theatre – such as technical gremlins or set/costume malfunctions!

WLT's next play, the musical *A Man of No Importance*, directed by Barbara Hughes with musical direction by Janet Provan, is set in conservative, Catholic Dublin back in 1964 where Alfie Byrne, our man of no importance, is a closeted homosexual living with his spinster sister. By day a bus conductor, his well-being is sustained by the importance of his evening role as the artistic director of the St Imelda's Players. The musical's title is a nod to Oscar Wilde's play, *A Woman of No Importance*, as Alfie hero-worships Wilde and his determination to stage Wilde's contentious and erotic *Salomé* sets off a train of life changing reactions.

A Man of No Importance requires a cast of seventeen, whose success requires quality work by both the principals and those playing cameo roles. Jennifer Paragreen thought they had all succeeded. On direction, Paragreen commented:

Taking on a full-length musical with seventeen on-stage performers (most with double or even triple roles) within the small confines of the Little Theatre is a herculean task requiring a huge amount of ingenuity, creativity, commitment and organisational skill. Director, Barbara Hughes, has clearly understood that this is an intimate character driven musical and ensured every member of her wonderful ensemble thoroughly understood the nature and motivation of the character being played. Musical Director, Janet Provan, rose to the challenge of training them to sing in character. The singing, whether solo or complex harmonies, was exceptional.

She ended with: Choreography by Jacqui McCallum benefitted from an inventive restraint to look effective while tuned to the dimensions of the WLT stage. Fitting all the St Imelda's Players onto the tiny stage within the stage was no mean feat.'

On 23 June 2019, three days before opening night, Robert Harsley noted in a Facebook post that the production was a sell-out.

Directed by Shirley Sydenham, the following play *Strawberry* was a special event for the Theatre, since its author, Kerry Drumm, had been an active member of the WLT community since 2015 when, newly arrived in Williamstown, she was exploring her new neighbourhood, found Williamstown Little Theatre's door was open, and walked right in, saying that she would like to help out. Famously, she was responsible in 2016 for the 70th anniversary mural which patrons saw as they entered the theatre. Early in 2019 she contributed her skills to developing a special social media campaign[144] focused on recruiting young people for backstage roles.

In 2017 Drumm's short piece *Half of Me* was shown at Gasworks Studio Theatre in Albert Park as part of Shannon Woollard's Play Six festival, which, as noted in Chapter 6, was first staged at WLT at the end of 2006. *Half of Me* tells the story of Helen, who became one of the central characters in Kerry's first full length play, *Strawberry*, which premiered as WLT's fourth production for 2019. As only the second play by a WLT member to have been staged by the Theatre (the other being Gillian Wadds' *Who Cares?* in 1990), *Strawberry* became a real 'whole of theatre' event. *Cues and News* reported extensively on the play's progress through the year, through auditions, casting, and first read through (where Kerry met the cast). As September 2019's *Cues and News* reported:

> *You couldn't get a seat in the dining room of the Prince Albert Hotel at seven o'clock on a Wednesday night in September. But you could get a drink and sit with a playwright as her heart pounded more quickly and loudly than yours. And you could run across the street in the rain which ruined your hair and your curls to a rapidly filling foyer. Filling with people who had been in the pub mere moments earlier. Or people who lived next door to you. Or people you'd seen a hundred times before in that self-same foyer or perhaps had stood behind in a queue at the post office or walked past in the supermarket. Local people at their local theatre to watch another play written by another*

---

144   *Cues and News*, February 2019.

local. To be the very first audience to watch the play.

And watch it they did. Enthralled with the story that one of them had written and another of them had directed.

And when it was over and tears were dried and hugs exchanged, everyone stayed to enjoy the supper catered by Robert Harsley and Peta Ripper before making the short journey home.

The focus of *Strawberry*[145] is Tabitha (Tabs), a feisty, confident fifteen-year-old who has been raised since toddlerhood by single dad Adam. A typical teen: outspoken, messy, glued to her smartphone, listening to music and constantly messaging. Out of the blue, her mother makes contact and against Adam's will, Tabs determinedly leaves for a short stay where her world is turned upside down. How does Tabs deal with the truth of her story? Deborah Fabbro, reviewing the play for *Theatrecraft*, had clearly enjoyed it:

This was a very satisfying piece of theatre and I commend WLT for producing a new work which will hopefully go on and be produced elsewhere.

On the quality of the script, Fabbro commented:

Although there are some heavy and dark issues put forth in this play, Ms Drumm's compassionate writing handles them with sensitivity and the moments of humour, which are nicely interspersed throughout the play, give us, the audience, a little breathing space. We laugh, cry and feel hope.

Although a little slow to start and with some extended pauses early on, the pace picked up to take us on a roller coaster ride and totally engrossed us in the story.

Fabbro thought that director Shirley Sydenham had 'assembled a very

---

145   This description of the play is taken from the audition notices which appeared in *Cues and News* in April and May, 2019.

Strawberry September 2019
Liam O'Kane as Adam, Tamar Collier as Helen and
Maxime Palmerston (seated) as Tabitha.

strong cast (Maxine Palmerson as Tabitha, Tamar Collier as her mother Helen and Liam O'Kane as Adam), and guided them superbly through this moving and emotional play, eliciting performances that convey the moving, and sometimes harrowing, stories with conviction'. Production values were also good: 'a pleasing, suitable and workable set designed by Dion Sexton with Les Hart' which was 'appropriately dressed by Celia Meehan, Greta Doell and Maria Haughey,' and 'enhanced by lighting designed by Craig Pearcey'. Sound cues and subscript music designed by Nelson Clemente did exactly what it should do, it enhanced the action of the play without being distracting.

Drawing from the experience gained a few years earlier during *If I Should Die Before I Wake*, Kerry Drumm was persuaded, along with the cast, to participate in a Q&A session with the audience after one of the Saturday night performances. Participants raised a number of topics such as the playwriting process, the workshopping of new plays and how the actors approached their roles.

It is worth noting that WLT followed up on this successful production by hosting a workshop on *Brothers*, Ms Drumm's next play, then still in development. The workshop was organised by Emma Hunt, under the auspice of her production company Little Red Fox productions. Kerry was very nervous but pleased with the outcome noting that the actors Daniel and Liam O'Kane (the latter from *Strawberry*) had showcased 'their instinct, especially as they were reading their script for the first time'. Cooperation between Ms Drumm, Ms Hunt, Peter Newling and the O'Kane brothers continued, and, after a two-night preview season at WLT, *Brothers* debuted at the 2022 Adelaide Fringe Festival. All involved were delighted that a strong contingent of WLT stalwarts made the trip to Adelaide to see the show – including WLT legend Laurie Gellon, now ensconced as an SA resident.

The venture to the Adelaide Fringe proved a great success. One reviewer described the show as 'classy'. The *Stage Whispers* reviewer had praise for the actors, the writer, and the director in turn. In summary:

Real life brothers Daniel and Liam O'Kane are magnificent as Matt and Jay… Both O'Kane's work brilliantly together … keeping the audience on their toes to bring all the detail together. Writer Kerry Drumm's words are terrific. She knits together the triggers and outcomes of the two brothers – dealing with domestic abuse, premature death, teenage hormones, and Nan's spam sandwiches. Peter Newling's direction is tight, squeezing heartfelt emotion and manic physicality from his performers.

Brothers would go on to be performed at the Edinburgh and Melbourne Fringe Festivals in 2022.

But back to 2019. Williamstown's final presentation that year was a Gaetano Santo directed 'Double Bill', *Black Comedy* by Peter Shaffer and *The Real Inspector Hound* by Tom Stoppard, the authors being 'two of Britain's most decorated writers, both recipients of knighthoods, multiple Tony Awards and an Academy Award among other accolades'.

WLT had first staged *Black Comedy* back in 1970.[146] As Jennifer Paragreen noted in her review: '

---

146   See page 86.

Williamstown Little Theatre

'Black Comedy' and 'The Real Inspector Hound' fit together well in light heartedness, place and time but what makes the combination even more appealing is that both plays require a cast of eight, five men and three women, and in this production each actor is called upon to perform in both plays. This sets a challenge for the actors and provides an extra frisson of excitement for the audience, wondering how well they will cope. The gales of laughter issuing from the audience throughout the evening provided testament to the success of this ploy.

Paragreen thought that all the actors acquitted themselves well. There is a lot of 'silliness and mistaken identity in these plays' which were brilliantly orchestrated by director, Gaetano Santo, who was also responsible for the clever set design. Moreover:

The production looked really impressive with appropriately lavish furniture and realistic props including exploding Buddhas and a dead body intelligently sourced by Deborah Fabbro, Peter Newling and Tony Tartaro. Brindsley's strange sculptures and other artworks were created by George Tranter, Ian Green and Janine Evans to remarkable effect. Costumes designed by Karin Bouvin and Chelsea Maron with Tony Tartaro set the era back to the 1960's and beyond with styles tailored to the status of the wearers and their machinations...

In the technical department Patrick Slee's audio design and lighting design by Craig Pearcey were crucial to setting the atmosphere of the plays. The reverse lighting plot needed in Black Comedy meant when the lights were on in Brindsley's apartment there was no lighting on stage and vice versa so the audience had a full view of everything happening supposedly in the dark. The really tricky part happened when a match was struck on stage or a torch turned on so that the light dimmed in proportion. Congratulations to Patrick Slee and Robert Edwards whose audio and lighting operation consistently maintained the illusion. In fact, congratulations to all involved in bringing these thoroughly entertaining and clever comedies to the Williamtown stage, whetting our appetites for more to come in 2020.

Sadly, as we all know, due to the Coronavirus, the 'more to come' hoped for by Jennifer Paragreen for 2020 became very little.

In February 2020, the Theatre presented the Jo Dipietro play *The Last Romance*, the third play by this playwright performed at WLT - the previous being *I Love You, You're Perfect, Now Change* in 2005, and *Over the River and Into the Woods* in 2015. Both David Collins in *Theatrecraft* and Jennifer Paragreen were impressed:

> Collins: *Opening WLT's account for 2020, The Last Romance by Joe Di Pietro is a story about love and loyalty told with uncomplicated beauty in what was a delightful production by all involved.*

> Paragreen: *Congratulations to the director, the three older actors and the young singer who made the most of DiPietro's engaging script. All involved should feel justly proud of their efforts in bringing this delightful comedy to the Williamstown Stage.*

The play centres on Ralph, an eighty-year-old widow with a crush on Carol whom he sees in the park with her dog, Peaches. Ralph and Carol gently strike up a friendship. This while Ralph's sister Rose is struggling with her own loneliness after her husband walked out on her twenty years earlier to live with another woman, but, being a good Catholic, she has steadfastly refused to divorce him. As Paragreen reported:

> *Director, Keith Hutton, has assembled a splendid cast to bring this charming play to life and their well-honed efforts have been enhanced by the attention to the detail in the work of the supporting technical team.*

On the acting Collins and Paragreen agreed, praising the work of Robert Harsley as Ralph (Collins: 'a first-rate performance that held the audience's attention'), Sandy Green 'who bustles in with impeccable comic timing and line delivery as the conniving sister' (Paragreen), and Janet Provan (Collins thought her performance 'sweet') and James Madsen-Smith. Special words were reserved for Daisy Provan-Koch playing the dog Peaches, 'a glorious and-well behaved performance' according to Collins, with Paragreen elaborating:

The Last Romance February 2020
Sandy Green as Rose Tagliatelle, Robert Harsley as Ralph Bellini,
anet Provan as Carol Reynolds, and Daisy Provan-Koch as Peaches.

'With an amazing biography almost as big as the dog, Daisy delighted many in the audience and never put a foot wrong all night.'

Janet Provan had an additional role in the production being, as Paragreen put it 'a major contributor to the musical aspects of the play', who, working with Sorcha Delaney, 'ensured that James Madsen-Smith was well trained to sing the required operatic interludes and nicely backed by a supportive piano accompaniment'.

Evidence of the Coronavirus COVID-19 began to emerge in Australia in February 2020, just as WLT was performing its first season for the year. The WLT Committee,[147] like those of many other organisations, reacted cautiously and hopefully at first, postponing its second scheduled production, *The River*, already in rehearsals, to 1-18 July of that year and asking the Play Selection Committee to slot the third play of the year, *The Raft*, into the 2021 season, indicating that anyone holding tickets for the proposed July 2020 production would receive a refund.

---

147   The balance of this paragraph is based on material in *Cues and News*, March and April 2020.

Before the end of March, however, as the Covid-19 situation deteriorated, the Committee had decided that the best and safest option was to cancel the rest of the 2020 season, issuing a special issue of *Cues and News* on 31 March to communicate that decision to the WLT community. As the Committee explained:

The ever-changing situation indicates that it is unlikely that we will be able to present any of the four remaining plays and we don't want to stay in the limbo of 'maybe play 3…4…5.

The Committee also indicated its intention to refund tickets for plays 2-5, but dared to suggest that 'if you wish to do so, you may choose to forego the refund and donate to WLT all or part of that money. This would be gratefully received to cushion the heavy financial loss to the company - but it is just a suggestion.' By mid-April, ticket secretary Robert Harsley was able to report that 'I have had over sixty people contact me to donate the rest of their year's subscriptions back to the theatre'.

Given that *The Last Romance* was to become WLT's final production until life could return to normality in 2022, and that this book is covering the period up to the Covid-19 era, it is appropriate that I give my usual summary of WLT's 8th decade, such as it was, here.

Since 2017, WLT has continued its tradition of what management jargon now refers to as 'internal capacity building', that is, using its own internal 'experts' to train and mentor new people to develop the 'non-acting' skills essential to presenting quality theatre. Thus in 2018 and 2019 through the efforts of Alex Begg and Emma Hunt, WLT had a different Stage Manager and Assistant Stage Manager for each production with some people working as ASMs in 2018 stepping up to the Stage Manager's role in 2019. Likewise in those years, thanks to Tony Tartaro, each production had a different costume coordinator, some new to WLT. During 2019, Maria Haughey obtained a Hobsons Bay City Council Vibrant Communities Grant for in-house training in 2020. Emma Hunt used this grant to update Front of House training.

At the same time, the Theatre has continued to introduce 'new blood' into its operations. For example, in his President's Report to the 2019 AGM, Peter Newling noted that:

In 2018 we had three directors work with us who had not directed here before. Of the 22 people who appeared on our stage in 2018, 12 were doing so for the first time. We had new workers welcomed to the set building team, the costuming team, the backstage team and the Front of House team.

The Theatre has also continued its long-established practice of noting in *Cues and News* the deaths of long-standing members of the Theatre community, acknowledging their special contributions. Thus in 2017, for example, there were tributes for:

- Ella Bambery, 'our longest serving life-member ... the sort of person every community theatre loves to have around'. Ella's last public role at WLT was the unveiling of the '70th anniversary wall' mural at the 2016 AGM (see page 276);
- Ray Hare 'a WLT legend ... a member for nearly 40 years', who was involved in nearly every aspect of the theatre, 'a fixture at our January working bees' who also 'delighted (and occasionally horrified) us with his Mystery Movie nights'; and
- Doug Lindsay 'a mainstay of the Company from the early fifties to the mid seventies - and (like Ray Hare) he did everything. 'He and his wife Joan were the heart and soul of WLT.'

In the Covid-induced lockdowns, the Theatre has done three major things.

Firstly, it has maintained its well-established tradition of remembering important milestones in the lives of its significant players, whether they, like Mary Little, have been around 'for ever' (in Mary's case since 1952 when she was just twenty-two years old), or have only 'recently' arrived such as current in-house reviewer Jennifer Paragreen (who started the job in 2012). Mary turned 90 on 3rd January 2020 and Jennifer celebrated her fiftieth wedding anniversary in February, both receiving extended coverage in *Cues and News*.

Secondly, through *Cues and News*, it has invited people to contribute memories of things past, some of which I have used in this work. All this to keep as many members as possible engaged with the Theatre, while there were no productions happening.

Thirdly, looking to the future, the Theatre has taken the opportunity presented by the lockdown to undertake major renovations to its physical environs. Peter Newling has provided the following extended description of the background to, and scope, of the proposed works:

Back in 2015, WLT knew it had an important milestone on the horizon – 2016 would mark the 70th anniversary of the company. As the Committee's minds started turning toward how best to celebrate that milestone, some other important issues started to emerge. If there's one downside to owning your own property, it's that no-one else will provide the maintenance for it! It was becoming clearer that the facility was starting to show its age. Some of the walls had started to show cracks, and there were ongoing concerns in relation to asbestos and mould – and we knew that these were going to be expensive problems to solve.

The choices available to the Committee at the time were (a) to spend a significant amount of money fixing up the existing buildings, or (b) to spend a significant amount of money creating new facilities.

It was also not lost on the Committee that 2018 would mark fifty years since the first show was put on at Albert Street. We knew that our current enviable position as a theatre company was due entirely to the long-sighted and courageous decisions that led to the acquisition of the Albert Street facility in 1967. We started to ask - what could we do now that would mean that those running WLT in fifty years' time would benefit most from our actions.

Discussions started around a ten-year redevelopment plan for the WLT site. Early in 2016, Committee member Tony Tartaro ran a series of consultations, involving people who used the space regularly, including Committee members, directors, actors, stage managers, designers and set constructors. The consultation focused on two questions:

1. What aspects of the WLT facilities must we preserve? (i.e. what really works well for the company? What makes WLT uniquely WLT?)

2. Think about the things that you experience as you work on productions or other aspects of the company's business. What changes/additions/improvements to the buildings would make that work easier and better?

The sessions generated a myriad of ideas. The main things that attendees agreed were:

- The courtyard is a defining element of what makes WLT special;
- Onsite costumes and props storage is important;
- Onsite storage for set construction stuff is important;
- The smallness of the theatre is actually a good thing;
- We need better dressing room and backstage facilities;
- It would be great to be able to go from stage left to stage right without having to go outside;
- It'd be great to expand the foyer space, and to have 'indoor toilets' and all-abilities access; and
- We need better air-conditioning/heating.

From there, a small Refurbishment Committee commenced the task of drawing up plans for potential capital improvements. WLT was fortunate to have an architect within its membership, in the form of Gaetano Santo, and a qualified builder - Bevan Uren - who both gave their time freely to advise on the process. A two phase, ten-year plan was hatched:

Phase 1 (two to three years) - expand the foyer area, introduce a new kiosk/kitchen area, move the bathrooms to the other side of the courtyard and make them accessible from the foyer, include all abilities bathrooms, move the dressing room to where the old bathrooms were, and replace the air-conditioning and heating.

Phase 2 (seven to ten years) - enclose the back courtyard, add a second storey around the current costume and props storage area, add in a greenroom space upstairs and vastly expand storage. This would involve adding reinforcing walls, to take the weight off the existing brickwork.

2017 - 2021

Convert the current furniture bay into a set construction workshop. The Committee approved the budget for phase one in 2019 - of roughly $240,000. A fundraising committee was established to help pay for it, and the Committee started looking at government support, available grants and donor options.

After considerable delay in getting the requisite permits, and the impact of COVID-19 restrictions, work on Phase 1 of the plan started in early 2021. Intensive effort by a range of people, spearheaded by Shirley Sydneham, resulted in the work being largely completed by the end of the year, with the renovations being formally 'opened' by Tim Watts, MP for Gellibrand, on 12 December 2021. The opening ceremony had about fifty WLT stalwarts in attendance, along with State MP for Williamstown Melissa Horne and the Mayor of Hobsons Bay Cr Peter Hemphill.

At the opening ceremony, the WLT Committee departed from the long-established practice of announcing new life members at the Theatre's AGM, and conferred life membership on Gaetano and Bevan in recognition of their work in directing the theatre refurbishment project.

In September 2021, the Committee decided it needed to do something at the end of the year which would show off the refurbishments, re-engage

Hon. Tim Watts MP, Member for Gellibrand, cutting the ribbon on the new facility, December 2021.

people with the theatre after a two-year absence, and bring in some much needed funds (two years without income was a very difficult challenge for the company).

The Theatre, in December 2021 staged a revue entitled *Something Old, Somewhere New* which reprised some of WLT's past performances, continued both musical numbers and comedy sketches, and featured a nightly raffle. The cast included ten WLT legends: Barbara Hughes, Brian Christopher, Ellis Ebell, Janet Provan, Keith Hutton, Adrienne Williamson, Bernadette Wheatley, Andrew Wild, Peter Newling and Robert Harsley.

The introduction to the second act of the revue incorporated a special reflection on the Coronavirus pandemic, written and performed by Maria Haughey. It has been reproduced here in a slightly edited form.

Once Upon A Pandemic - Maria Haughey

Once upon a pandemic there was no live theatre.
Imagine that. All across the world - in small towns, huge conurbations and by the sea - for days, then weeks, then months: there was no live theatre.
Lines remained unlearned. Rehearsals remained undone. Auditoriums remained unfilled. Sets remained.
Imagine that. For days, then weeks, then months.
Things remained.

Once upon a pandemic there was no set construction.
Imagine that. All across the world - in small sheds, large warehouses and by the sea - for days, then weeks, then months: there were no sets constructed.
Plywood remained unshaped. Flats remained unpainted. Nails remained unhammered. Thumbs remained unharmed.
Imagine that. For days, then weeks, then months.
Things remained.

Once upon a pandemic there were no opening nights.
Imagine that. All across the world - in vast venues, tiny theatres and by the sea - for days, then weeks, then months: there were no opening nights.
Sandwiches remained unmade. Conversations remained unhad. Glasses

remained unclinked. Reviews remained unwritten.
Imagine that. For days, then weeks, then months.
Things remained.

Once upon a pandemic there were no production runs.
Imagine that. All across the world – on Broadway, in the West End and by the sea – for days, then weeks, then months: there were no production runs. Tickets remained unsold. Doors remained unopened. Programs remained unpublished. Posters remained unhung.
Imagine that. For days, then weeks, then months.
Things remained.

Once upon a pandemic there were no closing nights.
Imagine that. All across the world – in village halls, in magical marquees and by the sea – for days, then weeks, then months: there were no closing nights. Flowers remained undelivered. Ovations remained unstood. Hugs remained unembraced. Memories remained unmemorised.
Imagine that. For days, then weeks, then months.
Things remained.

Once upon a pandemic things remained.
Imagine that. All across the world – in back kitchens, in spare bedrooms and by the sea – for days, then weeks, then months: things remained.
Meetings remained convened. Plans remained planned. Play bills remained developed. Dates remained agile. Hands remained washed. Songs remained sung.
Laughter remained loud. Lights remained on.
So that once upon a time when there would be no more pandemic things would remain.
Imagine that.

Chapter Nine

Looking Back on 75 Years

For much of the first seventy-five years of its existence, Williamstown Little Theatre has been considered as one of the better of Melbourne's non-professional theatre groups. It showed this promise in the 1950s by having several of its productions nominated by *The Listener-In* critics as amongst the best amateur productions of the year. Laurie Landray first explicitly stated the broader view in 1970, and it has been repeated regularly since by a diverse range of people reviewing for *Applause Applause*, *Curtain Up* and *Theatrecraft*. More recently, WLT's standing amongst its peers has been confirmed by its performance in the annual VDL Awards. In the first decade of these awards between 1997 and 2006, WLT received at least five award nominations in all but two of those years. In the subsequent decade WLT averaged seven award nominations per year.

This high standing amongst its peers has been reflected in WLT's ability to attract patrons. Except for five years after the advent of television in Melbourne in 1956, from the time it went 'all local' in 1952, the Theatre has managed to attract good audiences, even in its most troubled years during the mid 1970s. Barbara Hughes noted in 2002 the embarrassment of riches represented by the Theatre's growing subscriber base. Most years since 2007, 70% or more of tickets available for WLT's five annual productions have been sold before the first opening night of the year in mid-February. The most 'embarrassing' year was 2018 when the Ticket Secretary reported in January that only eighteen tickets were left for productions that year.

Clearly WLT has largely succeeded in presenting plays of sufficient interest and quality to satisfy its patrons, and to keep them coming back for more. For this credit is due to successive play selection committees and their chairpersons. The theatre has perhaps been fortunate that their patrons generally have had very broad tastes, evident from its earliest audience survey in 1951. But the theatre has also extended its patrons' interests by regularly staging premieres of plays. This practice started with the first play in its first All-local season in 1952, Joan Temple's D*eliver My Darling*, but has continued ever since - 'recent' examples being Hugh Whitemore's *Breaking the Code* in 1996, John Misto's *The Shoe-Horn Sonata* in 2003, and Lauren Gunderson's *Silent Sky* in 2018.

Another factor contributing to WLT's success is its willingness to be adventurous and innovative in its programming. The adventure came mostly from its choice of individual plays, some controversial because of their subject matter, others because of their casting challenges, *The Women* and *Lysistrata* with their all-female casts being the stand-out examples of the latter. Examples of innovation include the design of annual playbills with themes for example the staging of only Australian plays in 1988 and a Year of Comedy in 1994, and the planned staging of groups of plays over successive years: The Doll Trilogy over three years from 1999 to 2001, and then Neil Simon's semi-autobiographical trilogy from 2004 to 2006.

The theatre has always been able to attract competent directors for its plays. A consistent pattern, occurring perhaps as much by happenstance as by design, has been the use of a core group of directors over extended periods of time - Paul Hill, Alan Money and David Reid in the 1950s and 1960s, Vin Foster and Grahame Murphy 'forever', and Ian Walker, who directed ten plays between 1978 and 1986. More recently the Theatre benefited regularly from the directing talents of Laurie Gellon (from 1973 to 1996), Brian Crossley (from 1985 to 1999), Barbara Hughes (from 1997 to present), Bryan Thomas (from 1988 to 2007), Gordon Dunlop (from 1991 to 2001), Chris Baldock (from 2000 to 2016), Ellis Ebell (from 2005 to present) and Peter Newling (from 2006 to present).

Clearly, directors have been fortunate in being able to attract to WLT actors with the talent and capability to perform their allocated roles effectively. Over seventy-five years there have been so many of these that it is invidious to single out individuals in this conclusion. Suffice to say that the winners of the Cordell and Win Stewart Awards and (from 1968 to 1976) the Craven Award listed in Appendix 2 represent just a sample of the many good actors who have graced WLT's stages.

A feature of WLT's practice has been its willingness to try something different to promote appreciation of its work, and of theatre more broadly:

touring productions in the 1950s, a series of pantomimes authored by Gillian Wadds in the early 1960s, a children's theatre and a youth theatre in the early 1970s, the Instant Theatre Marathon in 1974, the development of Gillian's play *Who Cares* in the 1980s, Play Six from 2006 to 2012, and, most recently support for the work of Kerry Drumm starting with *Strawberry* in 2019.

In relation to the technical aspects of production, two areas in which WLT has long performed well are set design and costuming. As regards set design, two names stand out: Trevor McKay for his sets at the Mechanics' Institute, and David Dare for his on the much smaller stage of WLT's home since 1968. A team led by Nell Colville was responsible for many of the costumes at the Mechanics' Institute, but it was Pat Day from the 1970s who established WLT's enviable reputation for costumes, creating a major challenge for her successors now led by Tony Tataro and Barbara Hughes.

The Theatre has always been conscious of the need to build the capabilities of its members to undertake the on and off-stage tasks essential to its effective running. In the early days there was a focus on developing performers' knowledge and skills through play readings and produced play readings. Occasionally programs of lectures were held for the same purpose. Later, starting with Laurie Gellon's organising of a training program for backstage crew in 1978, the theatre has organised various specialised workshops, for example on lighting. This has continued through the last decade: in 2014 Alex Begg and Neil Williamson ran two 'technical workshops' on backstage work; in 2015 Tony Tartaro began conducting workshops on costuming. One result has been that from 2018 the theatre has been able to designate, at the start of the year, the production coordinators, stage managers and costume coordinators for all of the year's productions.

Less recognised perhaps as a factor in generating the spirited commitment required to successfully develop and maintain any organisation run largely by volunteers is the role of informal events. Again, WLT has a long tradition in this regard, starting with picnics annually in the 1950s, the occasional progressive dinner, theatre parties, meals at various restaurants around Melbourne, film nights and the regular gatherings at Ray and Roscmary Hare's residence in January.

As Brett Randall observed in 1946, WLT began its career with a significant advantage - access to the Williamstown Mechanics' Institute, with its large stage, ample storage and proscenium arch. This was not quite as good as having its own dedicated space - the Institute was managed by the Williamstown Council, and the Theatre had to share it with the Williamstown Light Opera Company. But since securing its own theatre in 1968, WLT has enjoyed the multiple benefits associated with that relatively unusual circumstance for amateur theatre companies.

Having your own theatre of course brings two specific challenges:
1. maintaining it, and
2. upgrading it as necessary to meet changing community standards.

Especially since 1980, the theatre has undertaken a continuous program of works to fulfil these requirements. Sometimes the jobs (e.g., repainting walls or replacing wearing carpets) can be seen as routine. Other tasks (e.g., upgrading of fire equipment) have been necessary to meet the requirements of regulators and/or insurers.

All such maintenance work has required significant effort by members. Sometimes the work has had to be done quickly to take advantage of unexpected opportunities - there were two to improve seating for patrons: in January 1981 (involving a remake of the auditorium) and again almost twenty years later when the seats installed in 1981 were replaced.

Other major works have included the construction of a new stage in 1998, the replacement of the stairs to the upstairs area (where the Theatre stores its collection of costumes and props) in 1989, and the air-conditioning/heating of the auditorium in 2002.

A more long-term problem began to emerge early in the 2000s when cracks began to appear in the walls of the building. Some of these were easily repaired but more significant work was required on the east wall of the foyer and the north wall of the furniture bay, requiring the expenditure of $47,000 over two years.

WLT has often found it difficult to attract sufficient members/volunteers to undertake the many 'non-glamorous' roles required to stage shows and ensure the theatre's continuing operation. Margaret Hetherington first drew attention to this problem in 1958, but it has recurred regularly since, for example in the mid 1970s. The Theatre hasn't often been IN CRISIS as Judi Clark headlined her plea for more backstage crew, set designers and set construction people in *Cues and News* in February 1990, but finding set builders remained difficult for much of the next two decades. Sometimes there were wider shortages: hence Barbara Hughes confessing in her report to the 2003 AGM to feeling 'a bit like a cracked record talking about a lack of production personnel'.

WLT has, almost since its beginning, been fairly systematic in its approach to management. Currently, at their first meeting of the year, committee members take responsibility for overseeing sixteen separate aspects of the theatre's operations. In many ways, however, this practice can be traced back to the system set up after the move into 'The Bakery' in 1968, itself a refinement of the first formal constitution adopted in 1952 and revised in 1961.

The Theatre has been particularly effective in its financial management, perhaps because many of its treasurers have served for long, often continuous, periods. The stand-out case is current treasurer Brian Christopher who has occupied the position for more than twenty-five years, but Amy Grove-Rogers did the job continuously for ten years up to 1990-1991, and before that Ivor Porter served for a total of sixteen years over four terms. Careful husbanding of resources has characterised the theatre from the beginning. This was particularly important in the period leading up to the purchase of the theatre in 1973, and more recently as the theatre has dealt with the range of problems caused by the aging of 2 Albert Street.

There has been, of course, a lot of learning by doing. Two elements of 'best theatre practice' - a subscription scheme and an audience survey - were introduced as early as 1951, but formal production meetings were not introduced until 1963, and, though suggested by Margaret Hetherington in 1958, budgeting for individual productions did not become common until the 1980s.

As it has done in the past, WLT has turned the challenge arising from an unexpected external threat - in this case the advent of the coronavirus in Victoria in February 2020 - into an opportunity, by undertaking a major refurbishment of its premises (almost everything except the actual theatre itself). The successful completion late in 2021 of phase one of the ten-year plan hatched in 2016 has laid the foundations for WLT to continue being one of Melbourne's leading amateur theatres, in a setting which is both more functional and comfortable for actors and crew, and more comfortable for patrons who no longer have to brave the elements to go to the loo!

Looking Back

Not only has Williamstown Little Theatre looked after its patrons' comfort inside and outside the theatre for seventy-five years, but it has also trained up generations of theatre practitioners, while serving up sustenance for the minds and hearts and theatrical appetites of its loyal followers from near and far.

APENDICES

Appendix 1:	Productions of Williamstown Little Theatre	297
Appendix 2a	Winners of the Cordell Award	310
Appendix 2b	Winners of the Win Stewart Award	314
Appendix 2c	Winners of the Craven Award	317
Appendix 3	Winners of the Grahame Murphy Award for Excellence	321
Appendix 4	Williamstown Little Theatre and the Victorian Drama League Awards	323
Appendix 5	Presidents, Secretaries and Treasurers of Williamstown Little Theatre	331
Appendix 6	Life Members Williamstown Little Theatre	335

Appendix 1:

Productions of Williamstown Little Theatre 1948-2022

Set out below is a complete list of the productions, with relevant directors, staged by Williamstown Little Theatre in the period between November 1948, when it staged its first production, and December 2021. *One-act plays are denoted by an* *
(Before 1948 WLT imported productions, a practice which continued until 1951).

Year	Production	Director
1948	*The Man of Destiny*	Alf Davidson
1949	*People at Sea*	Alf Davidson
	And No Birds Sing	Alf Davidson and Alec Doig
1950	*Poison Pen*	Alf Davidson
	Lovely To Look At	Alf Davidson
	A Murder Has Been Arranged	Alec Doig
1951	*This Happy Breed*	Alec Doig
	The Chiltern Hundreds	Alec Doig
	Mystery at Greenfingers	Neville Thurgood
1952	*Deliver My Darling*	Neville Thurgood
	Blithe Spirit	Ron Little
	A Touch of Silk	Ron Little
	Arms and the Man	Paul Hill
1953	*Young Mrs. Barrington*	Paul Hill
	Duet for Two Hands	Paul Hill
	Mountain Air	Alan Money
	Bonaventure	Alan Money

Appendix 1: Productions 1948-2021

Year	Production	Director
1954	*French for Love*	J. Tyrrell
	Ladies in Retirement	Ron Little
	Without the Prince	Paul Hill
	Still Life & Red Peppers	Alan Money
	Remember Caesar	Paul Hill
1955	*Lace on Her Petticoat*	Paul Hill
	Our Town Alan Money	Alan Money
	You Can't Take it With You Granite	Alan Money
		Paul Hill
1956	*Pygmalion*	Alan Money
	Night Must Fall	Alex Munro
	Widows are Dangerous	Veranne Irving
	Pacific Paradise	David Reid
1957	*Murder at the Vicarage*	David Reid
	Major Barbara	Alan Money
	Orchard Walls	Paul Hill
	My Three Angels	Victor Haywood
1958	*Bell Book and Candle*	Margaret Hetherington
	Small Hotel	David Reid
	The Heiress	Margaret Hetherington
	Book of the Month	David Reid
1959	*Suspect Neville Thurgood*	Neville Thurgood
	Goodness How Sad	Neville Thurgood
	The Women	David Reid
	The Importance of Being Earnest	Lorna Kirwood-Jones
1960	*Trespass*	Vin Foster
	The Match-Maker	Lorna Kirwood-Jones
	Johnny Belinda	Vin Foster
	The Bride and the Bachelor	David Reid

Appendix 1: Productions 1948-2021

Year	Production	Director
1961	Rape of the Belt Separate Tables Summer of the Seventeenth Doll Only an Orphan Girl	Margaret Hetherington Mavis Calder Gwladys Winfield Vin Foster
1962	See How They Run Multi-coloured Umbrella She Stoops to Conquer Harvey	Paul Hill Gwladys Winfield Mavis Calder David Reid
1963	Dracula Ring Round the Moon The Same Sky The Ballad of Angel's Alley	Paul Hill Lorna Kirwood-Jones Ron Little Vin Foster
1964	Dear Charles The Man The Chalk Garden The Boyfriend	Paul Hill Vin Foster Gwladys Winfield Grahame Murphy
1965	Hobson's Choice A Dead Secret Thieves' Carnival	Paul Hill Grahame Murphy Gillian Wadds
1966	The Sleeping Prince Sailor Beware The Glass Menagerie The Price of Perfection* Auto-Da-Fe* Collect Your Hand Baggage*	Grahame Murphy Vin Foster Gillian Wadds Gillian Wadds Grahame Murphy Grahame Murphy
1967	The Little Hut The Happy Journey Something Unspoken The Mother	Frank Wadds Ron Delaney Frank Wadds Gillian Wadds

299

Appendix 1: Productions 1948-2021

Year	Production	Director
1968	*Barefoot in the Park*	Vin Foster
	A Loss of Roses	Gillian Wadds
	The Miracle Worker	Ron Delaney
	The Miser	Grahame Murphy
	A Taste of Honey	Frank Wadds
	Make Me an Offer	Grahame Murphy
1969	*Come Blow Your Horn*	Vin Foster
	Gaslight	Vin Foster
	Diary of Anne Frank	David Connor
	The Recruiting Officer	Eric Donnison
	Rattle of A Simple Man	Loris Blake
	Odd Man In	Grahame Murphy
1970	*White Liars/Black Comedy*	Vin Foster
	Woman in a Dressing Gown	Loris Blake
	The Duenna	Grahame Murphy
	Five Finger Exercise	Bob Karl
	Semi-Detached	Maggie McInnes
1971	*The Grass is Greener*	Grahame Murphy
	Summer and Smoke	Bob Karl
	The Knack	Frank Wadds
	Wait Until Dark	Loris Blake
	The Happiest Days of Your Life	Rex Callinan
1972	*The Odd Couple*	Loris Blake
	The Shifting Heart	Doug Lindsay
	The Lion in Winter	Grahame Murphy
	The Prime of Miss Jean Brodie	Vin Foster
	Relatively Speaking	Loris Blake

Appendix 1: Productions 1948-2021

Year	Production	Director
1973	Goodnight Mrs Puffin Eden House Juno and the PaycockLes Terrill Cages	Loris Blake Lorna Kirwood-Jones Les Terrill Laurie Gellon
1974	What the Butler Saw A Funny Thing Happened on the Way to the Forum Enemy The Gazebo	Loris Blake Grahame Murphy Val Lehmann Gwladys Winfield
1975	Charley's Aunt A Man for All Seasons The Alchemist* Impromptu* Mutatis Mutandis* Lysistrata A Thousand Clowns	Kevin Good Grahame Murphy Doug Lindsay Peter Cheaseley Laurie Gellon Gillian Wadds Frank Wadds
1976	Ten Little Niggers The Slaughter of Saint Teresa's Day Hotel Paradiso A Bunch of Ratbags Butterflies are Free	Lorna Kirwood-Jones Doug Lindsay Ted Smeed Vin Foster Ewan Crockett

1977	Loot
	Look After Lulu
	The Philanthropist
	Ritual for Dolls*
	
	Say Who You Are
		Val Lehmann
		Ted Smeed
		Gillian Wadds
		Ian Jones and
		    Laurie Gellon
		Ewan Crockett and
		    Doug Lindsay

Appendix 1: Productions 1948-2021

Year	Production	Director
1978	*Goody Gumdrops*	Peter Black
	Rebecca	Peter Cheaseley
	The Gingerbread Lady	Loris Blake
	The Last of the Knucklemen	Ian Walker
	Simon and Laura	Laurie Gellon
	A Flea in Her Ear	Grahame Murphy
1979	*Not Now Darling*	Bob Karl
	Trap for a Lonely Man	Loris Blake
	Wind in the Branches of Sassafras	David Dare
	The Anniversary	Vin Foster
	Hay Fever	Gillian Wadds
1980	*The Ballad of Angel's Alley*	Grahame Murphy
	Don's Party	Ian Walker
	The Ghost Train	Vin Foster
	Journey's End	Laurie Gellon
	Not Even a Mouse	Laurie Gellon
1981	*Equus*	Grahame Murphy
	Don't Just Lie There, Say Something	Ron Little
	The Killing of Sister George	Ian Walker
	President Wilson in Paris	Ian Walker
	Only an Orphan Girl	David Dare
1982	*Travelling North*	Ian Walker
	The Second Mrs. Tanqueray	Brian Crossley
	King Lear	Ian Walker
	Dusa, Fish, Stas and Vi	Laurie Gellon
	It's a 2'6" Above the Ground World	Vin Foster

Appendix 1: Productions 1948-2021

Year	Production	Director
1983	In For The Kill The Removalists Flexitime A Boy for Me, A Girl for You Celebration	Richard Keown Ian Walker Alan Lee Laurie Gellon Judith Muir
1984	A Night in the Arms of Raelene Antigone The Elephant Man Jam Tomorrow Move Over Mrs. Markham	Ian Walker Vin Foster Grahame Murphy Laurie Gellon Amy Grove-Rogers
1985	See How They Run Gulls Present Laughter Lamb of God On Our Selection	David Ashton Ian Walker Brian Crossley Laurie Gellon Chris Waters
1986	Absurd Person Singular Another Country On Golden Pond Stevie The Bandwagon	Ian Walker Vin Foster Grahame Murphy Judith Muir Amy Grove-Rogers
1987	84 Charing Cross Road Filumena The Dresser Murder by Natural Causes Bedroom Farce	Vin Foster Doug Bennett Grahame Murphy Brian Crossley Amy Grove-Rogers
1988	In Duty Bound On the Wallaby The Shifting Heart A Pair of Claws The Club	Les Terrill Brian Crossley Bryan Thomas Amy Grove-Rogers Ray Hare

Appendix 1: Productions 1948-2021

Year	Production	Director
1989	*I'll Be Back Before Midnight* *The Winslow Boy* *The Happy Haven* *Pack of Lies* *Then Unvarnished Truth*	Henry Ismailiw Brian Crossley Laurie Gellon Les Terrill Judi Clark
1990	*Morning Sacrifice* *Noel Coward in Two Keys* *Whose Life is it Anyway?* *Who Cares?* *A Lovely Sunday for Creve Coeur*	David Dare Brian Crossley Les Terrill Gillian Wadds Wayne Pearn
1991	*Wings* *Uncle Vanya* *Bazaar and Rummage* *Amongst Barbarians* *Farewell Brisbane Ladies*	Ron Little Gordon Dunlop Wayne Pearn Grahame Murphy David Dare
1992	*Master Class* *Fallen Angels* *The Rivals* *Serious Money* *Table Manners*	Grahame Murphy Brian Crossley Gordon Dunlop Wayne Pearn Bryan Thomas
1993	*Mass Appeal* *Relative Values* *Mrs. Klein* *True West* *Sailor Beware*	Les Terrill Brian Crossley Gordon Dunlop Richard Chevalier Judi Clark

Appendix 1: Productions 1948-2021

Year	Production	Director
1994	*Same Time Next Year* *An Ideal Husband* *On Top of the World* *Money and Friends* *Season's Greetings*	Bryan Thomas Brian Crossley Gordon Dunlop Ray Hare Gordon Dunlop
1995	*Coralie Lansdowne Says No* *Waiting in the Wings* *Groping for Words* *Oleanna* *Cosi*	Gordon Dunlop Brian Crossley Judi Clark David Dare Maurie Johns
1996	*Death and the Maiden* *Breaking the Code* *Hay Fever* *Wallflowering* *Brilliant Lies*	Grahame Murphy Laurie Gellon Brian Crossley Bruce Wapshot David Dare
1997	*Lost in Yonkers* *A Woman of No Importance* *The Road to Mecca* *Sufficient Carbohydrate* *Something's Afoot*	Bryan Thomas Brian Crossley Gordon Dunlop Damien Coffey Barbara Hughes
1998	*Deathtrap* *The Sisters Rosenweig* *Private Lives* *Good Works* *Steaming*	Mel De Bono Brian Crossley Mark Robins David Dare Doug Bennett
1999	*Kid Stakes* *Lady Windermere's Fan* *Speaking in Tongues* *The John Wayne Principle* *Hysteria*	Bryan Thomas Brian Crossley Paul King David Dare Damien Coffey

Appendix 1: Productions 1948-2021

Year	Production	Director
2000	Other Times	Bryan Thomas
	Terra Nova	Chris Baldock
	Bruce Wapshot	Bruce Wapshot
	The Birthday Party	Paul King
	The Venetian Twins	Barbara Hughes
2001	Summer of the Seventeenth Doll	Bryan Thomas
	Amy's View	Gordon Dunlop
	Chilling and Killing My Annabel Lee	Paul King
	Master Class	Chris Baldock
	Born Yesterday	Ray Hare
2002	W;t	Liz Lipski
	Alarms and Excursions	Damien Coffey
	Blood Brothers	Chris Baldock
	Hate	Paul King
	Tons of Money	Maggie McInnes
2003	Quartet	Bryan Thomas
	The Shoe-Horn Sonata	Chris Baldock
	Silly Cow	Jill Clague
	Buried Alive	Paul King
	Lucky Stiff	Barbara Hughes
2004	Brighton Beach Memoirs	Bryan Thomas
	Three Days of Rain	Chris Baldock
	How the Other Half Loves	Shirley Sydenham
	Macbeth	Shannon Woollard
	Daisy Pulls it Off	Jill Clague

Appendix 1: Productions 1948-2021

Year	Production	Director
2005	Biloxi Blues Scenes from a Separation The Glass Menagerie Dealer's Choice I Love You, You're Perfect, Now Change	Bryan Thomas Shirley Sydenham Ellis Ebell Chris Baldock Janet Provan
2006	A Happy and Holy Occasion Broadway Bound Old Wicked Songs Copenhagen 'Allo 'Allo	Vicki Smith Bryan Thomas Chris Baldock Paul King Peter Newling
2007	Steel MagnoliasBryan Thomas Beyond Therapy Honour Gross Indecency Bullshot Crummond	Bryan Thomas Brett Turner Ellis Ebell Peter Newling Janet Provan
2008	The Drawer Boy Another Antigone The Cemetery Club Dancing at Lughnasa Honk!	Chris Baldock Juan Modinger Bernadette Wheateley Ellis Ebell Barbara Hughes
2009	Life x 3 A Few Good Men Rough Crossing Kindertransport Ruthless	David Dare Shane Ryan Peter Newling Chris Baldock Janet Provan
2010	Role Play Skylight Glorious Hotel Sorrento Habeas Corpus	Gaetano Santo Bernadette Wheatley Doug Bennett Ellis Ebell Lois Collinder

Appendix 1: Productions 1948-2021

Year	Production	Director
2011	*Two Weeks with the Queen*	Shirley Sydenham and Bob Harsley
	Not About Heroes	Shane Ryan
	Come Back to the Five and Dime Jimmy Dean, Jimmy Dean	Peter Newling
	The History Boys	Bruce Akers
	Play it Again Sam	Gaetano Santo
2012	*Moonlight and Magnolias*	Alan Burrows
	Compleat Female Stage Beauty	Chris Baldock
	God of Carnage	Bruce Akers
	Doubt, A Parable	Ellis Ebell
	The Dixie Swim Club	Lois Collinder
2013	*Talking Heads*	Shirley Sydenham
	33 Variations	Chris Baldock
	The Beauty Queen of Lehane	Ellis Ebell
	Morning Departure	Gaetano Santo
	A Funny Thing Happened on the Way to the Forum	Barbara Hughes
2014	*Almost Maine*	Kris Weber
	Proof	Jeff Saliba
	Six Dancing Lessons in Six Weeks	Alan Burrows
	Farragut North	Peter Newling
	The Kitchen Sink	Lois Collinder
2015	*Other Place*	Kris Weber
	Visiting Mr Green	Brett Turner
	Time Stands Still	Ellis Ebell
	Buffalo Gal	George Werther
	Over the River and Through the Woods	Helen Ellis

Appendix 1: Productions 1948-2021

Year	Production	Director
2016	Sweet Road The Nance If I Should Die Before I Wake Sitting Pretty London Suite	Peter Newling Chris Baldock Ellis Ebell Robert Harsley Gaetano Santo
2017	Bad Jews When I Was Five Vincent in Brixton The Seafarer The 39 Steps	Tess Maurice Ryan Brett Turner Shirley Sydenham Bruce Akers Barbara Hughes
2018	Mr Bailey's Minder Stones in his Pockets Under Milk Wood Silent Sky The Complete Works of William Shakespeare (Abridged)	Deborah Fabbro Travis Handcock Sandy Green Ellis Ebell Peter Newling
2019	Body Awareness The Exorcism A Man of No Importance Strawberry Black Comedy/The Real Inspector Hound	Kris Weber Les Hart Barbara Hughes Shirley Sydenham Gaetano Santo
2020	The Last Romance No further productions as Theatre closed due to Covid-19	The Last Romance
2021	No productions as Theatre closed due to Covid-19	

309

Appendix 2a: Cordell Award

The Cordell Award was established by the Theatre Board of Directors late in 1961 as a memorial to Ted and Alice Cordell. Ted had died suddenly from a heart attack whilst jogging in September 1961, only thirteen months after the death of Alice from cancer in August 1960. The award commemorates their work in the foundation and development of the Theatre and is awarded annually to the actor who is deemed to have given the best performance in a lead role in any of Willamstown's productions during the year.

Best Performance in a Lead Role

Year	Award Winner	Role and Play
1962	Gary Metcalf	Ben Donnelly in *The Multi-Coloured Umbrella*
1963	Lorraine West	Esther Brodsky in *The Same Sky*
1964	Lorraine West	Madame De in *Madame De*
1965	Vin Foster	Hobson in *Hobson's Choice*
1966	Ngaire McCutcheon	Emma Hornet in *Sailor Beware*
1967	Gillian Wadds	Cordelia in *Something Unspoken*
1968	Helen Koefedthe Park	Corrie in *Barefoot in the Park*
1969	Les Terrill	Percy in *Rattle of a Simple Man*
1970	June Lownds	Louise in *Five Finger Exercise*
1971	Lorraine West	Susie in *Wait Until Dark*
1972	June Lownds	Jean Brodie in *The Prime of Miss Jean Brodie*
1973	Steven Moore	The Man and John in *Cages*

Appendix 2a: Winners of the Cordell Award

Year	Award Winner	Role and Play
1974	David Bradshaw	Ken in *Enemy*
1975	Les Terrill	Sir Thomas More in *A Man for All Seasons*
1976	Peter Cheaseley	Don Baker in *Butterflies are Free*
1977	Bill Martin	Philip in *The Philanthropist*
1978	Lorraine West	Evy Mears in *The Gingerbread Lady*
1979	Lorraine West	Judith Bliss in *Hay Fever*
1980	Les Terrill	Osborne in *Journey's End*
1981	Carmel Behan	Edith Wilson in *President Wilson in Paris*
1982	Marian Sinclair	Paula Tanqueray in *The Second Mrs Tanqueray*
1983	Norah Toohey	Janet in *A Boy for Me, A Girl for You*
1984	Neil Modra	John Merrick in *The Elephant Man*
1985	Mary Little	Ruth in *Lamb of God*
1986	David Trendennick John Chilton	Judd in *Another Country* Guy Bennet in *Another Country*
1987	Marian Sinclair	Filumena in *Filumena*
1988	Shirley Cattunar	Sylvia Swift in *A Pair of Claws*
1989	Fransina Voorpostel	Catherine Winslow in *The Winslow Boy*
1990	Matthew McConnon	Brian in *Who Cares?*
1991	Laurence Mooney Jason Hopkins-Gamble	Brian in *Amongst Barbarians* Ralph in *Amongst Barbarians*

Appendix 2a: Winners of the Cordell Award

Year	Award Winner	Role and Play
1992	Bryan Thomas	Stalin in *Masterclass*
1993	Louise Whiteman	Melanie Klein in *Mrs Klein*
1994	Christine Andrew	Doris in *Same Time Next Year*
1995	Paula McDonald	Coralie in *Coralie Lansdowne Says No*
1996	Ian Grealy	Alan Turing in *Breaking the Code*
1997	Paula McDonald	Elsa Barlow in *The Road to Mecca*
1998	Kyria	Josie in *Steaming*
1999	Moira Smith	Emma Leech in *Kid Stakes*
2000	Michael Bingham	Torino/Laneto in *The Venetian Twins*
2001	Paula McDonald	Maria Callas in *Master Class*
2002	Jane Lindill	Vivian Bearing in *W;t*
2003	Ellis Ebell	Wilfred Bond in Quartet
2004	Kate Bowers Anthony Wright	Nan/Lina in *Three Days of Rain* Pip/Theo in *Three Days of Rain*
2005	Ellis Ebell	Stephen in *Dealer's Choice*
2006	Ellis Ebell	Professor Joseph Markham in *Old Wicked Songs*
2007	Nicola Wright	Shelby in *Steel Magnolias*
2008	Bruce Akers	Angus in *The Drawer Boy*
2009	Stephen Shrinkfield	Daniel O'Keefe in *A Few Good Men*
2010	Patricia McCracken	Florence Foster Jenkins in *Glorious*
2011	Andrew Mayes	Wilfred Owen in *Not About Heroes*

Appendix 2a: Winners of the Cordell Award

Year	Award Winner	Role and Play
2012	Scott Middleton	Edward Kynaston in *Compleat Female Stage Beauty*
2013	Julie Arnold	Dr Katherine Brandt in *33 Variations*
2014	Tim Constantine	Stephen Bellamy in *Farragut North*
2015	Rowan Howard	Nick in *Over the Rainbow and Through the Woods*
2016	Ziv Gordon	Ned in *The Nance*
2017	Mark Briggs	Richard Hannay in *The Thirty-Nine Steps*
2018	Liam O'Kane	Liam in *The Complete Works of William Shakespeare*
2019	Tim Murphy	Alfie Byrne in *A Man of No Importance*
2020	Not Awarded	Theatre closed due to Covid-19
2021	Not Awarded	Theatre closed due to Covid-19

Appendix 2b: Win Stewart Award

The Win Stewart Award was established in 1979 in memory of Win Stewart who had several stints as Theatre Secretary from 1947 until 1958.

It originally took the form of a scholarship to the Williamstown Youth Theatre but, following the demise of Youth Theatre in 1981, the award was given to the person who, in the opinion of the adjudicators, had given the best performance in a supporting role in any of the Theatre's productions each year.

Scholarship to Williamstown Youth Theatre

1979   Russell Collier
1980   Jacqui Tamlyn

Best Performance in a Supporting Role

Year	Award Winner	Role and Play
1982	Jim Ewing	Earl of Kent in *King Lear*
1983	Judi Clark	Mary Beckett in *Celebration*
1984	Sarah Ryan	Julia Colvin in *Jam Tomorrow*
1985	Derek Richards	Rev. Arthur Humphrey in *See How They Run*
1986	Norah Toohey	The Lion Aunt in *Stevie*
1987	Barbara Hughes	Rosalie in *Filumena*
1988	Anna Pianezze Barbara Hughes	Christine in *In Duty Bound* Various Roles in *On the Wallaby*
1989	Cae Rees	Julie Jackson in *A Pack of Lies*

Appendix 2b: Winners of the Win Stewart Award

Year	Award Winner	Role and Play
1990	Mary Little	Miss Gluck in *A Lovely Sunday for Croeve Coeur*
1991	Bryan Thomas Kate Llewellyn Katie Wright	`The Family´ in *Amongst Barbarians*
1992	Mary Little	Mrs.Malaprop in *The Rivals*
1993	Ellis Ebell	Crestwell in *Relative Values*
1994	Mary Little	Baby in *On Top of the World*
1995	Lena Fiszman	Cherry in *Cosi*
1996	Bryan Thomas	Brian in *Brilliant Lies*
1997	Judi Clark	Lady Manley-Prowse in *Something's Afoot*
1998	Oleh Kaowalyk	Mervyn Kant in *The Sisters Rosensweig*
1999	Ray Hare	Dr Yahuda in *Hysteria*
2000	Narelle Gillies Shannon Woolard	Beatrice in *The Venetian Twins* Florindo in *The Venetian Twins*
2001	Brian Christopher	Arthur Kitty in *Chilling and Killing my Annabel Lee*
2002	Judy Johnson	E.M. Ashford in *W;t*
2003	Fiona Hanrahan Dean Rogers	Rita La Porta in *Lucky Stiff* Various Roles in *Lucky Stiff*
2004	Paul Farrell Beth Klein	Jack Jerome in *Brighton Beach Memoirs* Sybil Burlington in *Daisy Pulls it Off*
2005	Peter Prenga	Ash in *Dealer's Choice*
2006	Janine Evans	Helga Gerhardt in *'Allo 'Allo*

Appendix 2b: Winners of the Win Stewart Award

Year	Award Winner	Role and Play
2007	Brian Christopher	Marquis of Queensberry in *Gross Indecency*
	Tim Constantine	Lord Alfred Douglas in *Gross Indecency*
2008	Melanie Rowe	Rose in Dancing at *Lughnasa*
	Lee Threadgold	Drake/Greylag in *Honk*
2009	Ian Grealy	Dvornichek in *Rough Crossing*
2010	Janine Evans	Arabella in *Role Play*
	Judi Clark	Mrs Swabb in *Habeas Corpus*
2011	Katherine Hubbard	Mona in *Come Back to the Five and Dime, Jimmy Dean, Jimmy Dean*
	Chris Perkins	Juanita in *Come Back to the Five and Dime, Jimmy Dean, Jimmy Dean*
2012	Emily Davison	Sister James in *Doubt: A Parable*
2013	Tim Barsby	Hysterium in *A Funny Thing Happened on the Way to the Forum*
2014	Janis Coffey	Multiple Roles in *Almost Maine*
2015	Stephanie Genilli	Mandy in *Time Stands Still*
2016	Cat Jardine	Sylvie in *The Nance*
2017	Liam O'Kane	Clown in *The 39 Step*
2018	Paula McDonald	Williamina Fleming in *Silent Sky*
2019	Venetia Macken	Margaret in *The Exorcism*
2020	Not Awarded	Theatre closed due to Covid-19
2021	Not Awarded	Theatre closed due to Covid-19

Appendix 2c: Craven Award

After the death of her husband Tom who was President on three occasions in the 1950s, Millie Craven endowed a perpetual trophy in his memory. Initially this was awarded to the most improved performer, but in 1973 was altered to be awarded to the best performance of the year in a supporting role. In 1977, the basis of the award was changed again. Since then, it has been awarded to the production considered by the judges to be the best overall in any year.

Most Improved Performer

1968	Ellis Ebell	La Fleche in *The Miser*
1969	Glenys Clodd	Lucy in *The Recruiting Officer*
1970	Christine Bambery	Pamela in *Five Finger Exercise*
1971	Stephen Moore	Tom in *The Knack.*
1972	Christine Saunders	Sandy in *The Prime of Miss Jean Brodie*

Best Performance in a Supporting Role

1973	Jim Shaw	Joxer in *Juno and the Paycock*
1974	Michael Walker	Hysterium in *A Funny Thing Happened on the way to the Forum*
1975	Nancy Gantner	Sandra in *One Thousand Clowns*
1976	Lyndall Heiner	Thelma Maguire in *The Slaughter of St Teresa's Day*

Appendix 2c: Winners of the Craven Award

Best Production

Year	Production	Director
1977	*The Philanthropist*	Gillian Wadds
1978	*A Flea in Her Ear*	Grahame Murphy
1979	*Hay Fever*	Gillian Wadds
1980	*Journey's End*	Laurie Gellon
1981	*President Wilson in Paris*	Ian Walker
1982	*Dusa, Fish, Stas and Vi*	Laurie Gellon
1983	*A Boy for You, A Girl for Me*	Laurie Gellon
1988	*Elephant Man*	Grahame Murphy
1985	*Gulls*	Ian Walker
1986	*Another Country*	Vin Foster
1987	*The Dresser*	Grahame Murphy
1988	*On the Wallaby*	Brian Crossley
1989	*The Winslow Boy*	Brian Crossley
1990	*A Lovely Sunday for Creve Coeur*	Wayne Pearn
1991	*Amongst Barbarians*	Grahame Murphy
1992	*Master Class*	Grahame Murphy
1993	*Mrs Klein*	Gordon Dunlop
1994	*An Ideal Husband*	Brian Crossley
1995	*Waiting in the Wings*	Brian Crossley
1996	*Death and the Maiden*	Grahame Murphy
1997	*The Road to Mecca*	Gordon Dunlop

Appendix 2c: Winners of the Craven Award

Year	Production	Director
1998	*Steaming*	Doug Bennett
1999	*Speaking in Tongues*	Paul King
2000	*The Venetian Twins*	Barbara Hughes; Musical Direction by Chris Sluice
2001	*Master Class*	Chris Baldock
2002	*W;t*	Liz Lipski
2003	*Lucky Stiff*	Barbara Hughes; Musical Direction by Janet Provan
2004	*Three Days of Rain*	Chris Baldock
2005	*The Glass Menagerie*	Ellis Ebell
2006	*Old Wicked Songs*	Chris Baldock
2007	*Gross Indecency: The Three Trials of Oscar Wilde*	Peter Newling
2008	*The Drawer Boy*	Chris Baldock
2009	*A Few Good Men*	Shane Ryan
2010	*Glorious*	Doug Bennett
2011	*Not About Heroes*	Shane Ryan
2012	*Compleat Female Stage Beauty*	Chris Baldock
2013	*A Funny Thing Happened on The Way to the Forum*	Barbara Hughes; Musical Direction by Janet Provan
2014	*Farragut North*	Peter Newling
2015	*Over the River and Through the Woods*	Helen Ellis
2016	*The Nance*	Chris Baldock

Appendix 2c: Winners of the Craven Award

Year	Production	Director
2017	*The Thirty-Nine Steps*	Barbara Hughes
2018	*Under Milk Wood*	Sandy Green
2019	*Black Comedy and The Real Inspector Hound*	Gaetano Santo
2020	*Not Awarded*	Theatre Closed due to Covid-19
2021	*Not Awarded*	Theatre Closed due to Covid-19

Appendix 3: Grahame Murphy Award for Excellence

Year	Recipient	For:
2009	Janine Evans	Outstanding poster designs
2010	Neil Williamson	Superb sound designs over a number of years
2011	Roger Forsey	Technical innovations and improvements at WLT in 2011
2012	Neil Williamson	Excellence in design and execution of sound
2013	Alex Begg	For a wide range of contributions as Stage Manager, sound/light operator, caterer, bump ins and bump outs.
2014	Brian Christopher	20 years as treasurer ensuring WLT's ongoing sound financial status
2015	Graeme Cope	Many years of outstanding service (e.g. as Chair of the Play Selection Committee and as Secretary)
2016	Ray Hare	His huge contribution to WLT since 1978 as actor, director, former President and entertainment director of our mystery film nights
2017	David Dare	35 years as ticket secretary and outstanding contribution to WLT's high production standard
2018	Frank Page	For his development of an electronic version of *Cues and News*, and its posting by 15th of each month

Appendix 3: Winners Grahame Murphy Award for Excellence

Year	Recipient	For:
2019	Damien Coffey	For his work as Play Selection Committee coordinator 'he revolutionised the way it operates'
2020	Not Awarded	Theatre Closed due to Covid-19
2021	Not Awarded	Theatre Closed due to Covid-19

Appendix 4: WLT & the Victorian Drama League Awards

Williamstown Little Theatre has been an active member of the Victorian Drama League (VDL) since its formation in 1952. Since 1997, the VDL has sponsored an annual awards program where member companies nominate one production from their annual playbill[1] to be assessed by adjudicators appointed by the VDL. Set out below is a list of WLT's entries into the awards since 1997, and the outcomes (nominations and awards received - **winners being denoted by ***)[2]

1997 - *The Road to Mecca* (Drama) & *A Woman Of No Importance* (Comedy)

In 1997, the first year of the awards, no nominations were published. So only the Award recipients are listed here:

Best Set: *The Road To Mecca* * (Gold Award)
Best Costumes: *The Road To Mecca* * (Silver Award)
Best Costumes: *A Woman Of No Importance* * (Gold Award)
Best Lighting: *The Road To Mecca* * (Silver Award)
Best Supporting Actress: Marion Sinclair for *A Woman Of No Importance* * (Silver Award)
Best Actress: Paula McDonald and Mary Little for *The Road To Mecca* * (Gold Award)
Best Director: Gordon Dunlop for *The Road To Mecca* * (Gold Award)

---

1   The VDL initially allowed companies to nominate more than one production for assessment, (in 1998 twenty-three companies nominated thirty-six plays) but the workload proved too difficult for the VDL's small staff to manage, so that from 2001 companies were allowed to nominate only one production each year. See my *The Victorian Drama League 1952-2002*, pp.93-95.

2   The list is derived from that available on the WLT website, except that I have reordered that list to start in 1997 and conclude in 2018.

Appendix 4: Victorian Drama League Awards

Best Production: T*he Road To Mecca* * (Gold Award)
Best Costumes: *A Woman Of No Importance* * (Gold Award)
Best Lighting: *The Road To Mecca* * (Silver Award)

1998 - Good Works (Drama) & The Sisters Rosenweig (Comedy)

Best Costumes: *The Sisters Rosenweig*

1999 - *Speaking In Tongues*(Drama) & *Lady Windermere's Fan* (Comedy)

Best Sound: *Speaking In Tongues*
Best Lighting: *Speaking In Tongues*
Best Costumes: *Lady Windermere's Fan* * (Silver Award)
Best Supporting Actress: Carmel Behan for *Lady Windermere's Fan* * (Gold Award)
Best Actor: Paul Farrell for *Speaking In Tongues*
Best Actor: Brian Christopher for *Speaking In Tongues*
Best Director: Paul King for *Speaking In Tongues* * (Gold Award)
Best Production: *Speaking In Tongues* * (Gold Award)
Also Judge's Award for continuing to present contemporary Australian works.

2000 - *Terra Nova*

Best Sound in a Comedy or Drama
Best Lighting in a Comedy or Drama
Best Costumes in a Comedy or Drama
Best Supporting Actor in a Comedy or Drama: Shannon Woollard * (Gold Award)
Best Supporting Actor in a Comedy or Drama: Brian Christopher

2001 - *Amy's View*

Best Set in a Comedy or Drama: Doug Bennett * (Silver Award)
Best Lighting in a Comedy or Drama: Stelios Karagiannis

Appendix 4: Victorian Drama League Awards

Best Sound in a Comedy or Drama: Chris Boek
Best Costumes in a Comedy or Drama: Pat Day
Best Supporting Actress in a Comedy or Drama: Maggie McInnes
    as Evelyn Thomas * (Gold Award)
Best Actress in a Comedy or Drama: Kate Bowers as Amy Thomas
Best Actress in a Comedy or Drama: Louise Whiteman as Esme Allen
Best Director of a Comedy or Drama: Gordon Dunlop
Best Production of a Comedy or Drama

2003 - *The Shoe-Horn Sonata*

Best Sound Design in a Comedy or Drama: Neil Williamson and John O'Brien-Hall * (Gold Award)
Best Actor in a Minor Role in a Drama: Brian Christopher as
    The Voice of Rick
Best Actress in a Drama: Shirley Cattunar as Bridie
Best Actress in a Drama: Mary Little as Sheila
Best Director of a Dram: Chris Baldock
Best Drama Production
Also, Judge's Award to Jill Clague for the program for *The Shoe-Horn Sonata*.
    in particular the historical background and photos of WWII.

2004 - *Brighton Beach Memoirs*

Best Set Design in a Comedy or Drama: David Dare
Best Supporting Actress in a Comedy: Suzanne Daley as Nora Morton
Best Supporting Actor in a Comedy: Paul Farrell as Jack Jerome
Best Actress in a Comedy: Helen Mutkins as Kate Jerome
Best Director of a Comedy: Bryan Thomas
Best Comedy Production

2005 - *The Glass Menagerie*

Best Set Design in a Comedy or Drama: David Dare * (Silver Award)
Best Lighting Design in a Comedy or Drama: Maureen White

Appendix 4: Victorian Drama League Awards

Best Sound Design in a Comedy or Drama: Neil Williamson * (Silver Award)
Best Costume Design in Comedy or Drama: Maggie McInnes
Best Supporting Actress in a Drama: Sophie King as Laura Wingfield
Best Supporting Actor in a Drama: Blake Testro as Jim O'Connor
Best Director of a Drama: Ellis Ebell
Best Drama Production

2006 - *Old Wicked Songs*

Best Set Design in a Comedy or Drama: David Dare * (Gold Award)
Best Lighting Design in a Comedy or Drama: Stelios Karagiannis * (Gold Award)
Best Sound Design in a Comedy or Drama: David Dare and Chris Baldock * (Gold Award)
Best Costume Design in Comedy or Drama: Pat Day
Best Actor in a Drama: Tim Constantine as Stephen Hoffman
Best Actor in a Drama: Ellis Ebell as Professor Josef Mashkan *
Best Director of a Drama: Chris Baldock *
Best Drama Production *

2007 - *Gross Indecency: The Three Trials of Oscar Wilde*

Best Set Design in a Comedy or Drama: David Dare
Best Lighting Design in a Comedy or Drama: Stelios Karagiannis
Best Costume Design in Comedy or Drama: Pat Day
Best Actor in a Minor Role in a Comedy or Drama: Brad Lowry as Narrator, Alfred Wood and Moises Kaufman
Best Supporting Actor in a Drama: Ellis Ebell as Sir Edward Clarke
Best Actor in a Drama: Chris Baldock as Oscar Wilde
Best Director of a Drama: Peter Newling
Best Drama Production

Appendix 4: Victorian Drama League Awards

2008 - *Dancing at Lughnasa*

Best Sound Design in a Comedy or Drama: Ellis Ebell
Best Costume Design in Comedy or Drama: Pat Day
Best Set Design in a Comedy or Drama: David Dare
Best Supporting Actress in a Drama: Katherine Hubbard as Maggie *
Best Actress in a Drama: Gail Bradley as Kate
Best Director of a Drama: Ellis Ebell
Best Drama Production
Also a Judge's Award to Eve Park for the Irish vocal coaching for *Dancing At Lughnasa*

2009 - *Kindertransport*

Best Set Design in a Comedy or Drama: David Dare
Best Lighting Design in a Comedy or Drama: Jason Bovaird
Best Sound Design in a Comedy or Drama: Neil Williamson and Chris Baldock * (Gold Award)
Best Costume Design in Comedy or Drama: Shirley Sydenham * (Silver Award)
Best Actress in a Minor Role in a Comedy or Drama: Katherine Hubbard as Helga
Best Actor in a Minor Role in a Comedy or Drama: Ellis Ebell as The Voice of The Ratcatcher and various roles
Best Supporting Actress in a Drama: Eileen Nelson as Lil
Best Actress in a Drama: Rebecca Jones as Eva
Best Actress in a Drama: Paula McDonald as Evelyn
Best Director of a Drama: Chris Baldock
Best Drama Production

2010 - *Skylight*

Best Set Design in a Comedy or Drama: George Tranter
Best Lighting Design in a Comedy or Drama: Craig Pearcey * (Silver Award)
Best Actor in a Drama: Barry Lockett as Tom Sergeant
Best Director of a Drama: Bernadette Wheatley

Appendix 4: Victorian Drama League Awards

2011 - *Not About Heroes*

Best Set Design in a Comedy or Drama: John Shelbourn * (Silver Award)
Best Costume Design in Comedy or Drama: Shane Ryan * (Silver Award)
Best Lighting Design in a Comedy or Drama: Gordon Boyd
Best Sound Design in a Comedy or Drama: Jeff Saliba

2012 - *Doubt: A Parable*

Best Set Design in a Comedy or Drama: David Dare * (Gold Award)
Best Lighting Design in a Comedy or Drama: Craig Pearcey * (Gold Award)
Best Sound Design in a Comedy or Drama: Neil Williamsonand and Ellis Ebell * (Gold Award)
Best Costume Design in Comedy or Drama: Shirley Sydenham
Best Actress in a Minor Role in a Comedy or Drama: Shelia Allen as Mrs Muller
Best Supporting Actress in a Drama: Emily Davison as Sister James *
Best Actress in a Drama: Marianne Collopy as Sister Aloysius *
Best Actor in a Drama: Tim Constantine as Father Flynn *
Best Director of a Drama: Ellis Ebell *
Best Drama Production *

2013 - *33 Variations*

Best Set Design in a Comedy or Drama: David Dare
Best Lighting Design in a Comedy or Drama: Jason Bovaird * (Silver Award)
Best Sound Design in a Comedy or Drama: Chris Baldock * (Silver Award)
Best Costume Design in Comedy or Drama: Tony Tartaro * (Gold Award)
Best Supporting Actress in a Drama: Kellie Bray as Dr. Gertrude Ladenburger
Best Supporting Actress in a Drama: Ella Harvey as Clara Brandt *
Best Supporting Actor in a Drama: Brian Christopher as Anton Schindler *
Best Supporting Actor in a Drama: Ellis Ebell as Anton Diabelli
Best Supporting Actor in a Drama: Lachlan Martin as Mike Clark
Best Actress in a Drama: Julie Arnold as Dr. Katherine Brandt
Best Actor in a Drama: George Werther as Ludwig Van Beethoven

Appendix 4: Victorian Drama League Awards

Best Director of a Drama: Chris Baldock
Best Drama Production

2014 - *Farragut North*

Best Sound Design in a Comedy or Drama: Bruce Parr and Jeff Saliba * (Silver Award)
Best Costume Design in a Comedy or Drama: Tony Tartaro
Best Actor in a Minor Role in a Comedy or Drama: Rowan Howard as Waiter/Frank * (Gold Award)
Best Supporting Actress in a Drama: Madeleine McKinlay as Molly Pearson; Melanie Rowe as Ida Horowitz
Best Supporting Actor in a Drama: Stephen Shinkfield as Paul Zara* (Gold Award)
Best Actor in a Drama: Tim Constantine as Stephen Bellamy
Best Director of a Drama Production: Peter Newling * (Gold Award)
Best Drama Production

2015 - *Visiting Mr Gree*

Best Set Design in a Comedy or Drama: George Tranter
Best Hand & Set Properties in a Comedy or Drama: Barbara Hughes & Maria Haughey* (Gold Award)
Best Actor in a Drama: Kieran Tracey
Best Drama Production*

2017 - *Vincent in Brixton*

Best Set Design in a Comedy or Drama: Kerry Drumm* (Gold Award)
Best Properties in a Comedy or Drama: Barbara Hughes and Maria Haughey * (Gold Award)
Best Costume Design in a Comedy or Drama: Tony Tartaro* (Gold Award)
Best Sound Design in a Comedy or Drama: Shirley Sydenham
Best Actor in a Leading Role in a Drama: Jonathan Best as Vincent Van Gogh
Best Actress in a Leading Role in a Drama: Cat Jardine as Ursula

Best Director, Drama: Shirley Sydenham
Best Drama Production

2018 - *Silent Sky*

Best Lighting Design in Drama or Comedy: (Silver Award): Jason Bovaird
Best Properties in a Comedy or Drama: Barbara Hughes, David Dare, and Dion Sexton
Best Supporting Actress in a Drama: Paula McDonald as Williamina Fleming * (Gold Award)
Best Director: Ellis Ebell
Best Drama Production

Appendix 5: Williamstown Little Theatre Presidents, Secretaries and Treasurers

Year/s	President
1947-1950	R. J. Long
1951-1954	Edward Cordell
1955 - 30/6/1958	Tom Craven
1958/59 - 1959/60	Win Stewart
1960/61	Ivor Porter
1961/62	Gwladys Winfield
1962/63 - 1967/68	Alec Colville
1968/69 - 1969/70	Doug Lindsay
1970/71 - 1971/72	Grahame Murphy
1972/73 - 1973/74	Doug Lindsay
1974/75	Gillian Wadds
1975/76 - 1976/77	Doug Lindsay
1977/78 - 1978/79	Pat Day
1979/80 - 1981/82	Laurie Gellon
1982/83 - 1983/84	Vin Foster
1984/85 - 1985/86	Ray Hare
1986/87	Vin Foster
1987/88	S. Baker
1988/89	Barbara Hughes
1989/90 - 1991/92	David Dare

Appendix 5: Presidents, Secretaries and Treasurers

Year/s	President
July 1992/Dec 1994	Laurie Gellon
1996 - Aug 2003	Celia Meehan
Aug 2003 - 2010	Bryan Thomas
2011 - 2012	Ellis Ebell
2013 - 2020	Peter Newling
2021 - 2022	Celia Meehan

Year/s	Secretary
1946/47	A. Sinclair
1947/48	A. Sinclair / Win Stewart
1948/49 - 1949/50	W. Ward / Win Stewart
July-Dec 1950	T McKay / Win Stewart
1951*	E. Black / Win Stewart
1952	Ivor Porter / Win Stewart
1953/54	Win Stewart / Ivor Porter
1955/56	Win Stewart
1957 - 30 June 1958	Nell Colville / Win Stewart
1958/59	Nell Colville / A. Cordell
1959/60 - 1960-61	Nell Colville / M. Hayes
1961/62 - 1965/66	Nell Colville
1966/67 - 1967/68	Nell Colville / June Lownds

Appendix 5: Presidents, Secretaries and Treasurers

Year/s	Secretary
1968/69	Nell Colville
1969/70	J. Mitchell
1970/71	J Mitchell / Nell Colville
1971/72 - 1972/73	Nell Colville
1973/74 - 1976/77	D. Joiner
1977/78	I. Jones
1978/79 - 1979/80	Amy Grove-Rogers
1980/81 - 1981/82	P. Lee
1982/83 - 1983/84	Frank Page
1984/85	A Hakk
1985/86	A. Hakk / L. Baker / Laurie Gellon
1986/87	Laurie Gellon / Grahame Murphy
1987/88	Barbara Hughes
1988/89	A. Hakk
1989/90 - 1990/91	Barbara Hughes
July1991 - Dec 1994	Graeme Cope
1995	Celia Meehan
1996	M Hammond
1997 - 2006	Barbara Hughes
2007 - 2008	Ness Harwood
2009 - 2021	Shirley Sydenham
2022	Peter Newling

Appendix 5: Presidents, Secretaries and Treasurers

Year/s	Treasurer
1946/47 - 1947/48	W. Ward
1948/49	W. Ward / H Conradi
1949 - Dec.1954	H. Conradi
1955 - June 1960	Ivor Porter
1960/61	Ella Bambery
1961/62 - 1967/68	Ivor Porter
1968/69	J. Mitchell
1969/70 - 1971/72	Ivor Porter
1972/73	Ella Bambery
1973/74 - 1974/75	Ivor Porter
1975/76 - 1976/77	Ella Bambery
1977/78 - 1979/80	Joan Lindsay
1980/81 - 1990/91	Amy Grove-Rogers
July 1991 - Dec 1993 1	Ellis Ebell
1994	Barbara Hughes
1995 - Present	Brian Christopher

Apendix 6: Life Members of Williamstown Little Theatre

Deceased

Ella Bambery O.A.M.
Alec Colville
Nell Colville
Ted Cordell
Tom Craven
Pat Day
Vin Foster
Amy Grove-Rogers
Ray Hare
Elsie Lang
Doug Lindsay
Ron Little
June Lownds
Gary Metcalf
Grahame Murphy
Dorothy Porter
Ivor Porter
Win Stewart
Bruce Wapshott
Lorraine West
Gwladys Winfield

Life Members 2022

Alex Begg
Brian Christopher
Judi Clark
Graeme Cope
Kerry Cordell
David Dare
Ellis Ebell
Roger Forsey
Laurie Gellon
Robert Harsley
Robyn Legge
Barbara Hughes
Joan Lindsay
Mary Little
Maggie McInnes (Maggie died on 14 August 2022)
Frank Page
Gaetano Santo
Gillian Senior (Wadds)
Shirley Sydenham
Bryan Thomas
Bevan Uren
Bernadette Wheatley
Neil Williamson
Mark Young

Bibliography

Newspapers and Magazines

Footscray Advertiser
Footscray Mail
Hobson's Bay Weekly
Sunshine Advocate
Star Advertiser
Stage Whispers
Theatrecraft
The Advocate
The Age
The Hearld
The Sun
The Listener-In
Listener-In TV
Western Suburbs Advertiser
Williamstown Advertiser
Williamstown Chronicle
VDL Newsletter

Books

Colin Badger, *Who Was Badger, Aspects of the Life of Colin Robert Badger, Director of Adult Education, Victoria,* 1947-1971
Harold Baigent, *Survey of Amateur Theatre in Victoria*, mimeograph, Melbourne, Council of Adult Education, 1965).
Geoffrey Blainey, *Our Side of the Country, The Story of Victoria*, (Melbourne, Methuen Hayes, 1984)
Peter Brook, *The Empty Space,* (London, Penguin Books,1990)
Judith Buckrich, *The Making of Us: Rusden Drama, Media and Dance 1966-2002*
Peter Cliff, *Dare to Dream*, (Melbourne, Brolga Publications, 2015)

Kate Crowl, *Famda's Frolics, A Potted History of Foster Amateur Music and Drama Association, 1953-2003*
John Elsom, *Theatre Outside London*, (London, MacMillan and Co., 1971
Doris Fitton, *Not Without Dust or Heat, My Life in Theatre*, (Sydney, Harper and Row, 1981)
Robert Glass, *The Victorian Drama League 1952-2002*, (Melbourne, Victorian Drama League, 2002)
James Joyce, *Portrait of the Artist as a Young Man*, (Penguin Edition, London 1992)
Mary Lord, *Hal Porter, Man of Many Parts*, (Sydney, Random House, 1993)
A L McLeod, *The Pattern of Australian Culture*, (Melbourne, Melbourne University Press, 1963)
Geoffrey Milne, *THEATRE AUSTRALIA (UNLIMITED), Australian Theatre Since the 1950s,* Monograph 10 in the Australian Playwrights Series (General Editor Veronica Kelly), (New York, Rodolpi, 2004)
Anthony Parker, *Amateur Theatre as a Pastime, A Comprehensive Guide to the Stage,* (London, Souvenir Press Limited, 1959)
Philip Parsons with Victoria Chance eds., *Companion to Theatre in Australia*, (Sydney, Currency Press 1995)
Susan Priestley, *Altona, The Long View* (Hagreen Publishing Company in conjunction with the City of Altona, 1988)
Robert Putnam, Bowling Alone, (New York, Simon and Schuster, 2000)
Leonard Radic, *The STATE of PLAY, The Revolution in the Australian Theatre since the 1960s*, (Ringwood, Penguin Books,1991)
Frances Reid, *Theatre Administration*, (London, Adam and Charles Black, 1983)
Kenneth Rowell, Stage Design, (London, Studio Vista, 1968).
Lynne Strahan, *At the Edge of the Centre, A History of Williamstown*, (Williamstown, Hagreen Publishing Company in conjunction with the City of Williamstown, 1994)
John Sumner, *Recollections at Play, A Life in Australian Theatre*, (Melbourne, Melbourne University Press, 1993)
J L Styan, *Drama, Stage and Audience* (Cambridge, Cambridge University Press, 1975)
Cheryl Threadgold, *In the Name of Theatre, The History, Culture and Voices*

of Amateur Theatre in Victoria
Neville Thurgood, *Good Evening, Ladies and Gentlemen*, (Richmond, Spectrum Publications, 1988)
Frank Van Stratten, *NATIONAL TREASURE, The Story of Gertrude Johnson and the National Theatre*, (Melbourne, Victoria Press, 1994)
David Williamson, *Home Truths*, (Sydney, Harper Collins, 2021)
Edwin Wilson, *The Theatre Experience*, 5th edition, (New York, McGraw Hill Inc., 1991)

www.ingramcontent.com/pod-product-compliance
Lightning Source LLC
Chambersburg PA
CBHW071954290426
44109CB00018B/2016